FLYING EQUIPMENT OF THE ITALIAN AIR FORCE

in World War II

Flight Suits • Flight Helmets • Goggles • Parachutes • Life Vests • Oxygen Masks • Boots • Gloves

Alberto Spaziani

SCHIFFER MILITARY HISTORY
Atglen, PA

Dedication
To Alessio, Andrea and Simone, from Dad

Where not specifically mentioned, the photos and objects are courtesy of the author, or private collection.

Acknowledgments
Ten years after my first work on World War II Italian radio communications equipped flight helmets, finally, thanks to the support and encouragement received from many people interested in, this new book is ready. Long time research and a significant archive of images, most of them unpublished, will help the readers identify the items in their collections, and to remember the brave airmen that used them. I hope that it fills a gap in the knowledge of Italian World War II Regia Aeronautica flight clothing and equipment.

I would like give a special thank to the following:

Italian Air Force Generals (retired): Emanuele Annoni, Umberto Bernardini, Raffaele Capaldo, Giosue' Carillo, Francesco Fagiolo, Silvio De Giorgi, Angelino Lo Vullo, Sergio Mazzerelli, Vittorio Merlo, Giuseppe Pesce, Costantino Petrosellini, Giuseppe Ruzzin, Potito Santoro, Giuseppe Scarinci.

Regia Aeronautica Pilots: Dante Mezzano, Attilio Sanson, Armando Galluzzi, Antonio Ragonese, Guglielmo Biffani, Guido La Ferla, Renato Chiri, Amleto Monterumici, Vannetto Cavicchioli, Luigi Di Cecco, Nino Laurencich, Leonardo Duminuco, Armando Mori, Giovanni Barcaro, Cesare Erminio,

Friends: Mrs. Anna La Ferla, Giovanna Roscigno, Lucio Biccolini, Elio Barbafina, Nicola Malizia, Nicola Virgilio.

ITAF Museum Staff Vigna Di Valle, Rome: Ten.Col.Pil. Massimo Mondini, Magg. Marco Bovesecco, Ten. Flavio Silvestrini, M.Lli Clementi, Rinaldi, Sanetti.

I am grateful to my collector friends: Franco Burgio, Claudio Canton, Pierluigi Castellani, Sergio Coccia, Stefano Crino', Luigi Di Gabriele, Athos Gaiani, Pierluigi Moncalvo, Flavio Pregnolato, Danilo Rao, Marco Rebosio, Stefano Santucci, P.Schifano, Gianni Tugliani, Remigio Zizzo, and to my friend Franco Manini for the translation.

A very special thanks to Captain G. Casolari, Director of Museo Dell'aviazione Di Rimini, and to Ivano Rossi Director of Museo Della Guerra Di Castel Del Rio.

Alberto Spaziani
Roma Gennaio, 2011

Library of Congress Control Number: 2013955266

ISBN: 978-0-7643-4377-3
Printed in China

Published by Schiffer Publishing, Ltd.
4880 Lower Valley Road
Atglen, PA 19310
Phone: (610) 593-1777; Fax: (610) 593-2002
E-mail: Info@schifferbooks.com

CONTENTS

FOREWORD

Alberto Spaziani's long awaited book plugs the wide gap in the history of Italian aviation regarding the flight gear of Italian aviators, a subject also neglected by Italian Aviation historians, their focus mostly on the events and aircraft.

At last, with this book, the gap between Italy, and other great countries that made the history of aviation, narrows. Those countries that understood, before us, the importance of the study, classification, and conservation of this branch of aviation history, wrongly considered "minor" for too long a time compared to the main stream of the historic planes collection followed by the museums, have consistently increased the knowledge and diffusion of the aeronautical culture. Hence, no longer only just a collector and militaria fair goer niche of interest, but history to be preserved as a testimonial of the technological progress that went together with other aviation components (systems, engines, avionics, etc.) in the "man-machine" relationship that makes the airplane a unique and fundamental weapons system.

I also want to mention that Alberto Spaziani, in addition to being a passionate aviation historian and collector, is a valid and active volunteer consultant to the ITAF Museum, specializing in the equipment and uniforms of the museum.

So I suggest everyone – historians and aviation history enthusiasts – have this book on their bookshelf, and to use it as the essential resource for Italian air force flight gear.

Lt.Col.Pil. Massimo Mondini
Director, ITAF Museum, Vigna di Valle, Rome
December 2013

PART 1: HISTORY

CHAPTER ONE

FLIGHT SUITS

The first flight suit "officially" accepted by the Regia Aeronautica (RA) to be used by flight crews, was the flight coverall made in gray moleskin, and was a direct derivative of the types used during and right after World War I.

Italian airman wearing an electrically heated flight suit, c.1916. Courtesy MUSAM-ITAF

This coverall was described in the RA document No.380, GURA (Giornale Ufficiale Regia Aeronautica) issue No.34 of November 20, 1926 in the chapter dedicated to, "additions and variations to the uniforms regulations," issued in the first 1923 "OD-4" (Official Document "Regolamento sull'Uniforme") edition. The same document also mentions a general "leather jacket" to be worn over the field uniform. A drawing of the jacket was also included.

The black leather jacket usually had a white fur lining with black fur collar and covered the wearer's knees.

The gray moleskin coverall had three external pockets, one on the left side of the chest and the others just above the knees.

It featured a collar, adjustment wrist and ankle straps made of the same material, a lap belt with metal buckle and a diagonal closure with six buttons. This closure was from just above the lap belt to the right shoulder.

Also established in the same document (GURA, November 20, 1926), was the position of the rank patches; a few centimeters above the wrists for the officers, on the shoulders for the warrant officers and on the sleeves for the sergeants and corporals.

Two World War II Italian airmen equipped with Roold flight helmets, and leather and electrically heated flight coveralls. Courtesy MUSAM-ITAF

Air Marshal Italo Balbo visiting Vigna di Valle seaplane base in 1927. Noteworthy are the black leather fur-lined flight jackets worn by the two airmen at left. Courtesy MUSAM-ITAF

Later on with a new official leaflet from the Air Ministry, published in the document No.213 of the GURA No.15 issue of May 6, 1927, it was stated what should be considered the mandatory and optional personal equipment.

Among the mandatory equipment there was a two-piece black leather flight suit to be worn as an alternative to the leather coverall, or a fabric blue-gray coverall, the latter to be used during the summer or in hot climate locations.

The leather jacket was intended to be worn over the field uniform, so it was oversized. The lining color was optional, but the collar was in mandatory black, as shown in period photographic evidence.

It also featured a lap belt, 5-6cm width, and three pockets, one on each side and a larger one on the chest side.

Rank badges were sewn in the same position as on the gray moleskin coverall.

MINISTERO DELL'AERONAUTICA

Supplemento N. 2 al

GIORNALE UFFICIALE

Roma, 23 Maggio 1929 - Anno VII

UNIFORME

Aggiunte e varianti alle disposizioni sull'uniforme per gli Ufficiali della R. Aeronautica

ROMA
STABILIMENTO COSTRUZIONI AERONAUTICHE
Laboratorio Fotocollografico
1929 - ANNO VII

Front cover of the May 23, 1929 issue of the Regia Aeronautica's official magazine GURA.

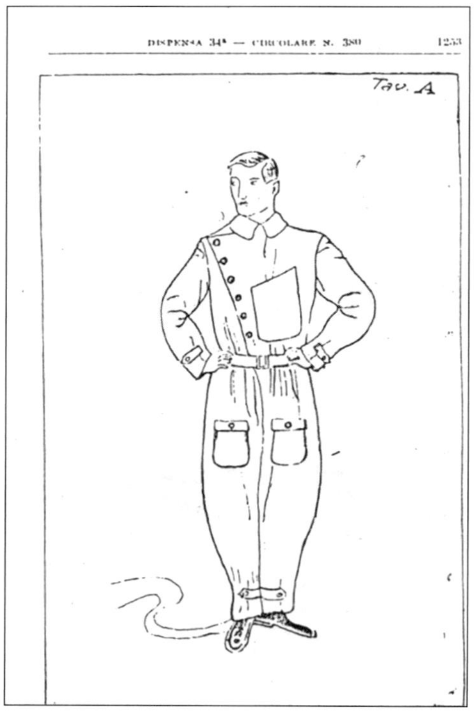

Reference drawing showing the first moleskin flight suit adopted in 1928.

Wearing the black leather jacket with the field uniform trousers was allowed, however, it was forbidden to wear the black leather trousers without the leather jacket.

The black leather trousers had two pockets just above the knees and featured a removable fur lining.

The leather, or the blue-gray, coverall were alternative to the flight suit and both featured a removable fur lining for use in various climates.

Above and opposite
Images taken from GURA magazine showing the fur-lined leather flight coverall. Note the two-piece version, and the correct position for the rank badges over the moleskin flight coverall.

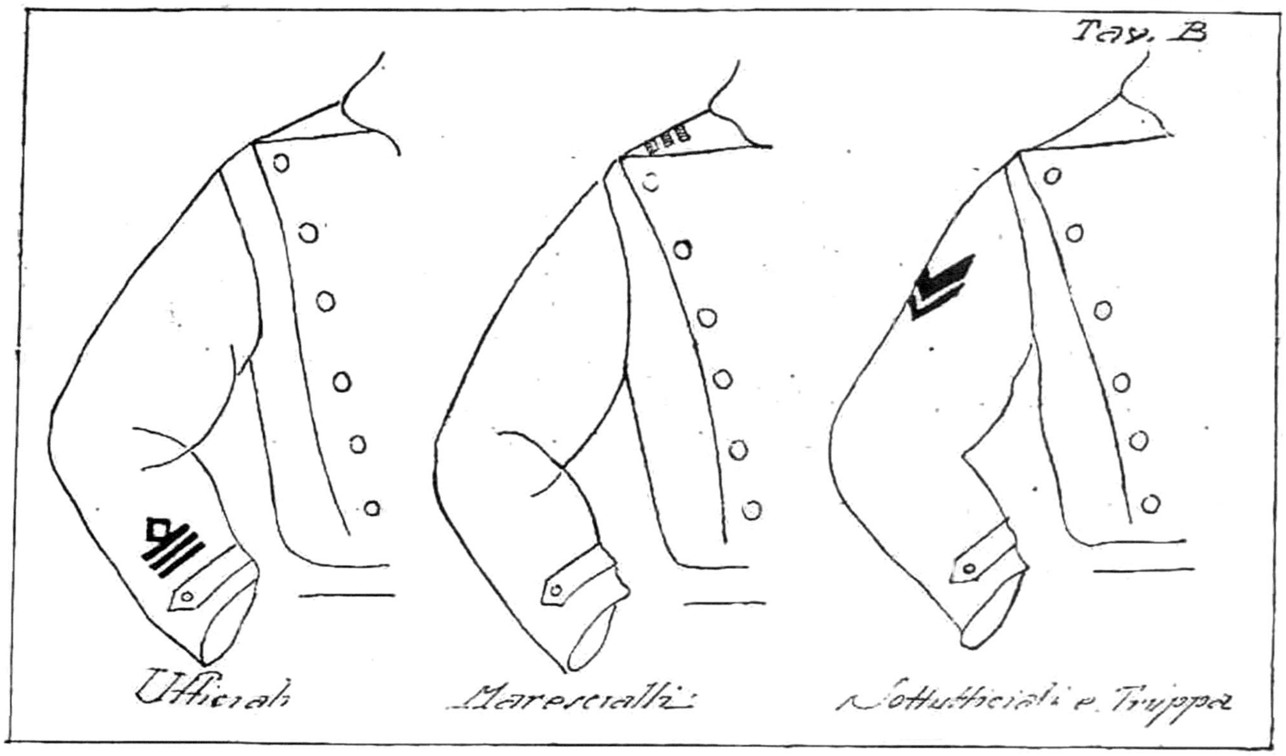

Guanti.

Di cuoio nero o marrone scuro, impellicciati o no.

Caschetto.

Di cuoio nero impellicciato e di foggia simile a quelli attualmente in uso.

Casco.

Per ora sarà della foggia simile a quello attualmente in uso.
In seguito sarà sperimentato un nuovo tipo di casco da adottarsi definitivamente.

INDUMENTI DI VOLO FACOLTATIVI.

Passamontagne.

Di lana grigio-azzurra.
L'apertura anteriore sarà tale da non disturbare la vista.

Occhiali.

Di foggia facoltativa.
Saranno muniti di cristallo o vetro bianco.

Gilet o cintura di salvataggio
(per il personale degli idrovolanti)

Di foggia facoltativa.

p. *Il Ministro*: Balbo.

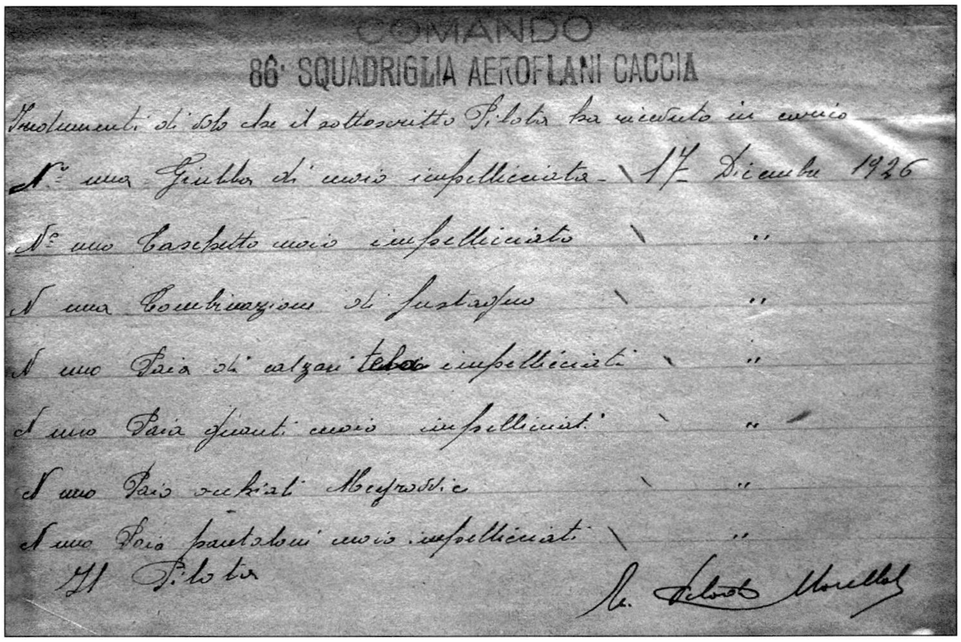

COMANDO
86ª SQUADRIGLIA AEROPLANI CACCIA

Indumenti di volo che il sottoscritto Pilota ha ricevuto in consegna

N° una Giubba di cuoio impellicciata \ 17 Dicembre 1926
N° uno Caschetto cuoio impellicciato \ "
N una Combinazione di fustagno \ "
N uno Paio di calzari tela impellicciati \ "
N uno Paio guanti cuoio impellicciati \ "
N uno Paio occhiali Meyrowsic \ "
N uno Paio pantaloni cuoio impellicciati \ "

Il Pilota

The personal logbook listed the flight gear delivered to each airman.

Airman with the two-piece fur-lined leather flight suit with flight boots. Courtesy MUSAM-ITAF

The use of the blue-gray flight coverall was soon confined to cadets of the RA flight schools only, until a new flight suit was adapted for air cadets. This flight outfit was composed of jacket and trousers, quite similar to the standard RA Model 40 flight suit but made of moleskin. Document No.6 of OD 4 1937, issued in June 1941 provides evidence of this.

Also on the flight coverall of 1927 (leather or blue-gray fabric) were three pockets, in the same position as the gray moleskin, with rank badges in the same position, although photos of that period show that rank badges were rarely fitted onto the leather coveralls.

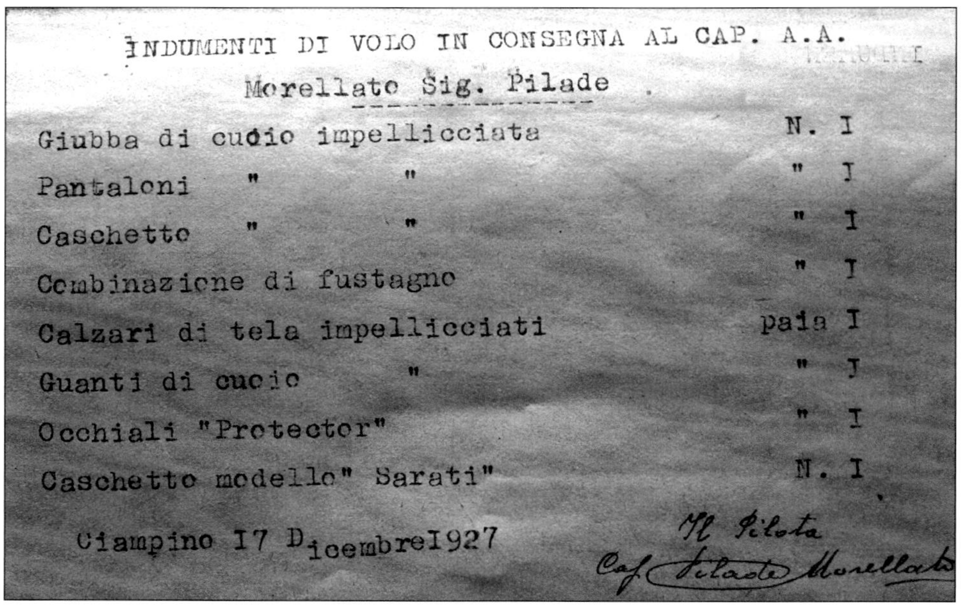

INDUMENTI DI VOLO IN CONSEGNA AL CAP. A.A.
Morellato Sig. Pilade

Giubba di cuoio impellicciata	N. I
Pantaloni " "	" I
Caschetto " "	" I
Combinazione di fustagno	" I
Calzari di tela impellicciati	paia I
Guanti di cuoio "	" I
Occhiali "Protector"	" I
Caschetto modello" Sarati"	N. I

Ciampino I7 Dicembre1927

Il Pilota
Cap. Pilade Morellato

Another example of the equipment list registered in the flight logbook. Note the mistaken "Sarati" instead of the correct "Saratti" for the protective flight helmet.

Airmen of the Colonial Air Force. The crewman on the left is wearing the standard leather jacket over the moleskin coverall. Courtesy MUSAM-ITAF

Drawing taken from the "Regia Aeronautica Uniform Manual Regulation" 1927 edition showing the standard issue leather jacket reference. Courtesy MUSAM-ITAF

In the same 1927 dated document, and for the first time, there is mention of an optional electrical heating device, though there is no technical description of it.

In this description there is no any specification about which closures were to be used. Buttons or zippers varied, depending on the manufacturer's choice.

Also on these models, the fitting of a black fur collar and the lap belt was mandatory.

From period photographic evidence, it is clear that there was no standard pattern for flight suits and only a "general" adherence to RA requirements.

In 1930 the RA adopted a standard flight coverall made of waterproof wool and known as the Model 30. It was made of olive drab or dark brown wool, with a detachable light brown wool liner.

Previous suits remained in use until stocks were depleted. Also, the early "protective" flight helmets were used until the new "SARATTI" model came into service in the flight schools.

In the 1930 model, the black fur collar was common to the inner liner and to the flight suit. In the first production batches, the liner had a black lamb fur collar.

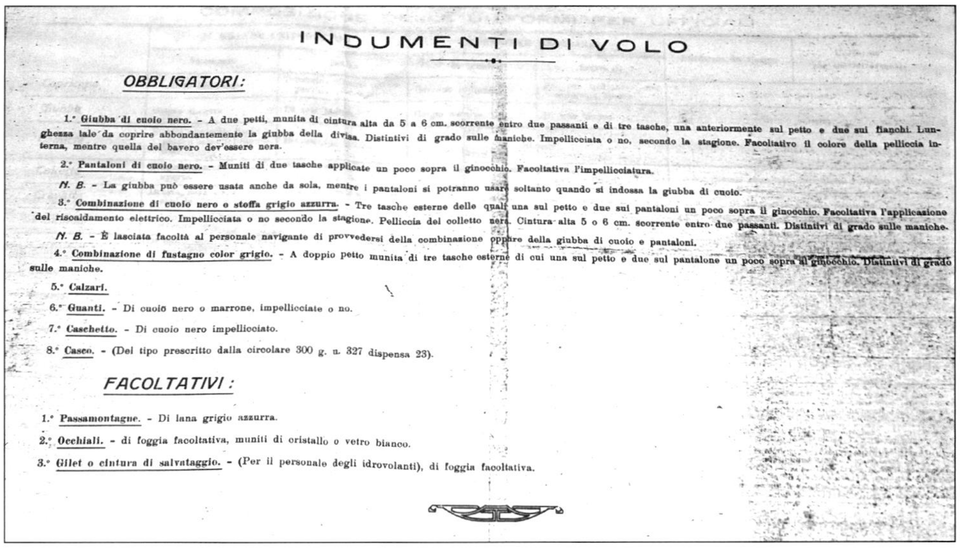

INDUMENTI DI VOLO

OBBLIGATORI:

1.° Giubba di cuoio nero. - A due petti, munita di cintura alta da 5 a 6 cm. scorrente entro due passanti e di tre tasche, una anteriormente sul petto e due sui fianchi. Lunghezza tale da coprire abbondantemente la giubba della divisa. Distintivi di grado sulle maniche. Impellicciata o no, secondo la stagione. Facoltativo il colore della pelliccia interna, mentre quella del bavero dev'essere nera.

2.° Pantaloni di cuoio nero. - Muniti di due tasche applicate un poco sopra il ginocchio. Facoltativa l'impellicciatura.

N. B. - La giubba può essere usata anche da sola, mentre i pantaloni si potranno usare soltanto quando si indossa la giubba di cuoio.

3.° Combinazione di cuoio nero o stoffa grigio azzurra. - Tre tasche esterne delle quali una sul petto e due sui pantaloni un poco sopra il ginocchio. Facoltativa l'applicazione del riscaldamento elettrico. Impellicciata o no secondo la stagione. Pelliccia del colletto nera. Cintura alta 5 o 6 cm. scorrente entro due passanti. Distintivi di grado sulle maniche.

N. B. - È lasciata facoltà al personale navigante di provvedersi della combinazione oppure della giubba di cuoio e pantaloni.

4.° Combinazione di fustagno color grigio. - A doppio petto munita di tre tasche esterne di cui una sul petto e due sul pantalone un poco sopra al ginocchio. Distintivi di grado sulle maniche.

5.° Calzari.

6.° Guanti. - Di cuoio nero o marrone, impellicciate o no.

7.° Caschetto. - Di cuoio nero impellicciato.

8.° Casco. - (Del tipo prescritto dalla circolare 300 g. n. 327 dispensa 23).

FACOLTATIVI:

1.° Passamontagne. - Di lana grigio azzurra.

2.° Occhiali. - di foggia facoltativa, muniti di cristallo o vetro bianco.

3.° Gilet o cintura di salvataggio. - (Per il personale degli idrovolanti), di foggia facoltativa.

Page taken from the "Regia Aeronautica Uniform Manual Regulation" 1927 edition describing the main items of RA personnel flight equipment.

1911 dated catalog of Giusti's flight gear production.

This coverall featured two large billowing pockets just above the knees, and two adjusting belts on both sides made of the same cloth (4-5cm width), each with a small metal buckle.

The torso section had two zips: the former on the right side from neck base to the crotch, the latter on the centerline from the crotch to the middle of the belly, about 30cm in length.

The trousers had lateral zips, from the ankles to the hips. These trousers were provided with two lateral openings in order to reach the pockets of the uniform trousers that were always worn under the flight suit.

All openings were provided with zips, and an electric heating device was among the options.

In this late-1930s photo note that the Lt.Col. at right is still wearing the moleskin flight coverall. Courtesy MUSAM-ITAF

Opposite
Air Cadets of the "LEONE" (LYON) class of the RA Academy, wearing the gray moleskin flight suit in 1931.

In this early-1930s photo note that the fur-lined leather jacket was still in use.

All the above descriptions are integrally taken from the RA document regarding the uniform regulations of 1930. There was a clear absence of precise manufacturing rules, so every maker, although following a general pattern, introduced "personal" interpretations of the RA rather general requirements.

Flt.Sgt. Francesco Fagiolo in his heyday wearing the Model 30 winter MARUS flight suit. He became a Lt.Gen. later in his career.

Advertisement from the "ALA D'ITALIA" ("Wing of Italy") magazine. Note that the famous sportwears tailor Giusti of Rome acted as agent and Rome depot for the MARUS factory of Turin in the early-1930s.

Above and right
The Countess Carina Negrone established a new altitude record flying a Caproni 113 on June 20, 1935, over Guidonia airfield. She wore an electrically heated Model 30 MARUS flight suit. Courtesy MUSAM-ITAF

This pair of student pilots wear the Model 30 MARUS flight suit. They hold the protective flight helmets of the Franco factory.

Above and below
Privately purchased flight suit – derivative of the Model 30 suit.

Advertisement leaflet for the MARUS factory.

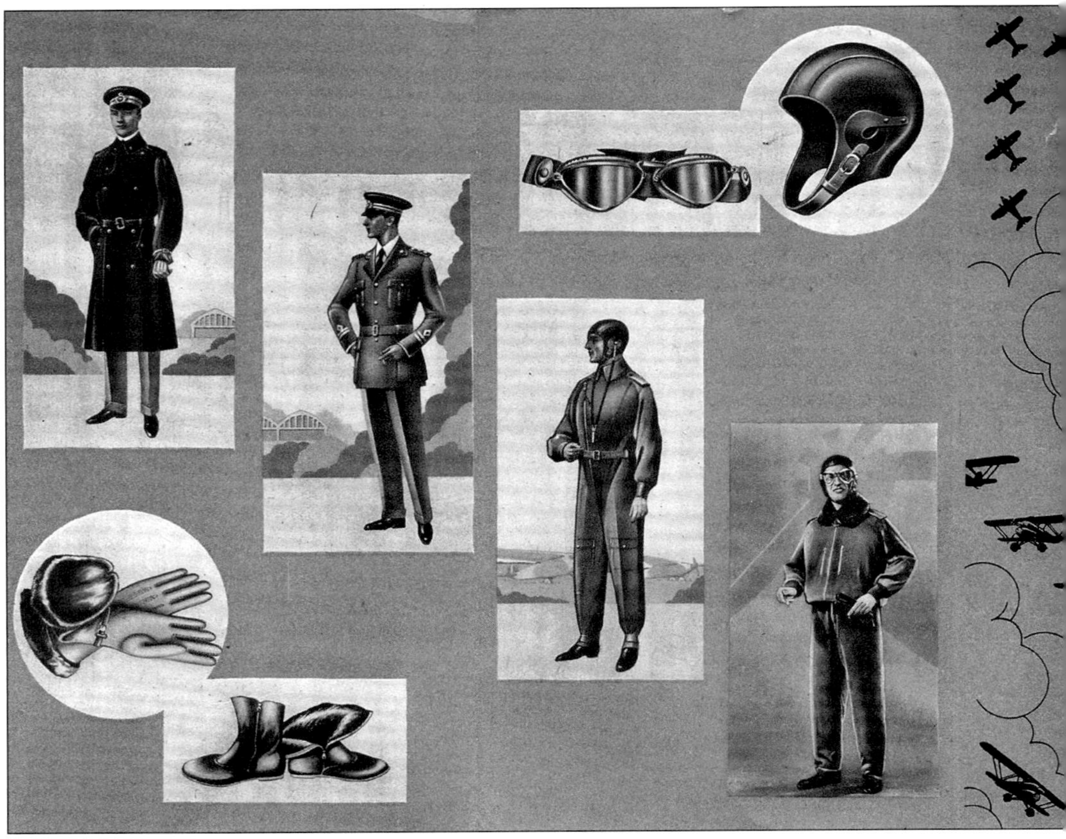

Gray moleskin flight suit – derivative of the Model 30 suit.

This random looking system looks quite different from the modern armed forces rigid specifications, TO and standard references, serial numbers, NUC etc.

In other countries like Great Britain, the United States, Germany, and Japan there was already a highly standardized classification system for military equipment.

For this reason, flight gear produced by these countries, after an accurate examination, shows minimal difference between the same types of items produced by different manufacturers due to their close respect to detailed rules issued by their HQs.

Through the years, the Model 30 flight suit was developed in several versions, including the electrically heated version produced by the MARUS factory. This version did not see widespread use, but was worn by Countess Carina Negrone during her record breaking high-altitude flight on June 20, 1935, flying a Caproni 113 over Guidonia airfield.

The final production batches had a fur collar brown or light brown, instead of the previous black fur. On the shoulders, two detachable epaulettes were provided, held by a button and a loop, the latter of the same cloth. There was also a lap belt held by two loops on both sides with a metallic buckle, and sometimes there was a horizontal pocket, 20cm wide, on the left side of the chest. Some suits were also produced using light brown moleskin.

The large pockets above the knees were always rounded in the lower section, and they were of the "billows" type with openings at the top. These pockets didn't lack the "Italian touch" showing variations like: straight openings, no billows, closed with or without a flap, with a central button or a zip. In Italy, the zips were called, "automatic denture catch."

Summer flight coverall made of light brown fabric – a Model 30 derivative.

In some commercial models, the inner lining was secured with buttons instead of strings, the latter typical of the MARUS factory.

The strings were sewn to the edges of the liner, then were laced up to the corresponding eyelets on the outer suit in order to link the inner lining to the outer. The system was reversed in some versions of the flight coverall named "Atlantica."

The detachable inner lining was made in various thicknesses, and in some versions there was option for an electrical heating system.

The MARUS factory developed an electrical heating system named "THERMOMAX" for the MARUS Model 40 flight suit; this system was chosen by other manufacturers for their flight suits.

Above and below
Model 30 winter MARUS flight suit.

The same airman shown opposite is now wearing the standard Model 30 MARUS summer flight coverall, and under it the winter liner with fur collar.

Summer Model 30 MARUS suit worn over the uniform. Note the shirt collar and tie overlapping the suit collar.

Privately purchased winter flight suit.

This system also provided heating for the flight gloves, flight boots and a skullcap worn under the flight helmet in lieu of the usual wool balaclava. The standard wool balaclava, as stated in RA OD 4, was made of blue-gray or light brown wool. It was common practice among RA flyers to use rice paper undercoats to protect themselves from windblast in open cockpit planes.

There were also "summer" versions of the Model 30 flight suit, in white or light brown fabric, and color depending on the manufacturer.

Both summer and winter models had, under the collar, a device to close the collar flaps around the wearer's neck for protection. This device was secured with a small buckle, hooks or buttons.

The Model 30 coveralls, although superseded by the more modern Model 40, was used throughout World War II by RA and ANR aircrew, and in the early postwar years.

The coverall Model 30 was confirmed with the same characteristic features along with a pictorial representation in the RA OD 4 in 1937.

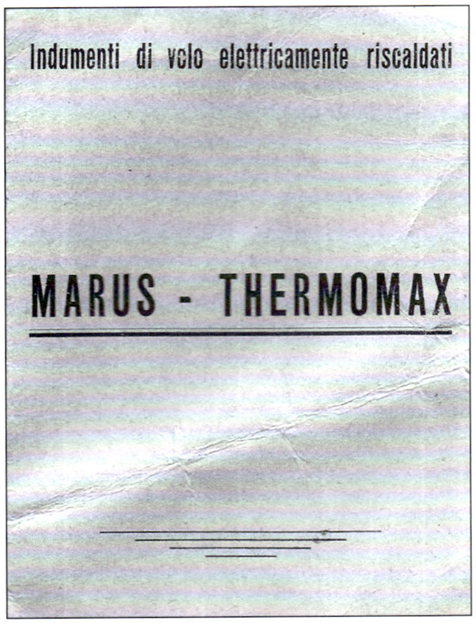
Indumenti di volo elettricamente riscaldati

MARUS - THERMOMAX

Reference and maintenance manual issued with the MARUS THERMOMAX electrical heating system kit used on flying suits.

Russian Front, summer 1941. Two variants of the summer flight suit.

1935. The airman at right is wearing the "ATLANTICA" flight jacket.

From 1930-1940, Italy gained war experience in Africa and the Spanish Civil War, in which the RA had a leading role.

Furthermore, the RA achieved worldwide appreciation with Italo Balbo's huge formation flights to Brazil and the United States, and with participation in the Istres-Damascus-Paris air race, won by the Italian SM.79 crews of the "Green Mice" team in 1937.

This period, rich with events and innovative technical achievements, also saw a strong impulse towards modernizing and updating flight gear.

Model 30 winter MARUS flight suit.

Left to right: winter "ATLANTICA," summer and winter Model 30 suit.

Image from the 1937 edition of the "Regia Aeronautica Uniform Manual Regulation" that still references the Model 30 suit.

The first versions of the MARUS two-piece flight suit were conceived by Italo Balbo for his Atlantic crossing flights during this period.

The basic pattern for the winter suit consisted of large trousers made of waterproof wool, large lateral pockets with straight or inclined openings (with or without zips). Sometimes these openings were provided only to reach the uniform trouser pockets, which was always worn under the flight suit. Color varied from medium brown to olive green.

There were zippered openings from the knees to the ankles with waist and ankles adjusting belts of the same cloth to adapt it to the aviator's body.

Model 30 winter by MARUS. Courtesy MUSAM-ITAF

Opposite
Model 30 derivatives.

Below
"ATLANTICA" winter jacket with slanted pockets.

Evidence of the RA's poor personnel flight gear standardization.

The winter flight jacket, made from the same wool cloth, also had a loose fit. The sleeves' attachments to the jacket's body were rounded. There were also variations in the position and shape of the pockets, in the collar fastener, and in the fitting of the inner liner: with strings (MARUS) or buttons (GIUSTI and GENNERINO).

Wool elasticated bands, 8cm in width, were sewn at the jacket waistline and wrists. Both trousers and jacket had a detachable light brown wool lining, similar to the Model 30 suit. Snug fitting was provided by a string and eyelet system. A large light brown fur collar was attached to the jacket inner lining. The jacket inner lining had sleeves, a feature abandoned in the Model 40.

Underneath the jacket main zip, there was a 2cm width flap to separate the zip from the underlying clothes.

In some versions of the "Atlantic" flight suit, there were detachable epaulettes, secured by a button, and also seen on the summer version, which was extensively used during the Spanish Civil War.

By the end of 1940, the RA began supplying a new winter flight suit model, consisting of jacket and trousers, to its flight crews.

At right
Top
MARUS "ATLANTICA" variant.

Middle
The "ATLANTICA" was used also in the Spanish Civil War.

Bottom
Flight engineer wearing a non-standard flight suit. Courtesy MUSAM-ITAF

Above
Another example of flight gear mixing in the same unit.

MARUS factory leaflet.

Uniformi per allievi delle Scuole di Pilotaggio

Uniformi varie

Durante le esercitazioni di volo s'indossano:
la combinazione di fustagno, in due pezzi, della foggia risultante dall'annesso figurino, gli stivali, il caschetto e gli occhiali.
I pantaloni della combinazione debbono essere introdotti negli stivali.

Durante le esercitazioni sportive s'indossano:
la maglia, i calzoncini e le scarpette sportive (pag. 116 ter).

Drawing from the O.D. of 1937 "Regia Aeronautica Uniform Manual Regulations" showing the student pilots' flight suit, that was similar to the Model 40.

Student pilots wearing the flight suit described above.

After earning his wings, this new pilot proudly shows the mint Model 40 jacket as a status symbol of his achievement.

The new trousers were tighter at the ankles and provided with the usual light brown wool liner system which was the same for the new jacket.

The jacket collar was made with short lamb wool sewn on the outer jacket. The jacket had a central zip, two "bean" shaped pockets and a elasticated waistband.

The sleeves had two elasticated wristbands, 6cm in length. The trousers had two unzippered, double billow front pockets, two upper lateral openings, two lower zippered pockets, and was provided with an internal elasticated belt and hook system, to sustain themselves on the front side (Patent No.365227). Electrical heating was optional. Notably, the inner wool liner was without sleeves. Some summer versions were made following the same general pattern as the winter version, but wrist and ankle adjustment was provided by two buttons.

In July 1942, the RA HQ, modifying the document No.590 of the GURA, stated that all Model 40 flight suits, as well as flight gloves and boots, had to be provided with electrical heating.

In 1941, with the same type of variations to the OD No.4 of 1937 edition, a new two-piece flight suit entered service. This suit was similar to the Model 40 but made of gray moleskin. This flight suit was conceived for RA student pilots during flight training. For the storage and transport of the flight clothes, a fabric bag was provided. This bag was waterproofed and had a closure device.

In the years prior to World War II, it was a common practice among RA student pilots to personally purchase items like flight suits, flight goggles, flight gloves, flight helmets, often directly in the RA flight schools from the sales agents of the manufacturers.

During World War II, the RA HQ stated clearly (at last!) rules for the supplying of flight gear. Flight gear was directly supplied by the administration and it fit two categories: individual and unit.

Flight clothes were provided in either mint or used condition. The minimum operational life of new gear was calculated to be three years (GURA 23rd issue, Document No.466, July 1942).

Indumenti di volo

Combinazione da volo estiva in due pezzi

Della foggia risultante dall'annesso figurino.
Di tela color avana chiaro.
È composta di una giacca e di un pantalone lungo rimboccato.
La giacca è munita di una chiusura automatica a dentiera, apribile; ha due tasche in alto e termina con una fascia elastica.
Le maniche si stringono in fondo con un polsino elastico, a due abbottonature.
Il pantalone ha, lateralmente e in alto; due tasche, un'apertura centrale con bottoni, due aperture in basso ai lati con chiusure automatiche a dentiera, fisse.
Il pantalone è provvisto di cinghia della stessa stoffa e termina con un polsino elastico, a due abbottonature.

Caschetto estivo

Di foggia uguale a quella del caschetto di cuoio (invernale).
Di tela color avana chiaro.

Indumenti di volo

Combinazione da volo invernale in due pezzi

Della foggia risultante dall'annesso figurino.
In tessuto di lana impermeabilizzata di color verde oliva.
È composta di una giacca e di un pantalone lungo, più stretto al fondo.
Sia la giacca che il pantalone sono foderati con tessuto di lana cammello e muniti di lacciuoli per l'attaccatura delle rispettive fodere.
Il collo della giacca è di agnello rasato, uso castorino ed è applicato sul tessuto esterno.
La giacca è munita di una chiusura automatica a dentiera, apribile; ha due tasche al centro, e termina con una fascia elastica.
Le maniche si stringono in fondo con un polsino elastico.
Il pantalone ha sul davanti due tasche sovrapposte a soffietto, due aperture laterali in alto e due in basso, con chiusure automatiche a dentiera, fisse, ed è inoltre provvisto di cintura elastica con gancio per sorreggere il davanti ribaltabile.
È facoltativo l'uso del riscaldamento elettrico.

Calzari

Della foggia risultante dall'annesso figurino.
Di pelle color marrone opaco.
Internamente sono impellicciati con agnellino, dello stesso color marrone.
Ampi in modo da potersi portare sopra le calzature.
Senza tacco.
Chiusura laterale a dentiera, fissa

Guanti

Della foggia risultante dall'annesso figurino.
Di cuoio color marrone, impellicciati o meno.

Caschetto

Della foggia risultante dall'annesso figurino.
Di cuoio color marrone, impellicciato o foderato con stoffa.

Casco di protezione

Del modello risultante dall'annesso figurino.
È ricoperto di cuoio color marrone scuro.
È costituito da 4 spicchi di duralluminio, indipendenti l'uno dall'altro, e posti su di un fusto di tela gommata; il tutto è sormontato da una crociera protettrice.
La base è costituita da 2 semicerchi imbottiti.

Passamontagne

Di lana color marrone.

Occhiali

Foggia facoltativa.
Con cristalli o vetri bianchi o colorati, o con altra sostanza trasparente.

Summer and winter Model 40 flight suits as depicted in the "Regia Aeronautica Uniform Manual Regulations."

DISPENSA 36ª — CIRCOLARE N. 663 — 1911

N. 663 – SERVIZIO DI COMMISSARIATO. — Varianti alla composizione delle serie di indumenti di volo ed alle norme relative alla loro costituzione ed amministrazione.

Il primo comma della circolare n. 466 del *Giornale Ufficiale della R. Aeronautica*, dispensa 23ª, in data 11 agosto 1942-XX è sostituito dal seguente:

« La composizione della serie di indumenti di volo di prescrizione per il personale della Regia Aeronautica è così stabilita:

1 caschetto conformato per l'applicazione di telefoni e laringofoni, munito di complesso per elettroriscaldamento;

1 paio di occhiali da volo con relativo astuccio;

1 combinazione di lana impermeabilizzata, provvista di fodera di pelo di cammello e di complesso per elettroriscaldamento;

1 paio di guanti provvisti di complesso per elettroriscaldamento;

1 paio di calzature di cuoio impellicciato, provviste di complesso per elettroriscaldamento;

1 sacco di tela di canapa impermeabilizzata, con chiusura per la conservazione degli indumenti di volo;

1 casco di protezione, per le sole dotazioni delle Scuole di 1° periodo ».

Il Sottosegretario di Stato: FOUGIER

p. Il Ministro: FOUGIER.

Dicembre 1942

Electrically heated flight suits were officially adopted in 1942 as stated in the December 1942 GURA.

Luglio 1942

DISPENSA 23ª — CIRCOLARE N. 466 — 1383

N. 466 – SERVIZIO DI COMMISSARIATO. — Composizione delle serie di indumenti di volo e norme relative alla loro costituzione ed amministrazione.

A modifica di quanto è stabilito dalla circolare numero 590 del *Giornale Ufficiale* della Regia Aeronautica per il 1937, la composizione della serie di indumenti di volo di prescrizione per il personale della Regia Aeronautica è così stabilita:

1 casco di protezione;

1 caschetto di cuoio impellicciato, munito di dispositivo per applicazione del telefono di bordo;

1 paio di sordine;

1 paio di occhiali da volo con relativo astuccio;

1 combinazione di lana impermeabilizzata, costituita di giubbetto e pantalone, provvisti di fodera di pelo di cammello e di complesso per elettro-riscaldamento;

1 combinazione di tela;

1 paio di guanti di cuoio impellicciato, provvisti di complesso per elettro-riscaldamento;

1 paio di calzari di cuoio impellicciato, provvisti di complesso per elettro-riscaldamento;

1 sacco di tela di canapa impermeabilizzata, con chiusura, per la conservazione degli indumenti di volo.

Le serie di indumenti di volo vengono fornite dall'Amministrazione e possono essere di dotazione individuale o di dotazione di Reparto.

Gli indumenti possono distribuirsi nuovi od usati.

Per gli indumenti distribuiti nuovi è prescritto un periodo di durata minimo di anni tre.

Per gli indumenti usati il periodo di durata minimo viene stabilito, a seconda del loro stato d'uso ed in ragione di 1/3 o di 2/3 di quello normale, dalle Direzioni di Commissariato, man mano che provvedono al relativo invio.

In this photo an Academy student pilot wears the standard issue sweater as flight gear.

Right and below
Two-piece Model 40 flight suits.

After the armistice of September 8, 1943, in the chaos following it and with the born of two Italian Air Forces, the so-called Cobelligerent Air Force in Southern Italy and the Fascist National Air Force ANR in Northern Italy, the flight gear situation became more complicated. The Cobelligerent Air Force continued to use the Model 40 flight suits along with British and American equipment. Studying World War II era photographic evidence shows that there was a mix of equipment with a progressive increase in use of Anglo-American gear, due to the exhaustion of original Italian items. Being that major manufacturers were located in Northern Italy, only GIUSTI in Rome provided some small supply quantities with great difficulty.

Bomber Wing crews showing non-standard personal flight equipment. Courtesy N. Virgilio, from "L'Aeroporto Fantasma"

For the Fascist National Air Force (ANR) there were supplies from the Luftwaffe for items such as flight suits and helmets, goggles, oxygen masks, boots and life vests.

The only exceptions during those difficult years, was a new flight suit similar to the Model 40 and to the "Atlantic" suit, produced for the ANR by MARUS and MITA. A particular flight suit, also a derivative of the Model 40, was produced by an anonymous factory (most probably Giusti of Rome) for the Cobelligerent Air Force and used mostly by Baltimore bomber crews. This suit had billowed pockets on the front of the trousers and close to the wristbands on the jacket sleeves, and classic inner liner of light brown wool.

The ANR flight suit was the two-piece type, jacket and large trousers, and was manufactured in greenish waterproof wool.

The jacket had the classic light brown wool lining with a large fur collar. The liner was detachable and fitted to the outer jacket with the usual string-eyelet system. There were two large lateral pockets, inclined rearward with metal inner buttons. The usual elasticated bands were fitted to the waist and wrists, the latter 7cm in length. There were detachable epaulettes on the shoulders.

The collar had two strips with buttons for tightening around the wearer's neck.

Two observer officers from the army wearing electrically heated Model 40 flight suits. Taken from "Nei cieli di Guerra"

Model 40 flight suits.

Courtesy A. Sanson

The trousers of the more recent pattern, had a practical zippered front opening 40cm in length, inclined to the right in the upper section, and finishing with a string and eyelet with button.

There were two adjusting belts provided on both sides of the waist, and two pockets with rear facing flaps and central button for closure.

These trousers had a 25cm zipper on the inner side of the ankles, with an adjusting string with a button in the lower part. There were two large billowed pockets just above the knees, similar to the old Model 30 suit, closed by an internal zip.

Notably, the old Model 30 suits were used by both RA and ANR crews until stocks were exhausted.

ANR two-piece flight suit produced by MARUS and MITA.

Italian pilots from a Bf 109 RA unit showing a mix of Italian and German equipment. Courtesy G. Carillo

ANR airmen.

Rare image of the Cobelligerent Air Force jacket – probably produced by Giusti.

By the end of 1944 in southern Italy, some Cobelligerent Air Force units received a new flight suit model, similar to the MARUS, with improvements in pocket design.

Supposedly, considering the geo-political situation of Italy during the late war years, and that Rome had been liberated by the Allies in 1944, this suit was manufactured by Giusti of Rome.

This late-war suit is nearly identical to the one produced by Giusti for the post-war Italian Air Force in the early-1950s, and used until the Giusti blue "BIS" type suit entered service in the late-1950s.

This rare and interesting photo sequence, showing the dressing of a 4th Fighter Wing pilot, allows an interesting view of his flight gear: electrically heated Model 40 flight suit, gloves and boots; Siemens flight helmet; Pirelli life vest; SALVATOR parachute; life raft; distress marker flares; oxygen mask. Courtesy Chianese

CHAPTER TWO

FLIGHT HELMETS

Since the beginning of aviation, flight helmets always represented the status symbol of being an aviator, much more than other flight gear components.

Flight helmets followed the evolution of aviation, starting as protective devices against cold air, relative wind, and noise. They evolved into very sophisticated gear, thus incorporating communication headsets, and later, in helicopter and jet helmets, visor data displays and gunsights.

Before the creation of the RA as an independent armed force, the various helmet types used by Italian flyers were basically the same as used at the beginning of aviation. There were two basic categories of flyers helmets: leather flight helmets, lined internally with fur or wool; and the hardshell crash helmets originally made in France by Roold and later reproduced locally. These were built using a cork shell, felt and other material covered with strong rubberized fabric, and were able to protect the flyer's head from moderate shocks.

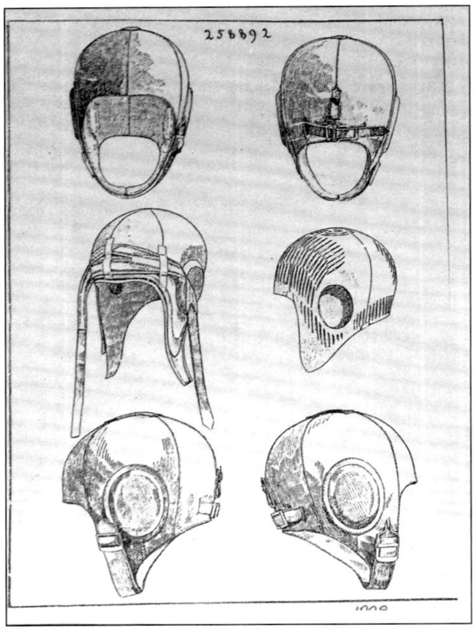

Commercial advertisements taken from magazines of the Italian aviation pioneer era, showing flight helmets produced by Vietti & Roncoroni of Milan.

It was common practice for aircrew to wear a wool balaclava underneath these helmets in order to improve the chill protection while flying in open cockpit aircraft.

The first models were not intended for military use as they were available on the civilian market, and produced by the most famous sportswear brands of that era.

Early flight helmets were used by aviators, auto drivers and bikers as well, so one can find leather helmets without aviation related utilities like goggles retaining straps and earphone holding cups.

In the early documentation of the newborn RA (1923), there are basic descriptions of flight helmets, and like the remainder of the flight gear, include descriptions of the type of materials to be used to manufacture them, like "soft leather" or "fabric," the color, and a basic pattern to be followed. This left some freedom to the makers to introduce variations to the standard outfit.

Moreover, particularly in the late-1930s, flyers were free to choose some items of their personal flight gear, like flight suits and goggles. Period images show the flight outfit customization carried on by Italian flyers of that era.

In addition to the various custom made flight helmets, the RA put into service two standard models of flight helmets: the former in soft calf leather produced in various shades of brown with light brown wool inner lining; and the latter in white, or hazel fabric, to be used for summer flying or in a tropical environment.

Both RA standard helmets shared the pattern with the leather "snails" on both sides for ear protection. These snails were closed by two snap buttons and contained two leather disks to reduce noise levels, or two earphone capsules, if the plane was radio equipped. Both models had a chinstrap with a small buckle and another small strap on the rear to hold the goggles elastic band.

The most widespread helmets of both versions were those produced by the Giusti factory in Rome. Giusti specialized in sportwears production, like the MARUS factory in Turin. In the early-1930s, Giusti was the MARUS products dealer for the Rome region, later on becoming an independent flight gear manufacturer.

With the GURA official document No.300 dated July 27, 1927 – signed off by Minister Balbo, and regarding RA uniform regulations, among other flight gear – there existed a new type of flight helmet produced by the Achille Saratti factory of Rome. This helmet was composed of four separated sections of aluminium fitted onto a thick rubber ring covered by brown leather. This helmet, named "protective helmet," although listed as standard equipment until 1930, was only used in RA flight schools and was later superseded by a new model produced by the Franco factory of Milan – the "Breda" flight helmet. The "Saratti" model was also produced by the Fumagalli factory of Milan.

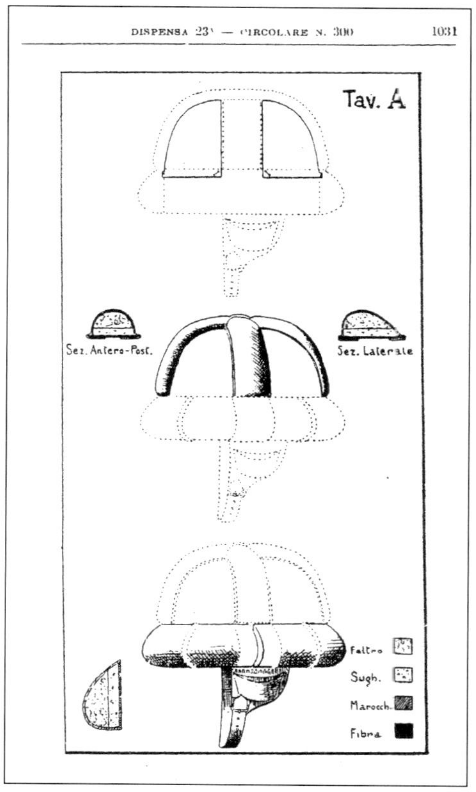

Page taken from the GURA document No.300, in 1927, with a description of the first type of protective flight helmet produced by the Saratti factory.

Early-1930s. The RA is now independent from the Italian Army. Several student pilots from one of the early RA Academy classes proudly pose for this group photo. Note the moleskin flight suits and the models Breda and Franco standard protective helmets. The photo at right was taken on October 7, 1931, the day of the first solo flight in a Breda A-4 of the RA Academy by Cadet Potito Santoro, who later became a general.

In GURA document No.590 of November 18, 1937, it states that all "fur lined flight helmets" were to be superseded by the new "earphone equipped flight helmets." And it's a matter of fact that until 1941, when a contract was signed with the MICROTECNICA factory in Turin, earphone equipped helmets were rare in the RA.

Another example of the early-1930s protective flight helmet. Courtesy MUSAM-ITAF

In 1942, with GURA document No.466, the RA Hardware Commissariat, among the flight gear listed, and although continuing to include the "protective helmet," stated that there was also a "leather fur lined helmet with provision for earphones." Later on in document No.663 of December 1942, signed off by Lt.Gen. Fougier, there was a further modification stating that the above mentioned helmet had to be provided with an electrical heating device.

No evidence exists that electrically heated helmets were ever put into active service by the RA, with exception of few French made electrically heated balaclavas captured during the French campaign in 1940.

Two VIPs: the Duke of Aosta and Ettore Muti, famous aviators of that period, showing what was then the standard Italian flight helmet – the famous Giusti flight helmet of Rome. Commander Muti's helmet shows the metal fittings for the "Gosport" intercom system.

Giusti flight helmet.

Guidonia Airfield, 1940. Colonel Pezzi, altitude record breaker for single-engined aircraft, is boarding his plane wearing the classic Giusti helmet.

The use of radiotelephonic helmets was strictly related to the presence of radio-equipped aircraft. Transport and bomber aircraft were usually equipped with a radio operated by a radioman. Conversely, single seat fighters were rarely equipped with a radio. It was common opinion among the fighter jockeys, that the radio was a useless additional weight and that it was an unaffordable device.

During the North African campaign in July 1942, the sixty MC.202s of the RA 4th Fighter Wing were radio equipped to allow them to fly interception missions with guidance provided by German Freya radar equipment. The radio equipment fitted to the outstanding MC.202 fighters was the Allocchio-Bacchini B-30 model.

After the armistice of September 8, 1943, there were two Italian Air forces: the Cobelligerent Air Force in southern Italy fighting on the side of the Allies, and the National Republican Air Force (ANR) in northern Italy fighting on the side of the Axis. Due to this situation, it was obvious that the use of RAF/USAAF flight helmets in southern Italy and Luftwaffe flight helmets in northern Italy.

Early Italian radiotelephonic flight helmets were usually normal leather/fabric helmets with field installed earphone capsules. In the late-1930s, some German derivatives were produced by various Italian manufacturers. During World War II, more advanced models

Radioman flight helmet with microphone and earphones, produced in 1930.

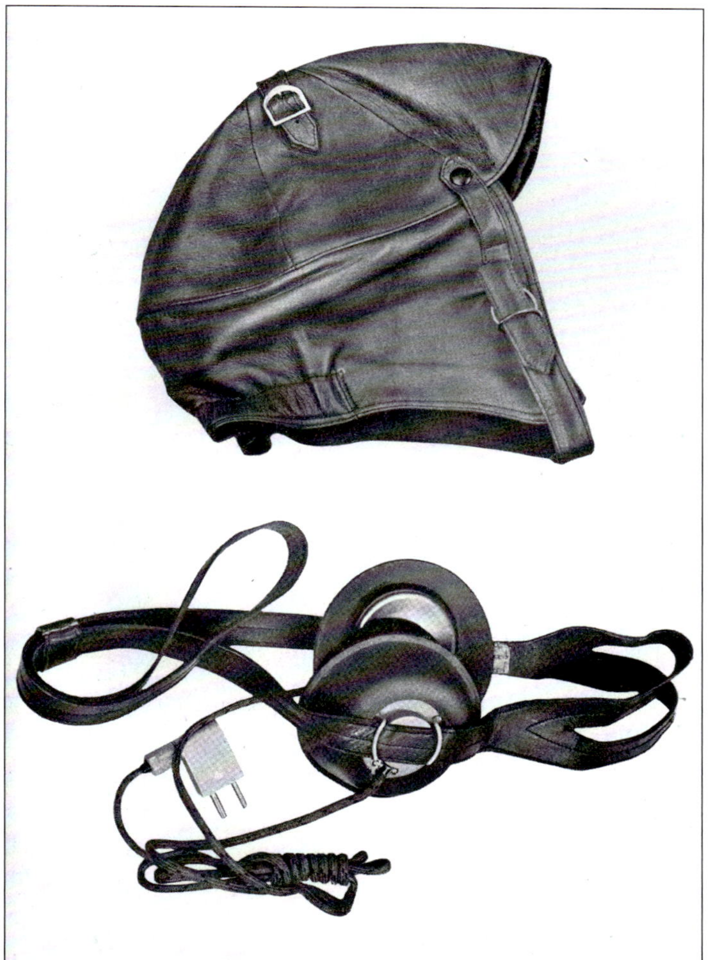

Fig. 31 - Casco telefonico.

Two radio headset variants for radiomen and usually delivered with the radio equipment.

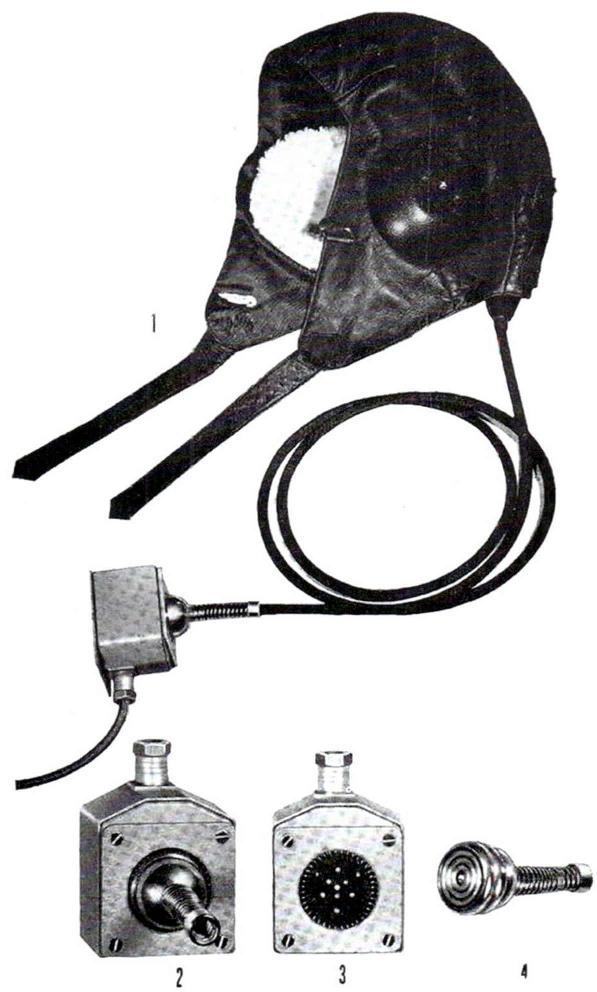

Fig. 16 - Complesso casco con spina a strappo: 1) Casco; 2) spina a strappo completa; 3) spina a strappo femmina; 4) spina a strappo maschio.

were produced in either leather or fabric. All of these models were equipped with earphones and throat microphones, either dynamic or magnetic. A rear communication cable ended with a plug that enabled easy disconnection from the plane in case of bail out. The main factories for these helmets were SAFAR, MICROTECNICA, the Italian SIEMENS and LESA. For a more detailed description of these helmets refer to, Caschi da Volo Radiotelefonici della Regia Aeronautica by this author.

Flight helmet with Siemens earphones.

Pilot Francesco Fagiolo onboard his MC.202 of the 51st Fighter Wing. He is shown wearing almost a bathing outfit with an Italian Siemens flight helmet.

These three fighter pilots are wearing the SAFAR winter helmets Model APP 8035, and summer fabric helmets Model 8120.

The two aircrew at left are wearing Microtecnica-Siemens flight helmets, and the one on the right wears a modified German LKpS 101 with the typical Italian radio plug made in different pattern by FEME and SAFAR. Courtesy P. Marzetti Archive

In addition to Italian models, the RA used large quantities of various German flight helmets, initially due to the use of Ju 87 and Bf 109 aircraft by the RA, and after September 1943 by the ANR (Lkpw-101, Lkps-101, Lkpn-101). The Cobelligerent Air Force in southern Italy used, along with surviving Italian helmets, RAF (C, D, E types) and USAAF (A-11, ANH-15) helmets.

SAFAR Model APP 8035 helmet with German oxygen mask Model HM-51.

The then Staff Sergeant Pilot F. Fagiolo is shown boarding his FIAT G.50 "Freccia" (arrow) fighter on a Belgian airfield during the Battle of Britain with the RA Expeditionary Air Corps (CAI). He is wearing a standard Giusti flight helmet.

During the early post-war period, a mixture of German and Anglo-American materiel was used by the newborn Italian Air Force (ITAF) until the mid-1950s to fly piston engined planes (Fiat G-46 and G-59, Spitfire, P-51, P-47) and early jets (DH-100). Some German flight helmets were converted to be used in Anglo-American planes, fitting suitable earphone capsules, throat microphones and connection plugs.

Early SAFAR winter flight helmet Model APP 7938. As discussed in this book, this fighter pilot of the 4th Fighter Wing has his name and rank (sergeant) painted on the earphones in white or yellow. Courtesy Chianese

Pilots of the 4th Fighter Wing ready for a unit transfer flight. They're all wearing SAFAR winter flight helmet. Courtesy Chianese

Above
Radioman onboard a multi-engined aircraft. He is shown wearing the white summer fabric flight helmet with a radio headset.

Top right
Fully garbed student pilot wearing a Saratti protective flight helmet.

Right
CR.42 fighter pilots ready for a mission. They are wearing SAFAR APR 8135 flight helmets, which means they're flying radio equipped CR.42s.

CHAPTER THREE

GOGGLES

In official documents, there exists evidence that the RA equipment service produced only a basic description of the flight goggles, although the relevance of these items as protective devices for the crewmembers requested more attention.

In the RA official journal GURA, with reference to uniforms regulations issue OD-4, it was reported: "... the flight goggles are of optional pattern, with crystal or glass lenses, either neutral or colored. Other types of transparent hardware (plastic) are allowed for the lenses."

This basic description allowed manufacturers to develop goggles according to their own specifications and for buyers to follow their personal taste.

The RA never standardized flight goggles for flight crews, although the most used models were those produced by the Ratti factory in Turin, particularly the "PROTECTOR" series.

There was also a limited use of French made (Cebè) and American made (Meyrowitz) goggles as well. Included in the personal logbooks of crewmembers was a list of flight equipment assigned, so it's possible to know the type of goggles used by the aviators.

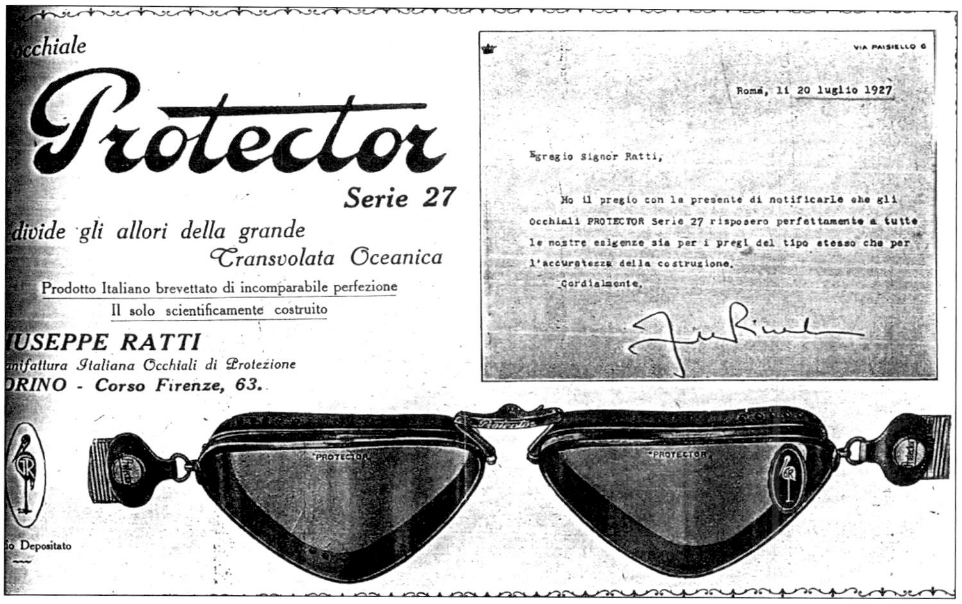

Commercial advertisement for the Protector Model 27 flight goggles from the magazine "L'Ala d'Italia" ("Wing of Italy").

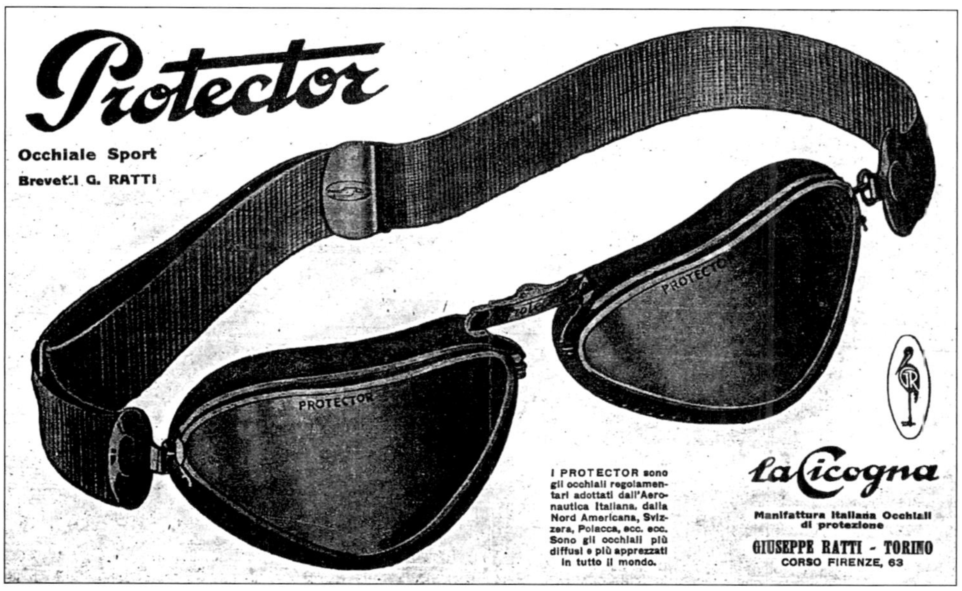

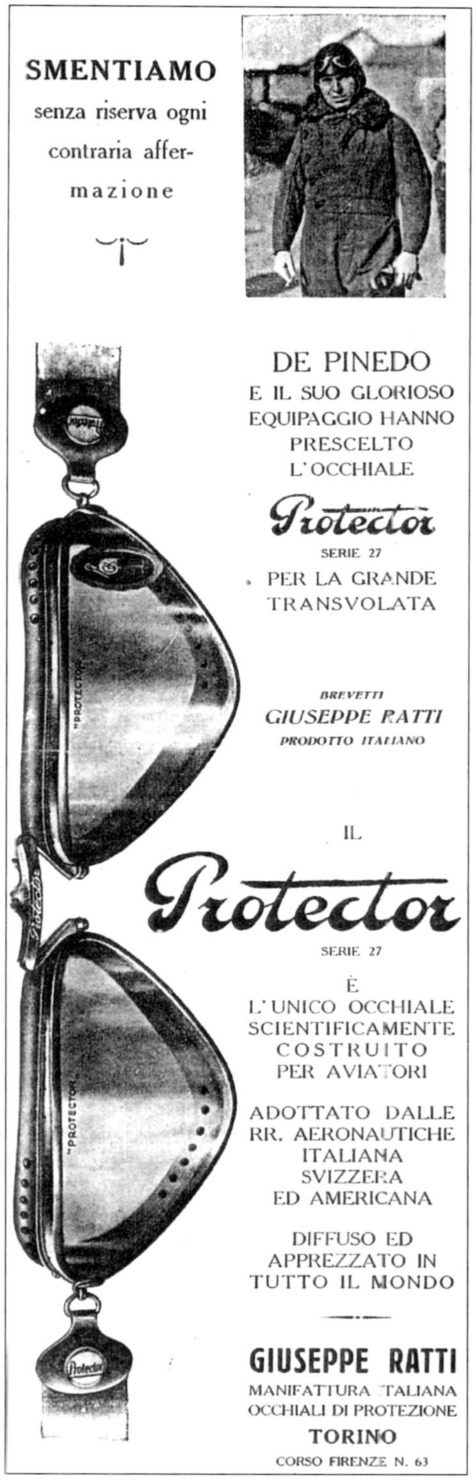

Protector Model 27 flight goggles with foam rubber cushions.

It was eventually deemed that flight goggles should meet some basic safety requirements like lightweight, handiness, resilience of frames and lenses, field of view width, anti-fog devices, etc.

In 1917, Giuseppe Ratti, owner of the BERRY optical factory in Caboto St. in Turin, started to produce goggles dedicated to sportsmen and aviators.

In 1927 Ratti created the first version of the PROTECTOR series with smoked lenses. They featured "cat eye" metal frames and lenses with soft facial rubber cushions incorporating small holes to avoid fogging.

An elastic headband provided easy wear on flight helmets and the RA immediately purchased large lots of these goggles. In several advertisements of that period, famous aviators, like F. De Pinedo, acted as testimonials for these successful goggles. Later on, several air forces of the world adopted the PROTECTOR goggles, including the USAAF. For this reason, even on batches produced during World War II, "MADE IN ITALY" is engraved on the frames.

The PROTECTOR model 27 was very similar to the following production batches; there were only little different details in the frame adjusting bridge, in the elastic band fittings and in the colors of the cushions, red or pale gray rubber. In the 1930s different models have been produced like the SUPER PROTECTOR with wider lenses and flat white rubber cushions instead of the PROTECOR 27 rubber tubes. This model featured an adjustable anti-fog system in the frame.

Advertisement for the Super Protector goggles.

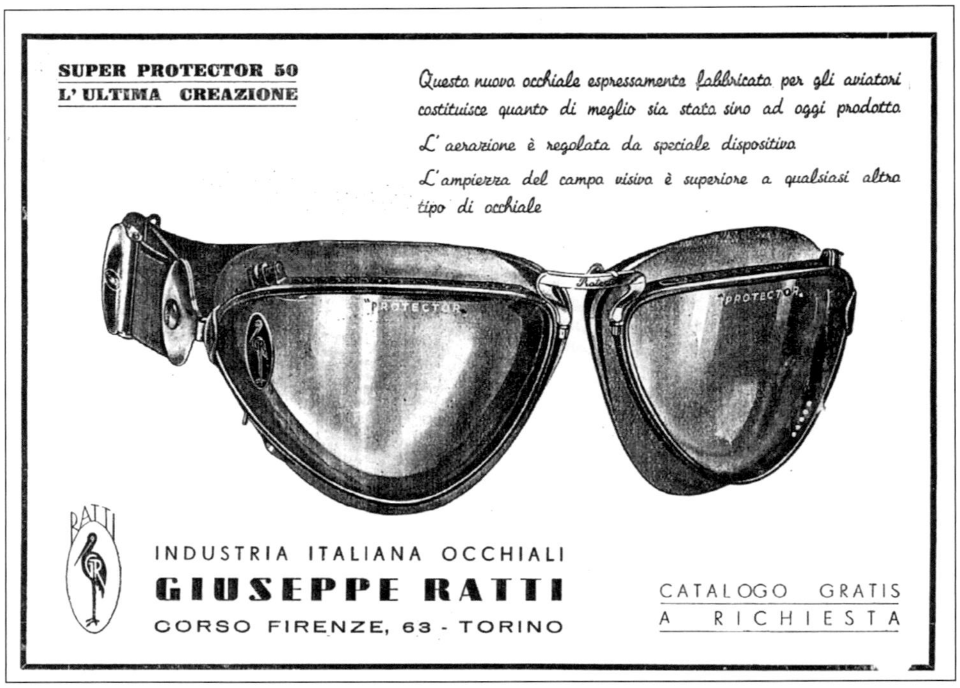

Advertisement for the Super Protector 50.

All of the models produced by Ratti feature the PROTECTOR logo engraved on the lenses, and on some goggles there is the famous "Chinese man with a Hammer" logo if provided with shatterproof lenses. Lenses could be made of glass, crystal, neutral or colored, curved or flat. Prescription lenses could also be fitted. Plastic lenses were fitted on cheaper models.

The various models in the PROTECTOR series were delivered in metal cases. These cases had various shapes and dimensions, depending on the model of the goggles. These little masterpieces are much appreciated by collectors.

In addition to the PROTECTOR series dedicated to aviation, the Ratti factory produced several other models such as the well known DICTATOR series. These goggles differed from the PROTECTOR series mainly in the bridge adjusting mechanism that used a small wheel fitted in the middle of the bridge, similar to the German Leitz models.

Another manufacturer was the FOPAIS Franchini factory (FOPAIS = FABBRICA OCCHIALI PER AVIAZIONE INDUSTRIA SPORT). Italian aviators greatly appreciated FOPAIS products and purchased a large quantity of these goggles as an alternative to the PROTECTOR models.

It was common practice that sales agents for the various flight gear manufacturers often loitered near RA flight schools to sell their flight suits, goggles, flight helmets and boots to student pilots at favorable purchase conditions.

The most famous FOPAIS goggles were the FRANCOR and VELTRIS models. The FRANCOR model had a rectangular frame, in aluminium or brass, with a solid bridge and two elastic headbands. The VELTRIS had "cat eye" lenses, similar to the RATTI models, and the bridge was either solid or adjustable. In the second case it featured a compass adjusting mechanism with central wheel or a sliding mechanism as well. The VELTRIS goggles were provided with a folding plastic sunshield. Also interesting is the adjustable anti-fog system with air filter used in the FOPAIS goggles series.

Also, the manufacturer delivered the more expensive models in metal cases, reserving paper boxes for cheaper models dedicated to the civilian and sports markets.

In addition to these widespread models, Italian flyers used many other goggle types conceived initially for auto drivers and bikers and modified for flight use, such as those produced by BARUFFALDI and IOPS and others.

This image was taken in the early-1950s showing student pilots during their training in the DH 100 Vampire. They're wearing Protector goggles over American A-11 leather helmets.

LINCE goggles used in Africa in the 1920s.

These two photos are from the early-1940s and show German goggles with velvet lined one-piece rubber cushions and large lenses.

Italian pilot wearing Protector goggles.

There is period photographic evidence of aircrewmen using Italian Army (Regio Esercito) anti-sand goggles normally used for desert operations along with tropical cork helmets, and particularly used in North Africa.

Furthermore, after the French campaign in 1940, the Italians captured large quantities of French materiel, including flight goggles produced by the OTO and CEBE factories.

RA crews, and later on ANR flyers, used large quantities of German goggles, particularly the NITSCHE und GUNTHER models. Sometimes Italian flyers traded these goggles with German flyers, a common practice among allies.

The Italian Cobelligerent Air Force in southern Italy used British flight goggles like the RAF Mk.VII and Mk.VIII. These were also used later by pilots in the 1950s when flying DH-100 Vampires in the new Italian Air Force.

CHAPTER FOUR

PARACHUTES

In 1928, the RA put its first parachute into service. The SALVATOR B model, it was conceived by Prospero Freri, a former World War pilot, and Giuseppe Furmanik, an engineer of Polish ancestry. They proposed their parachute to the new Italian Air Force in 1926.

The parachute as an emergency escape device for Italian aircrews was adopted by the RA due to Freri's insistence, tenacity, courage, and technical capabilities. He personally tested all his experimental parachutes and during his career logged 150 parachute jumps.

Freri's first prototype, the AERODISCENSORE ("air descender") was bulky and difficult to use. It was very similar to the parachute used by balloon crews during World War I. It was hefty and fitted to the fuselage skin of the aircraft and could be used only in a very limited flight envelope – definitely an impractical emergency device.

Left
Prospero Freri wearing the "AIRDESCENDER" harness. Courtesy MUSAM-ITAF

Right
Prospero Freri wearing the SALVATOR D-30 parachute. Courtesy MUSAM-ITAF

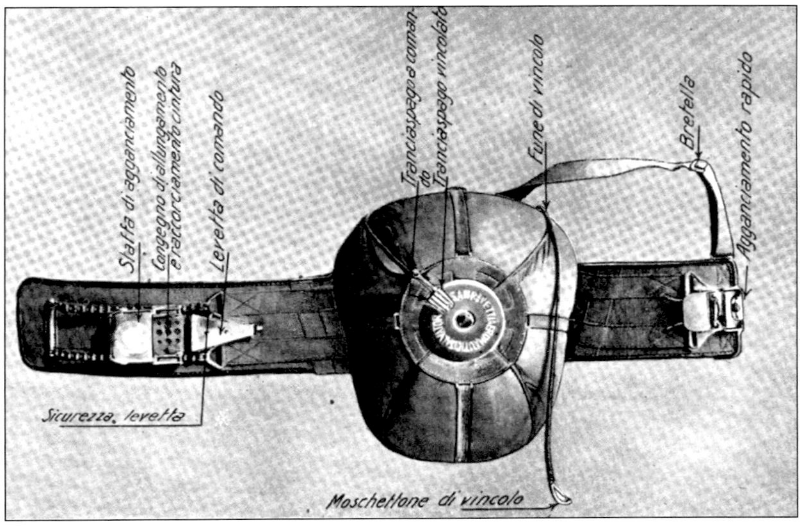

SALVATOR type B backpack parachute.

Rear view of the SALVATOR Model B parachute.

SALVATOR B in wear.

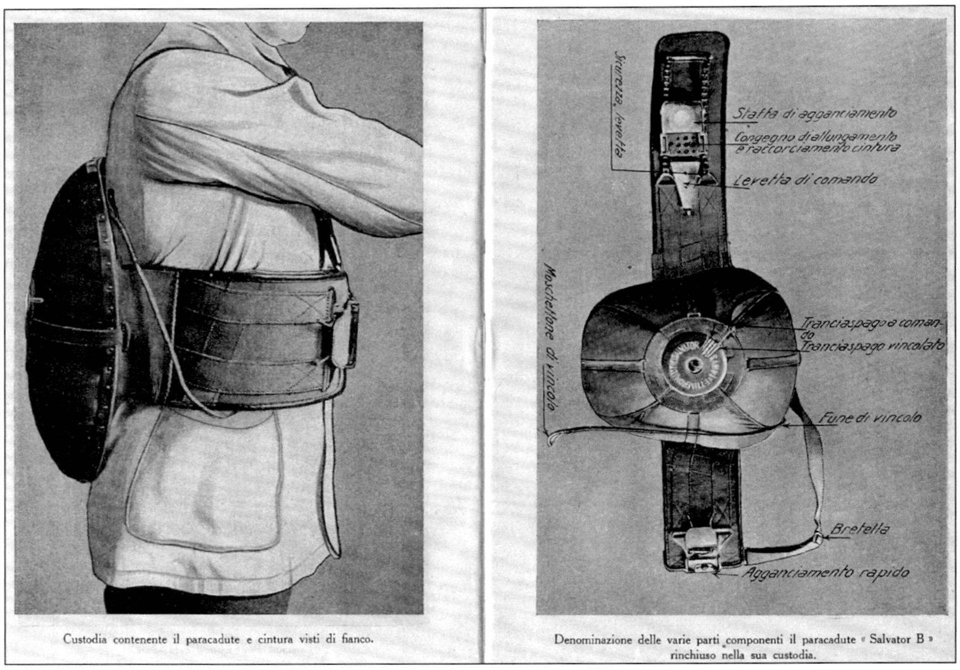

Image from the SALVATOR B operation manual.

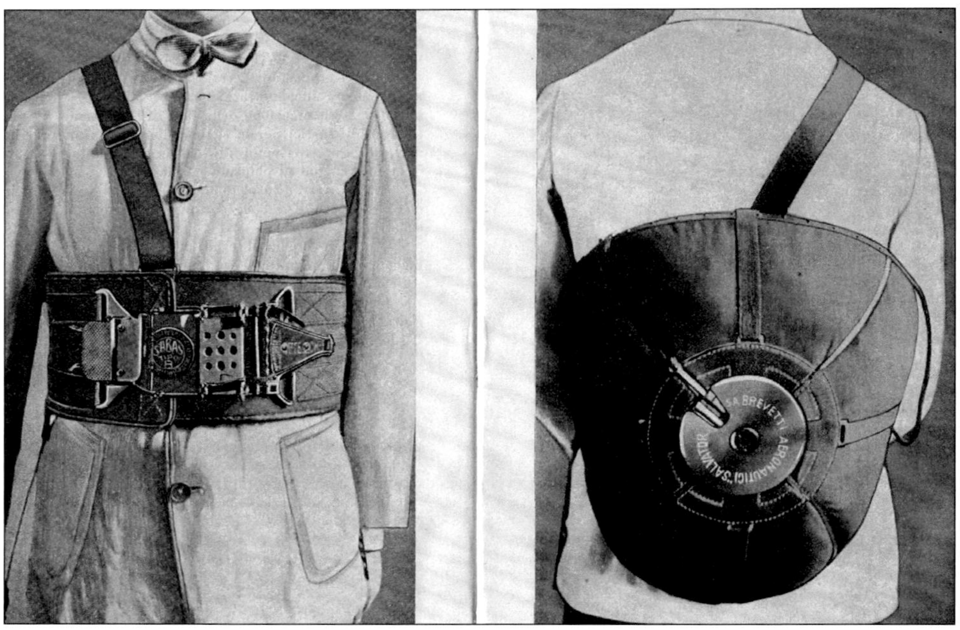

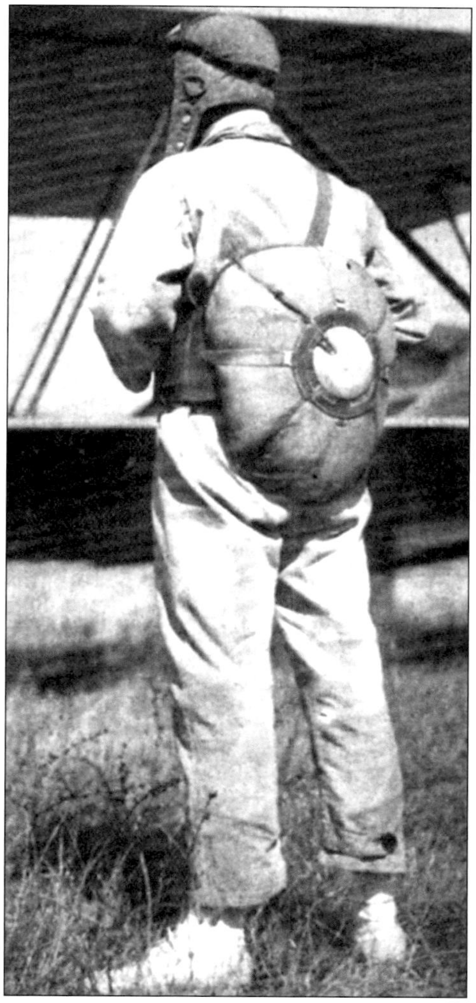

Left
Rear view of the SALVATOR B.

Right
RA pilot with SALVATOR B parachute.

Later on, Freri proposed to the RA Technical Bureau a new type named "SALVATOR A," which was basically the "air descender" with a few improvements. The real new development was the "SALVATOR B." Relatively light, 16.3kg, and small, it was a backpack type with a harness suitable to be donned easily over the flight suit. The new parachute could be opened manually via a pull handle or automatically with a lanyard hooked to the plane structure.

The lanyard for the automatic opening had a 350kg tensile strength and was hooked to the airplane structure with a metallic snap-hook. In case the airman could not open the parachute manually, the automatic device opened it after three seconds of free fall.

Development continued and a model "C" was created followed by a model "D," used also in the first postwar period, particularly in civilian flying clubs.

Many aviators' lives have been saved by the introduction of the parachute, however, unfortunate accidents occurred. On April 27, 1928, Lt.Gen. Guidoni died testing a SALVATOR parachute jumping over the Montecelio airbase, east of Rome. The airbase was renamed Guidonia to honor his memory.

Lt.Gen. Guidoni was an engineer on the RA technical staff, and was not sure of the affordability of the SALVATOR parachute. He decided to test it personally and died during the attempt. He wrote a letter before his fatal jump, with suggestions to improve the SALVATOR; this letter is now in the Italian Air Force Museum in Vigna di Valle near Rome.

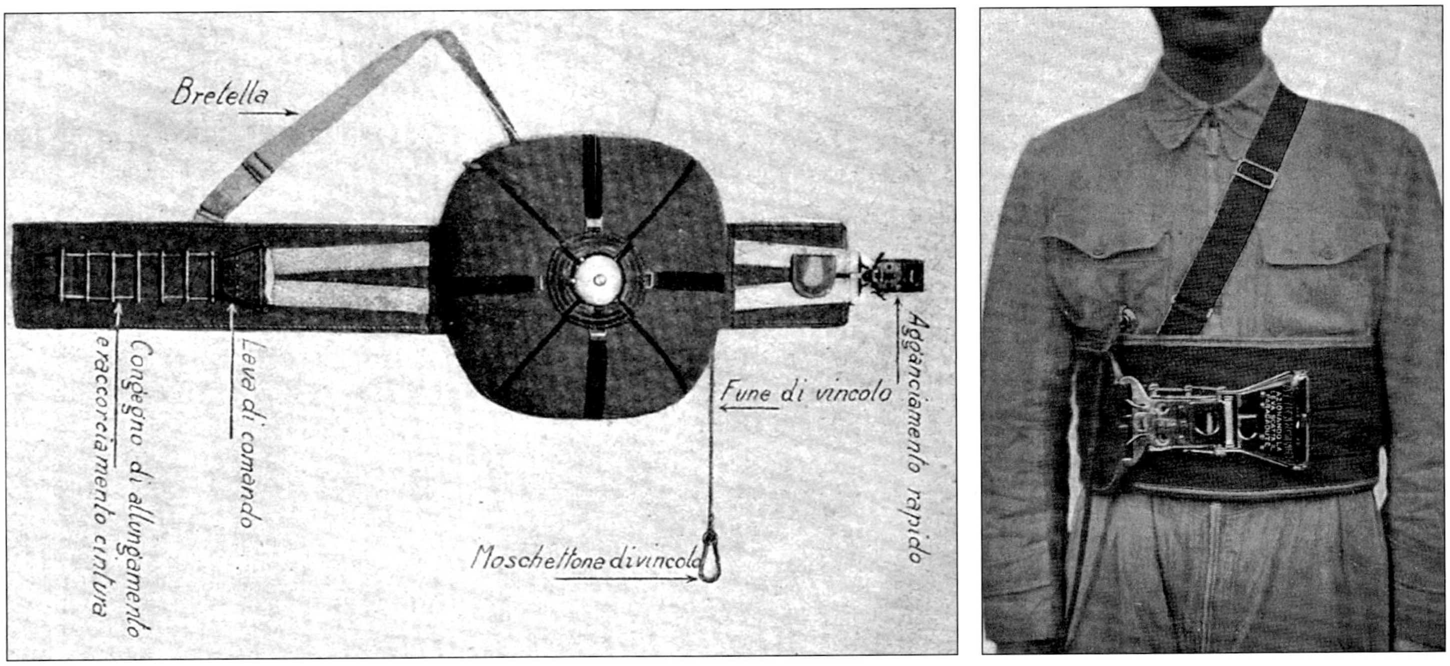

Operations manual image of the SALVATOR D-30.

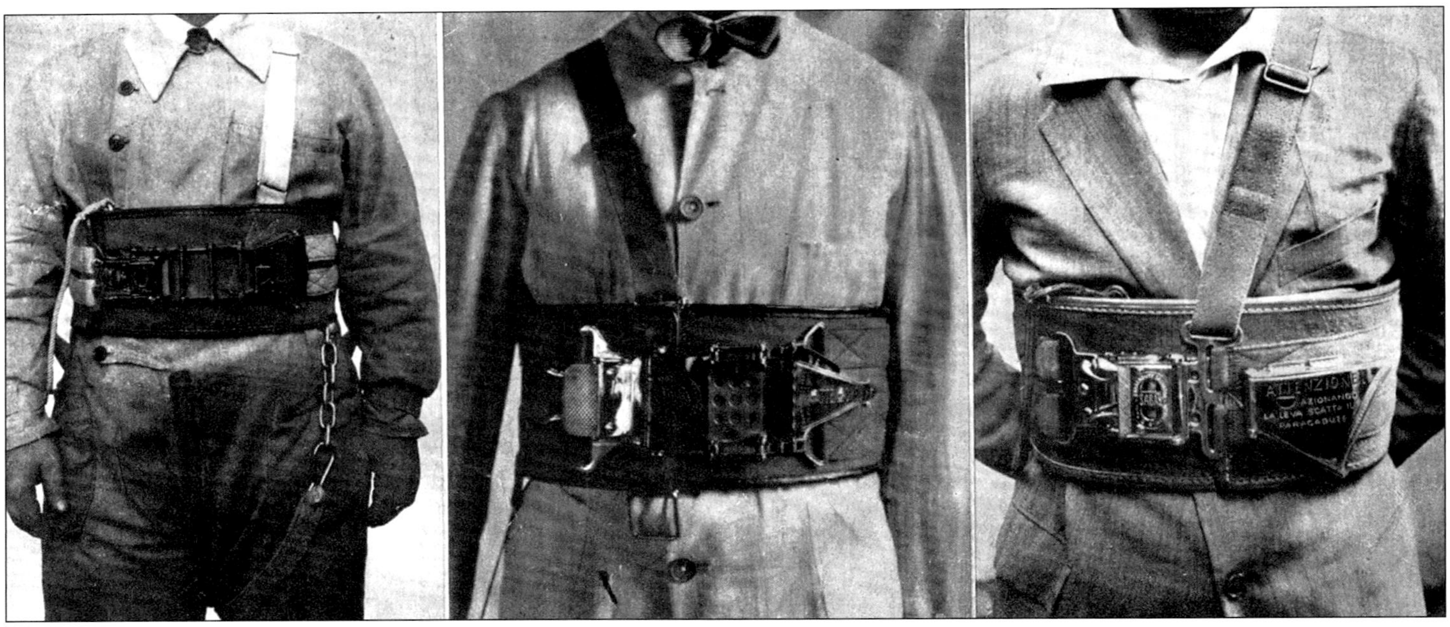

Harnesses of the parachute D-30, B and D.

Other singular accidents occurred during a mass dropping of troops over Libya. Several troops unbuckled from the parachute harness before reaching the ground, thus causing injuries and casualties. To this day the cause is unknown.

Due to several SALVATOR failures, many improvements were carried out on the parachute harness.

In the first models – until the Model 30 (the number stands for the entry year and the letters V, S, D stands for chest, seat, back type) – the harness was composed of a single thick leather chest belt with velvet inner lining holding the adjusting hook system and pull-handle, and by a diagonal belt passing over the right shoulder. Later on, the improvements were: an additional belt on the left shoulder, a crotch strap on the same side and later in the Model 39 these straps were doubled in order to have a symmetrical harness configuration.

It is possible to find in different production batches of the same model, a different harness configuration with snap hooks and blocking lever.

Parachutes were factory delivered with a carrying bag for transportation, a tool kit for the folding operation, and some spare parts.

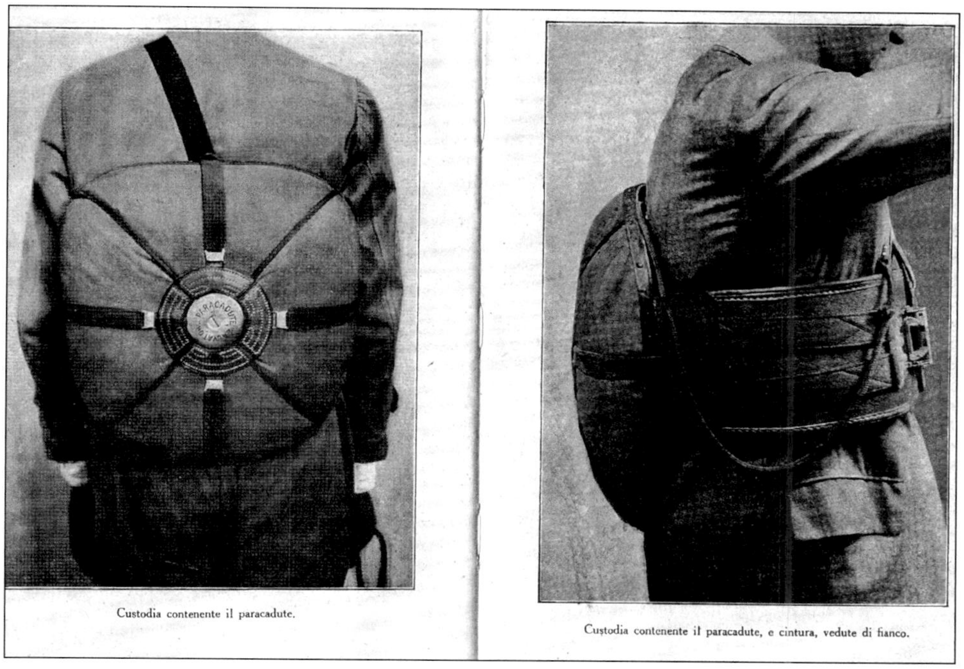

Operations manual of the SALVATOR D-30.

Left
Photo of a student pilot taken at Grosseto airfield. He is shown wearing the SALVATOR D-30.

Right
Detachable SALVATOR A-30 for use by aircrew.

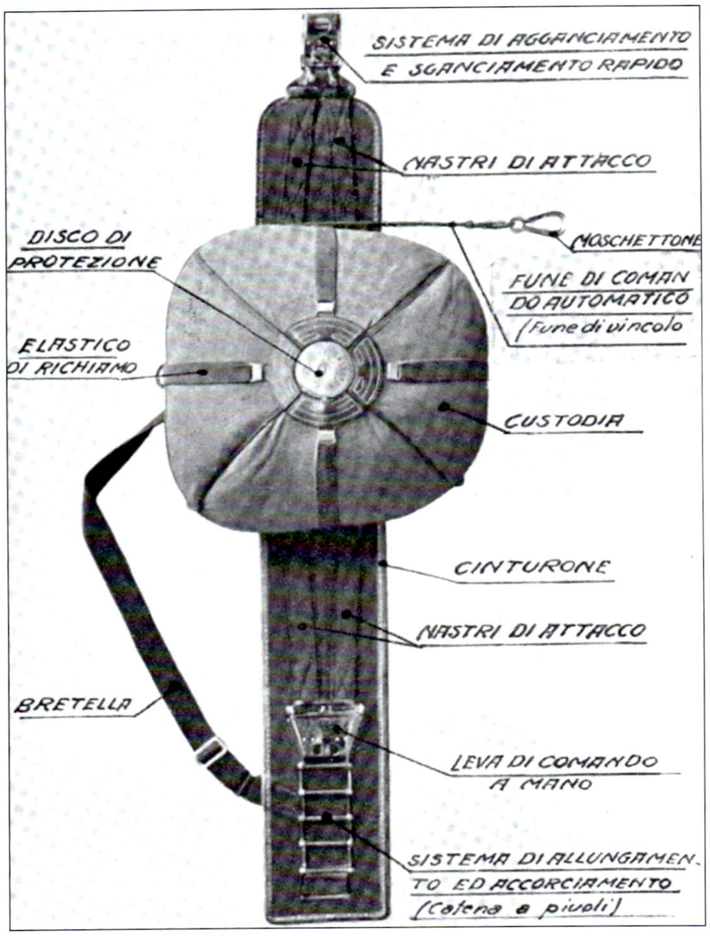

First variant of the SALVATOR D-30.

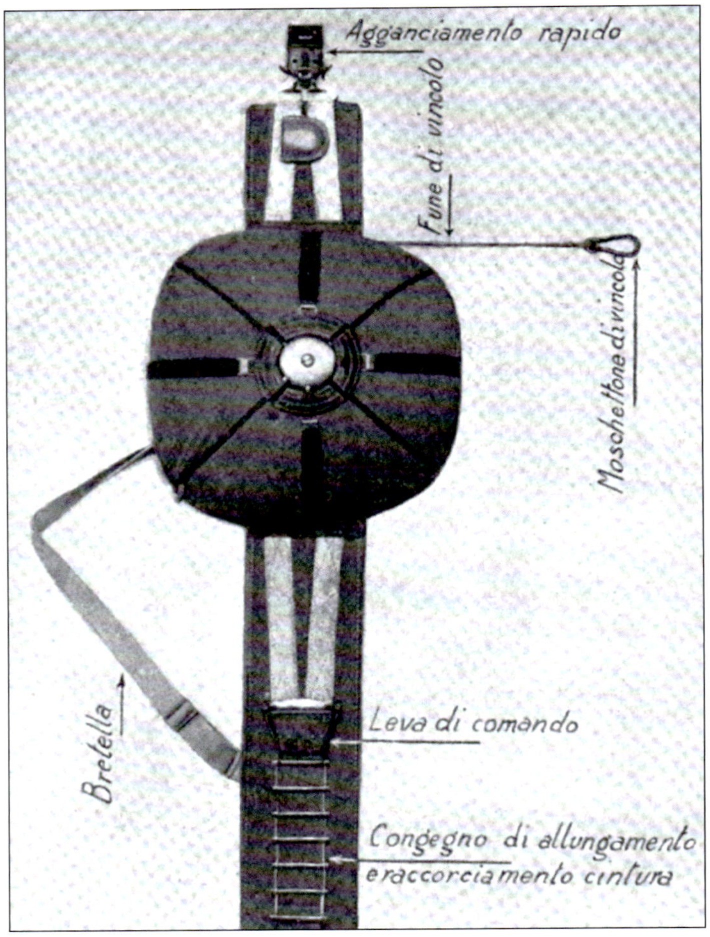

Second variant of the SALVATOR D-30.

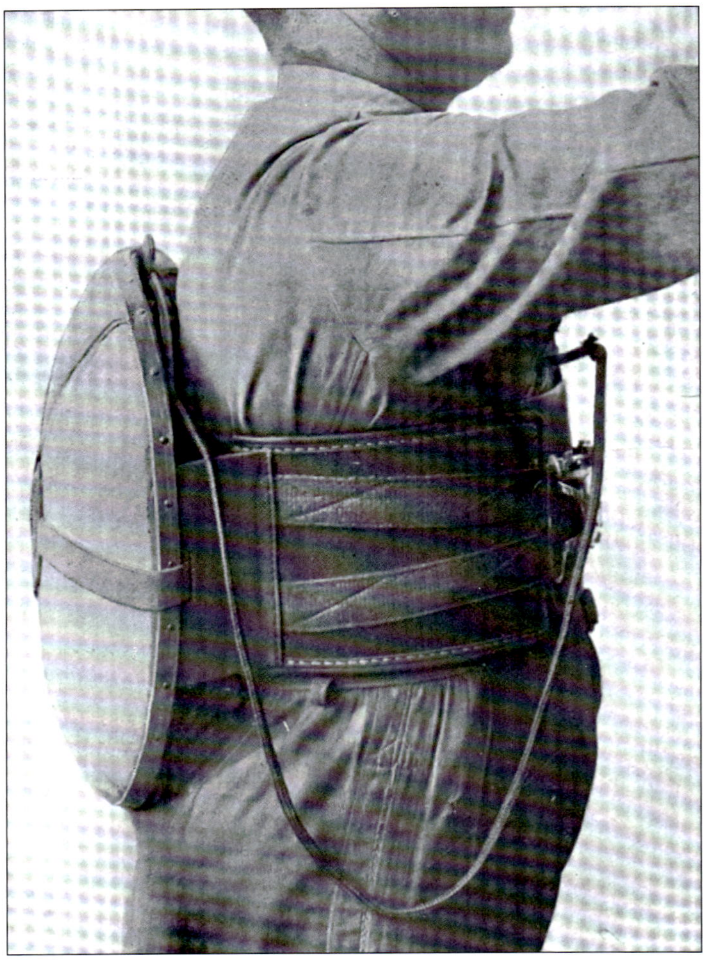

SALVATOR D-30 backpack parachute.

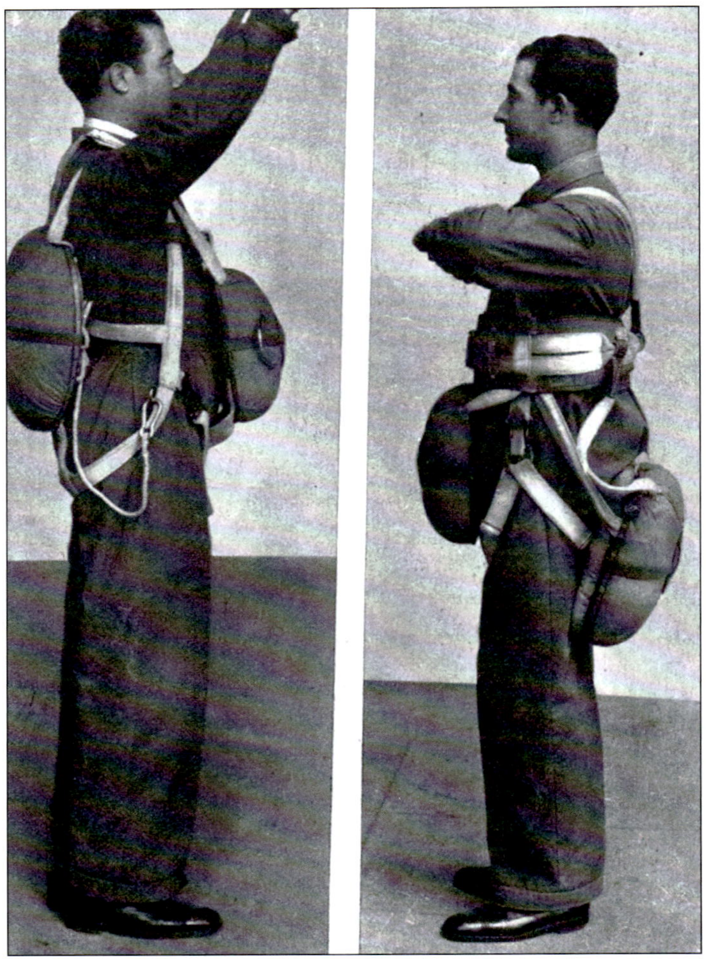

SALVATOR D.I. with harness and training strap.

The last series of the SALVATORs were affordable devices and their production continued until the early-1960s for the Italian Air Force.

Carrying bag and accessories for the SALVATOR parachute as depicted in the RA booklet "the Parachute."

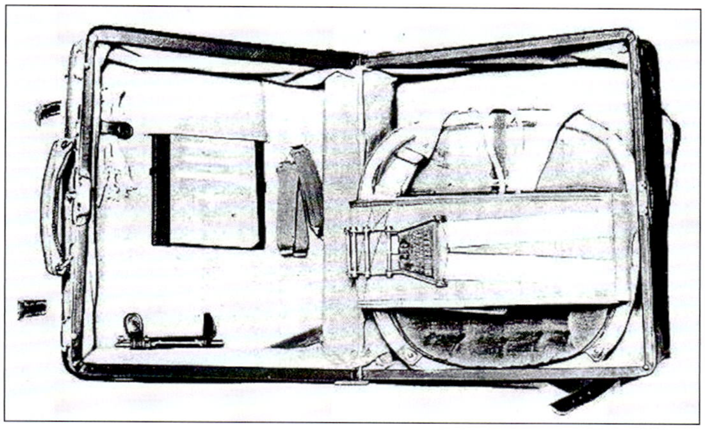

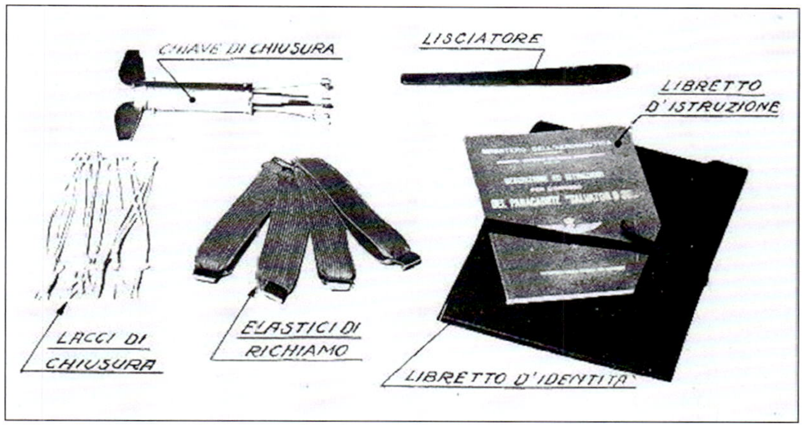

As for other parachute equipment used during World War II, the RA and ANR also used German and French parachutes, the Cobelligerent Air Force used British and American parachutes.

SALVATOR D-30 with strap.

SALVATOR S-30.

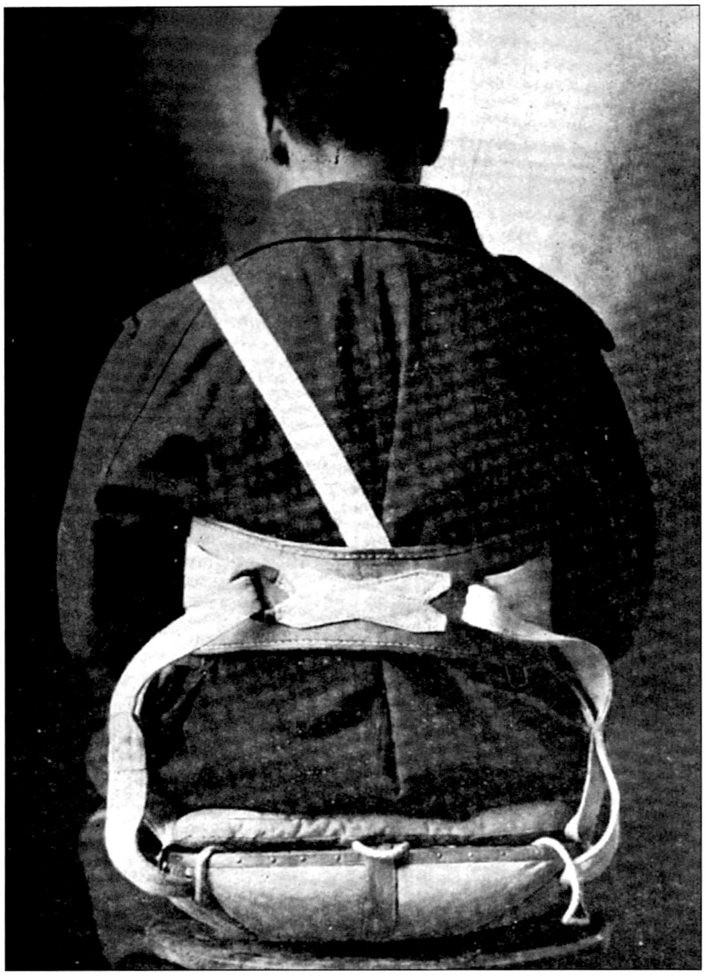

SALVATOR S-3 with padded container.

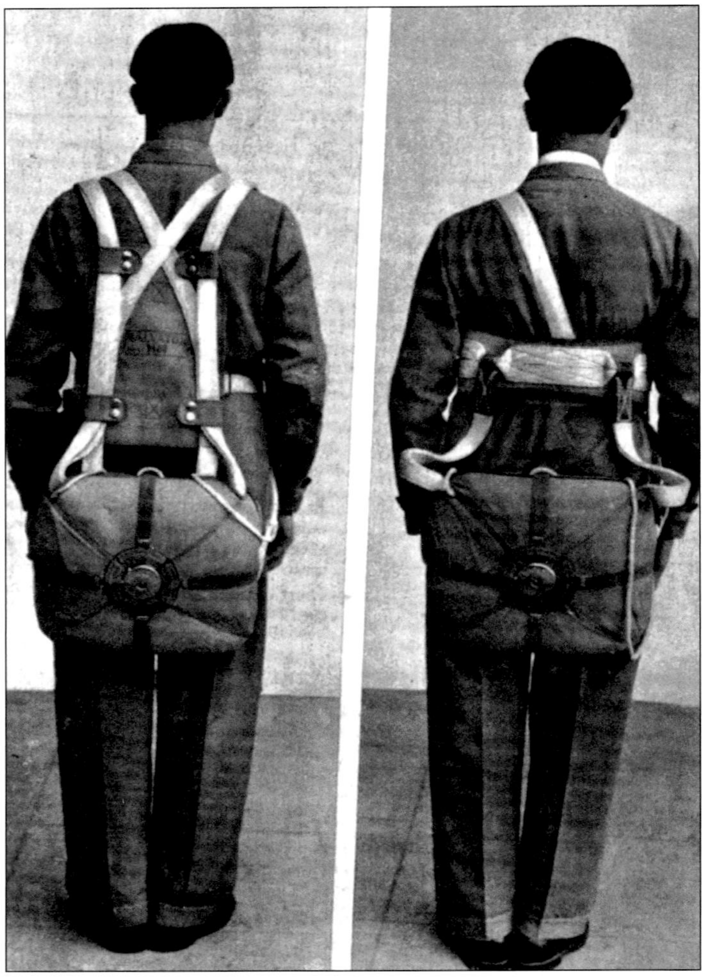

S-30 with harness and strap.

Pilots wearing SALVATOR D-39 parachutes.

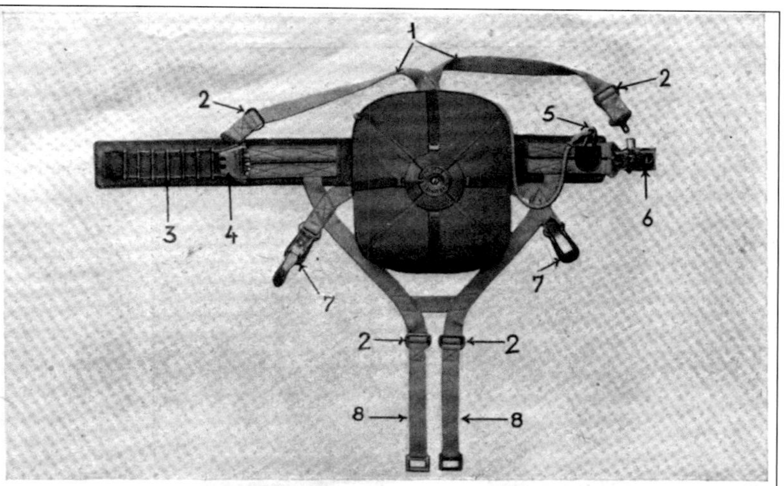

Denominazione delle varie parti componenti il paracadute *Salvator D 39* rinchiuso nella sua custodia. (Vista all'esterno).

1. Bretelle – 2. Fibbie di regolazione – 3. Congegno di allungamento ed accorciamento cintura – 4. Leva di comando – 5. Moschettone e fune di vincolo – 6. Agganciatura – 7. Ganci a scocco – 8. Cosciali.

Denominazione delle varie parti componenti il paracadute *Salvator D 39*, rinchiuso nella sua custodia. (Vista interna).

1. Bretelle – 2. Fibbie di regolazione – 3. Agganciatura – 4. Ganci a scocco – 5. Cosciali.

SALVATOR D-39.

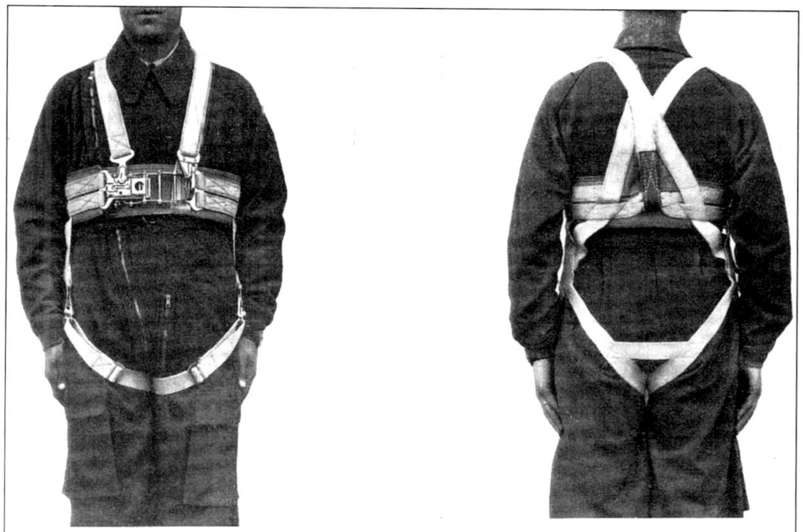

Salvator A 39 (senza custodia) visto davanti.

Salvator A 39 visto di dietro.

A-39 parachute harness.

CHAPTER FIVE

LIFE VESTS

Although this piece of flight gear has to be considered "vital" for the survival of downed aircrew at sea, the RA dedicated scarce attention to life vests.

During the RA's early years, the life vest, named "life jacket" by the RA, was intended for seaplanes crews only, so ground based aircrews did not receive this item as standard equipment, even if they flew overwater missions!

Very early examples were rather basic and were mere inflatable belts in order to reduce their dimensions. They could be orally inflated and donned with a harness or like a jacket. They were made with kapok or cork segments to permit buoyancy. Often they were the same models used by the RM (Royal Italian Navy). Due to their basic construction these life vests were bulky and impractical.

Seaplane bomber crews wearing kapok life preservers during the early World War II years. Courtesy L'Ala D'Italia and Nei Cieli di Guerra

Aircrewman of the 30th Wing at Sciacca airport in 1940, wearing the kapok life preserver and German LkpS 64 flight helmet. Courtesy N. Virgilio (L'Aeroporto fantasma)

In the mid-1930s, some experimental life vests were developed meeting aviation requirements, and suitable to be worn underneath a parachute harness.

In the following years, particularly at the beginning of World War II, and due to the challenging extended overwater missions required by the war scenarios (English Channel, and the Mediterranean), all possible live vest types were put into service by the RA

Initially, to deal with the unforeseen need for life vests, the RA adopted RM models, or their derivatives – mostly the kapok/cork types with "sausage" shaped padding.

As noted previously, they were bulky and impractical, limiting the mobility of crewmembers inside the aircraft. Major problems arose if a parachute harness should be worn over them.

These types were also produced with special shaped buoyancy segments with recessed spaces to accommodate the harness of the German seat type parachute delivered with Ju 87 aircraft. Also, the Luftwaffe kapok type vest entered into R.A service.

Along with the earlier bulky models, a model with oral inflatable bladders came into service. This type of life vest was made with yellow rubberized fabric and could be donned by putting the head in the upper hole of the jacket. Some models also had a lap belt.

In addition to the low effectiveness due to their poor wearing solution, it was impractical to orally inflate the bladders after getting rid of the parachute in the water or a life raft after ditching.

MC.200 fighter pilot wearing a kapok life preserver shaped in order to wear the SALVATOR D-39 parachute. Courtesy N. Virgilio (L'Aeroporto fantasma)

Several problems were reported by crews flying at high altitudes; they often experienced the inflation of their life vests due to the expansion of the residual air trapped inside the bladders, causing the seat and parachute harnesses to become intolerably tight. For this reason, crewmembers carried a knife or pointed tool to pierce the bladder. This operation, of course, damaged the vest and one could only hope not to have to use it during the remainder of the mission.

Above and left
Another type of kapok life preserver shaped to fit the SALVATOR D-30 parachute.

A Ju 87 pilot is shown putting on his German flight gear before a dive-bombing mission.

As for the kapok life vests, they were too stiff and if an aircrewman ended up in a facedown attitude drowning was possible due to the large rear collar of some of these models. This large collar was conceived to help maintain the wearer's head well above the water level if in a correct floating attitude.

The only inflatable models produced for the RA were the "jacket" type. The bladders could be inflated orally through a thin rubber tube that could be closed with a small cap or by folding it. There is no evidence of automatic inflatable life vests produced in Italy.

A FIAT CR.42 fighter pilot wearing a shaped kapok life preserver.

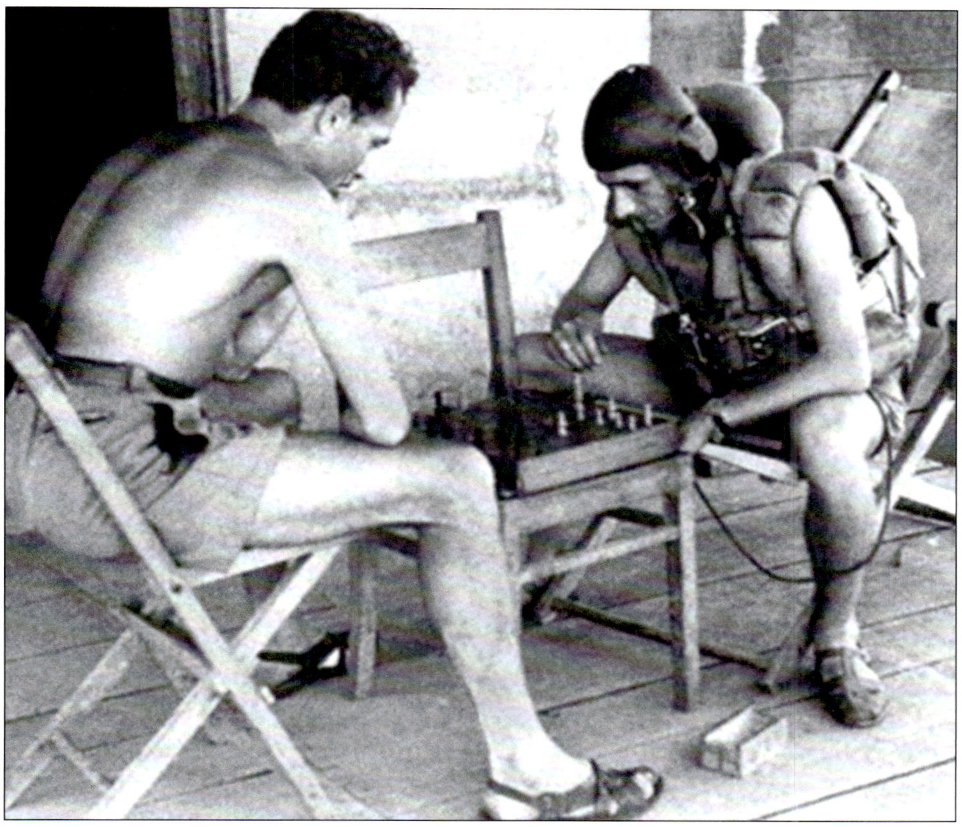

A ready alert pilot ready for take off in the hot Sicilian climate. He's almost in a bath outfit, but wearing his SALVATOR parachute and life preserver. Courtesy N. Virgilio (L'Aeroporto fantasma)

RA aircrew wearing different types of life preservers.

After September 1943, the ANR extensively used German automatic inflatable life vests, and the Cobelligerent Air Force used Anglo-American types.

Although not particularly known, the RA was involved in the Battle of Britain with an expeditionary force named the CAI, and was composed of a relatively small number of bombers and fighters.

Rare picture of the Pirelli collar life preserver. Courtesy Chianese

Right
Two airmen preparing for a mission wearing the most advanced Pirelli life preservers. Taken from Nei Cieli di Guerra.

Far right
These two airmen are wearing the most advanced Axis life preservers: the German SCHWIMMWESTE and the Italian SICURSALVA. Courtesy N. Virgilio. (L'Aeroporto fantasma)

The Germans, after seeing the inadequate equipment of Italian aircrews, supplied them with electrically heated flight suits, fur-lined flight boots, and life vests – the SCHWIMMVESTE Model 10-30B-2.

Another picture of the SICURSALVA life preserver. Courtesy Chianese

This pilot wears the first variant of the SICURSALVA. Courtesy Chianese

Additional pictures showing how the SICURSALVA was worn. Courtesy Chianese

This group of pilots shows a second lighter variant of the SICURSALVA; the front part is smaller in order to be more comfortable. Courtesy Chianese

CHAPTER SIX

OXYGEN MASKS

World War II era RA oxygen masks are very rare today, and quite difficult or even impossible to find on the collectors' market. Due to small production batches, few Italian oxygen masks survived after the end of the war.

The RA, though having oxygen systems fitted onboard its aircraft since early-1930s (reference here is a technical document of the OMI factory dated 1932), did not give priority to this important asset. This was due to the Italian aviation strategy of the period, the relatively low performances of the aircraft, and the rather basic industrial skills of the country.

With the exception of some cumbersome experimental oxygen delivery systems used for the altitude record breaking attempts – Donati 1934, Pezzi 1937, Negroni 1935 – the industrial standard systems were quite basic.

The standard oxygen system was a high pressure one. Oxygen was contained in a metal bottle and delivered to the mask through a thin rubber hose. There was a regulator that mixed and diluted the oxygen automatically or manually depending on the altitude.

Pilot Renato Donati at Guidonia airfield on November 4, 1934 after his altitude record-breaking flight of 14,433 meters flying a Caproni CA.113. He is wearing a MARUS Model 30 flight suit with electrical heating and an experimental oxygen mask conceived for the record attempt. Courtesy MUSAM-ITAF

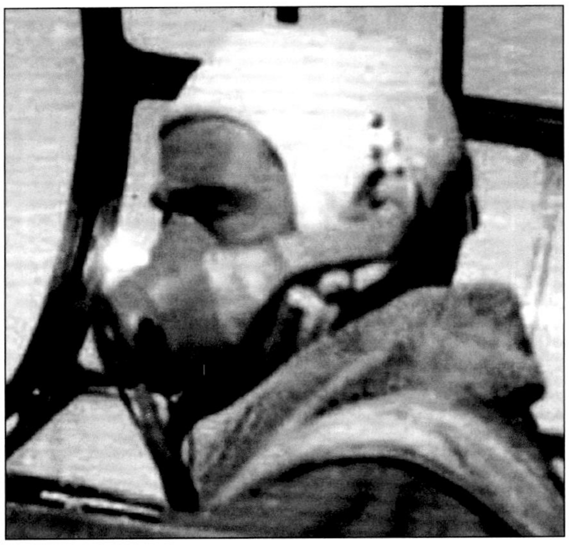

The standard oxygen mask produced by FILOTECNICA and nicknamed the "dognose." Courtesy Chianese

The RA standard oxygen mask was made of a gray-green rubber and covered the nose and mouth of the wearer. The face piece was shaped into a truncated cone, and because of its shape was nicknamed the "dognose" or "pignose by the aviators that used it. This mask was easily donned having only an elastic band to secure it around the head. The elastic band was riveted on both sides of the mask and an adjustment buckle was provided. On the rear side of the Giusti flight helmet, there was a leather strap to hold the mask band.

On the front of the mask, there was a large cylindrical cap about one inch thick, with a joint for the thin oxygen hose. The front cap could contain an electrical (de-icing) heater to avoid two problems:

1.) Icing of the residual moisture contained in the oxygen tank due to the rapid expansion of the oxygen inside the pressure regulator device, with ice build up inside the feeding lines.

2.) Condensation and icing inside the mask body due to the wearer's breathing. The mask did not have an exhaust valve and this caused several anoxia events. Improved Italian masks were tested, but being that the German Draeger system was more affordable, the decision was taken to use this system as the standard.

The first problem was fixed by inserting a small electrical heater in the pressure-reducing device. The icing inside the mask body was fixed clamping a small 12v/32w heater on the front cap, the wiring held along the oxygen hose by a tubular metallic net.

Conversely, as reported by some sources, it is now clear that Italian oxygen masks were never fitted with microphones – like German masks as well. The use of a throat microphone was standard for both air forces. Italian and German throat microphones were of two types: separate units, or placed within the flight helmets (only if these helmets contained a built-in earphone system). The Italian wired flight helmets were patterned after the Luftwaffe's.

It's clear that the shape of the mask and its rather basic donning system did not provide a good level of comfort and sealing, particularly during the high G forces involved in close combat.

During the 1930s, particularly in open cockpit aircraft (CR.32, CR.42 etc.), the majority of Italian fighter pilots preferred to use a bare oxygen tube held between their teeth. Sometimes a ceramic cigarette holder was used. This was a common practice in bomber crews as well. This practice was quite an impractical and unhygienic solution, as confirmed by veterans to the author. They said also that the oxygen hoses were often lying on the cockpit floor, so were dirty, and contaminated by oil, and grease.

Veterans also mentioned to the author that they used the mask with the flight goggles. The mask leaked so badly that the lenses of the goggles quickly fogged. In order to avoid this problem they again used the old "hose between the teeth" method – but the hose (with or without the mouthpiece) also froze up inside their mouths.

For these reasons, in open cockpit fighters and in the multi-crew aircraft, particularly during the first years of service with the oxygen systems, the use of the bare rubber tube held by the teeth was a wide spread practice among Italian aircrew. Icing apart, problems arose due to the careless usage.

During the following years, while more challenging tasks and increased aircraft performances required new oxygen technologies, there were few modifications to the standard "dognose" mask. Conversely, remarkable improvements were achieved on the side of the regulating devices for single-seat fighters and bombers.

The factories involved in oxygen systems production for the RA were: OMI (Ottica Meccanica Italiana, also producing optical equipment and almost the whole range of magnetic compasses), ISSA, FILOTECNICA, PIRELLI, and SALA-CIAMBERLINI, just to name a few of the more important firms.

The "dognose" mask was also produced in a portable version, suitable for fitting to a parachute harness in order to permit bomber crewmen movement inside the plane. This type was similar to the American "bail out" system.

In 1941 the RA aviation magazine "Rivista Aeronautica" published an article regarding the oxygen mask conceived by Prof. Margaria, produced by FILOTECNICA and PIRELLI and was named after its designer: the "Margaria type mask."

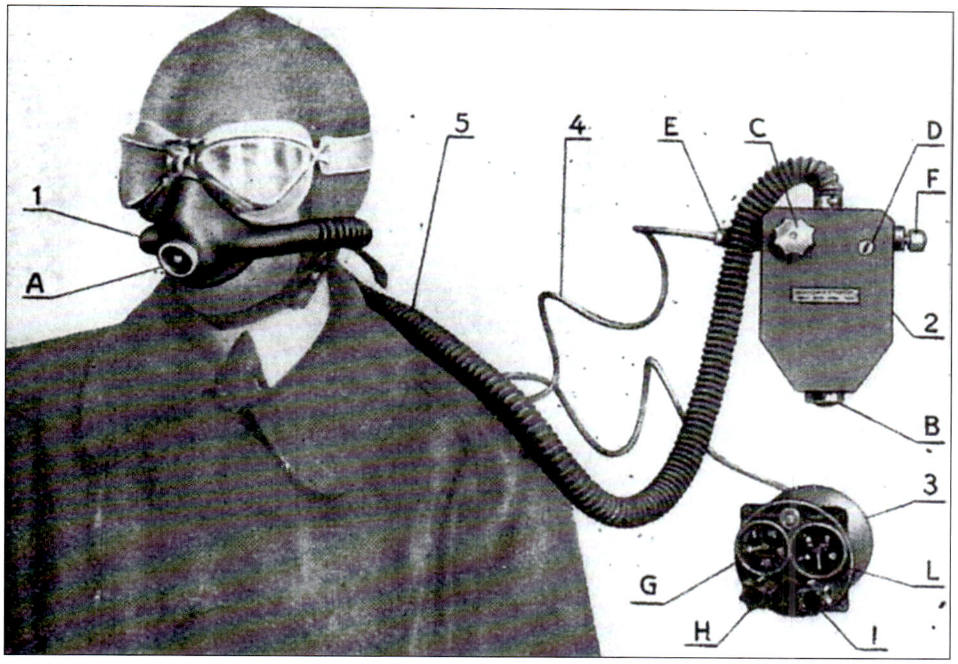

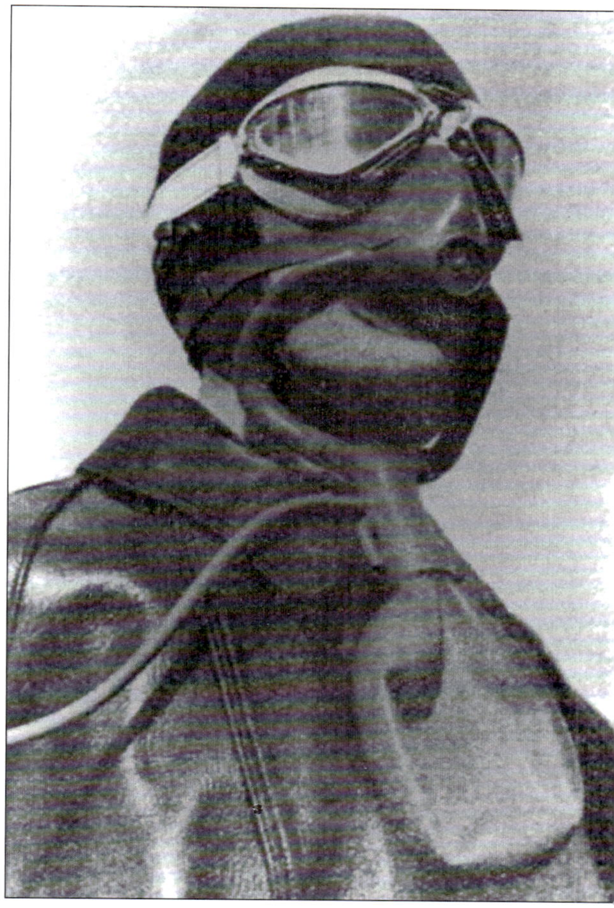

Two different models of the "MARGARIA" oxygen mask, named after its inventor Dr. Margaria.

Prof. Margaria was the head of the Guidonia Medical Research Center. He conceived a new type of oxygen system that enabled Italian flyers to deal with the decrease of the oxygen partial pressure at high altitudes in a better way. The new system also reduced oxygen consumption thus increasing endurance.

The new system was the first Italian "demand" type, meaning that the oxygen flow was regulated by the pilot's breathing rate and not a continuous flow of oxygen in the mask as in previous masks. The "demand" type was already in use in the USAAF, RAF and Luftwaffe.

In the rather basic continuous flow Italian systems, the flyer received a continuous flow of pure oxygen with a lot of waste. Some little improved systems mixed the oxygen with the air thus allowing an exhaled mixture to be rebreathed by the flyer and wasting part of the delivered oxygen.

The Margaria's system, showed here in a rare image, was available for a single pilot or multi-crew, and was composed by the mask body available in two versions: nasal and oronasal.

The mask had an exhalation valve (A). The oxygen flowed through the corrugated hose (5) to the "lung" contained in the box (2). At the bottom of the box, in communication with the lung, there was an inspiration valve (B). Through this valve passed the flow "on demand" to the flyer:

- By the box containing the rubber lung (in the first version it was fitted directly to the lower part of the mask, like the American A-8 model) linked to the mask by a corrugated hose.

- By the control box (diluter) from which the low pressure oxygen was delivered to the rubber lung in the box through the low pressure line; the box got the hi pressure oxygen from the oxy bottle through a second thin metal line. The control box enabled a further pressure reduction and adjusted the flow according to the flight altitude.

The control box had two gauges to check the system: the bottle high-pressure gauge and the flow meter. The system granted breathing sea level condition between 4,000 and 10,000 meters in altitude. This system has been deemed superior to the one developed in the U.S. by Boothby and Lovelace, scientists at Mayo clinic in 1940.

As stated previously, due to the tragic and repetitive failures of early Italian oxygen systems caused casualties and aircraft losses. In 1941, on new production aircraft, particularly the Macchi MC.202, Reggiane RE.2001 and in the forthcoming "series 5" fighters, new oxygen systems were fitted produced by the famous German DRAEGER factory.

Three photos showing details of the standard RA oxygen mask. Courtesy MUSAM-ITAF

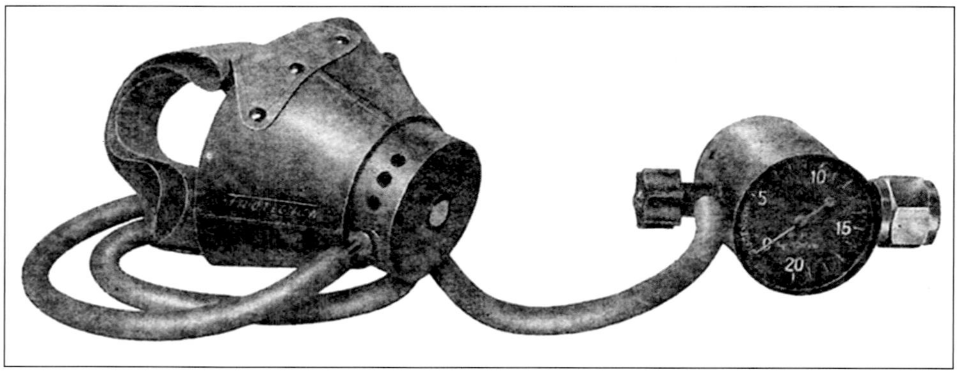

Oxygen system image taken from the FILOTECNICA catalog of 1941.

Crew of the 30th BW wearing the portable oxygen system. Courtesy N. Virgilio (L'Aeroporto fantasma)

Another photo of a 30th BW pilot. Courtesy Canton

German oxygen masks used by the RA with the DRAEGER systems were either "two hook" or "three hook" types. The Italian flight helmets were adapted for the use of these masks.

German types used by the RA were mostly the 6701, the HM-5, the 1067 and the 1069e, used until September 1943, and by ANR flyers in the Fascist Republic of Northern Italy until April 1945. There is no evidence that any of these masks were produced under license in Italy.

Airman wearing the portable oxygen system.

INALATORE DI OSSIGENO "I. S. S. A."
Mod. CIAMBERLINI

Figura 1.

Oxygen system produced by I.S.S.A.

Nice image of a MC.200 pilot ready for a high-altitude flight. Courtesy N. Virgilio (L'Aeroporto fantasma)

FILOTECNICA oxygen system as depicted in the 1941 catalog.

Radioman wearing the "dognose" oxygen mask.

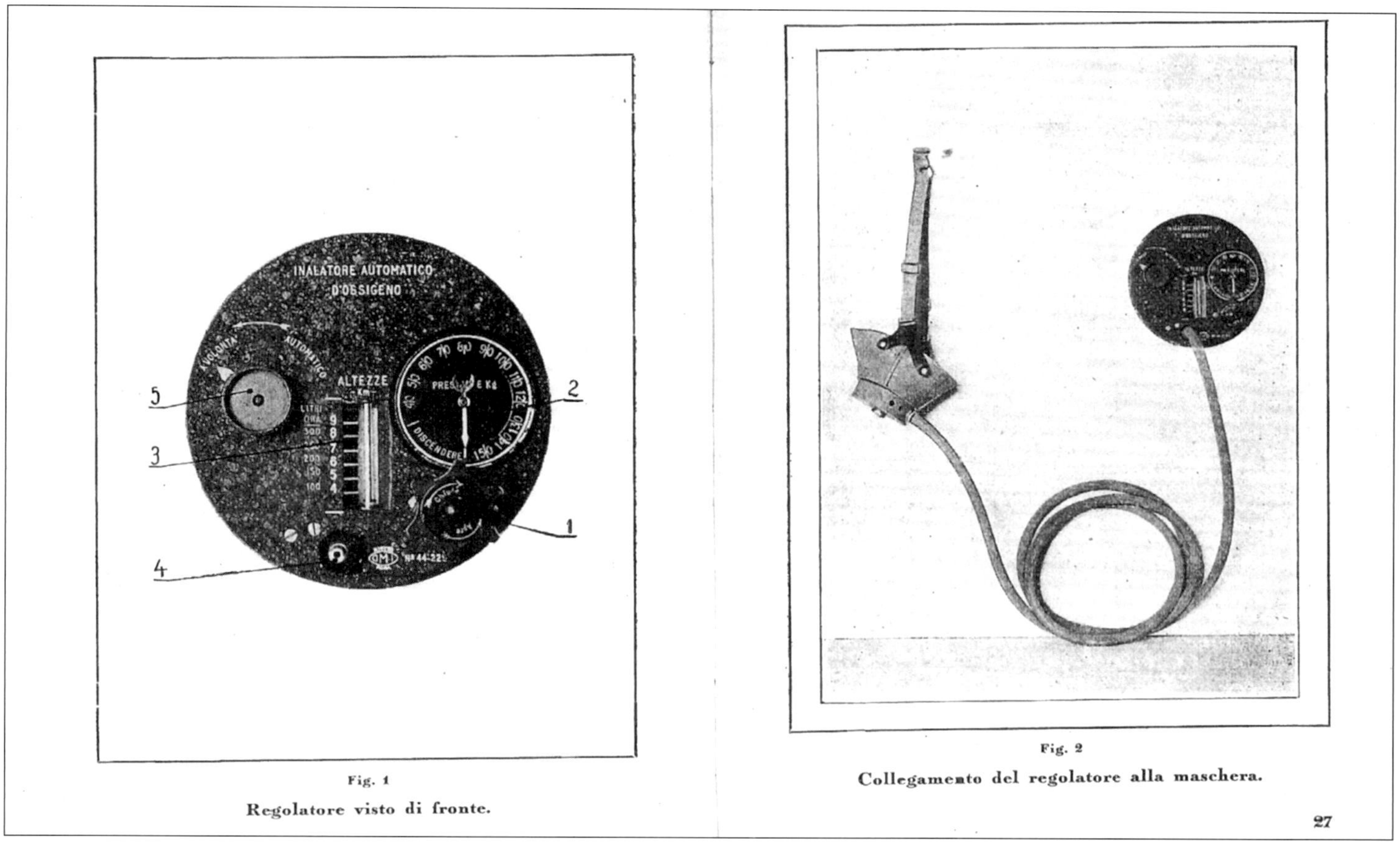

O.M.I. oxygen system.

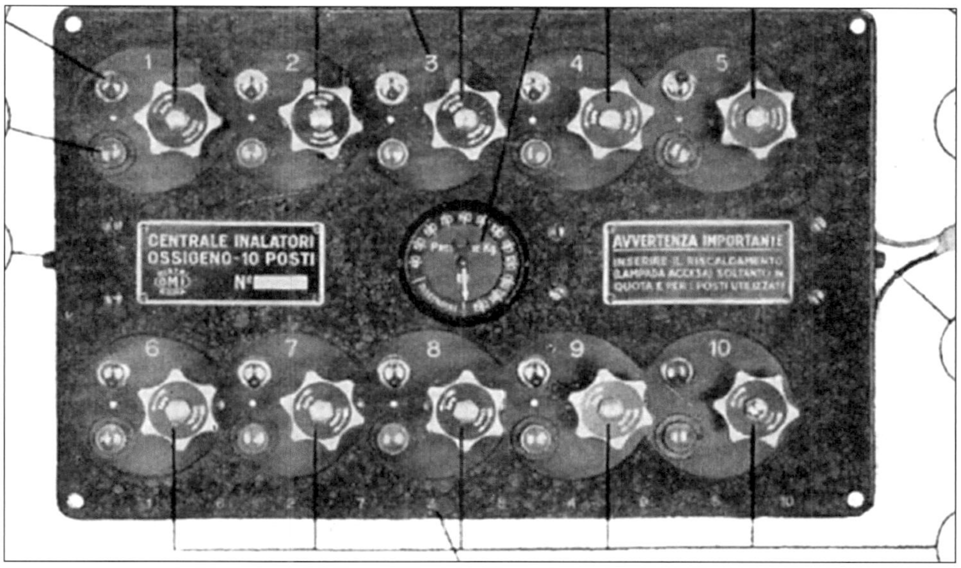

Oxygen system control panel as installed in multi-engine aircraft.

SM-79 crew.

Col. Pezzi wearing the experimental pressurized suit and helmet conceived and built in Guidonia for his record-breaking high-altitude flight. Courtesy MUSAM-ITAF

Another oxygen mask tested in Guidonia. Courtesy MUSAM-ITAF

Italian airman wearing the German AUER 10-6702 with three fitting hooks.

Italian fighter pilot wearing a mix of Italian and German flight gear. Courtesy C. Canton

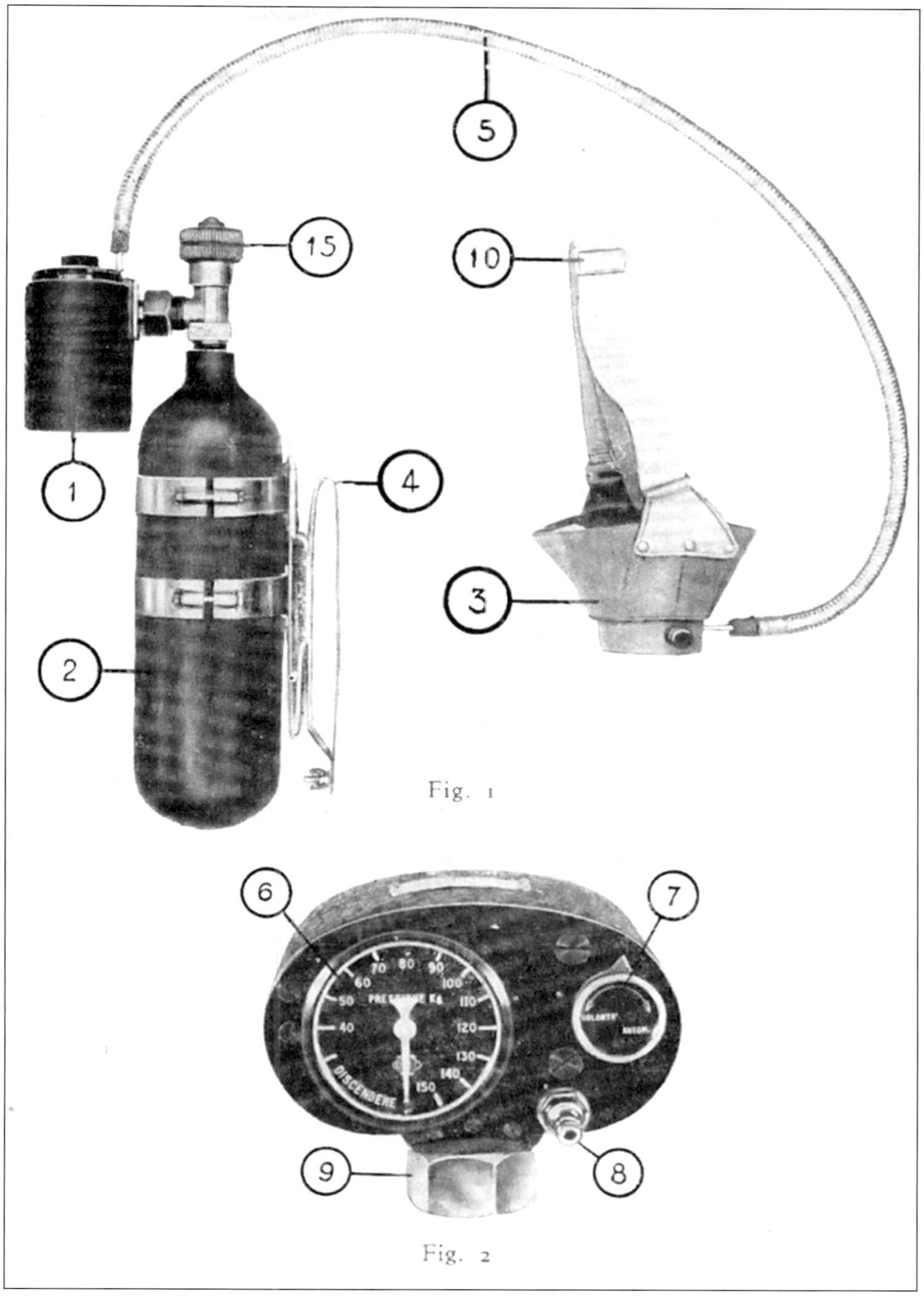

View of the O.M.I. portable system taken from its operation and maintenance manual.

PART 2: COLOR GALLERY

CHAPTER SEVEN

FLIGHT SUITS

Gray flight suit used during World War I. The 1928 model was a derivative of this suit. Courtesy S. Coccia

Fur-lined leather jacket used until the late-1930s. Courtesy MUSAM-ITAF

Regia Aeronautica's black leather trousers. Courtesy A. Gaiani

Standard leather jacket without collar belonging to an Italian naval aviator. Courtesy S. Coccia

Another fur-lined leather jacket used by the RA. Courtesy MUSAM-ITAF

First issued gray moleskin flight suit adopted by the RA in the second half of the 1920s.

Moleskin coverall of the early-1930s.

Summer fabric coverall, commercial issue.

MARUS 1930 model flight suit with electrical heating. Note the suit and gloves connecting plugs. Courtesy A. Gaiani

MARUS classic winter flight suit.

MARUS Model 30 variants. Courtesy MUSAM-ITAF

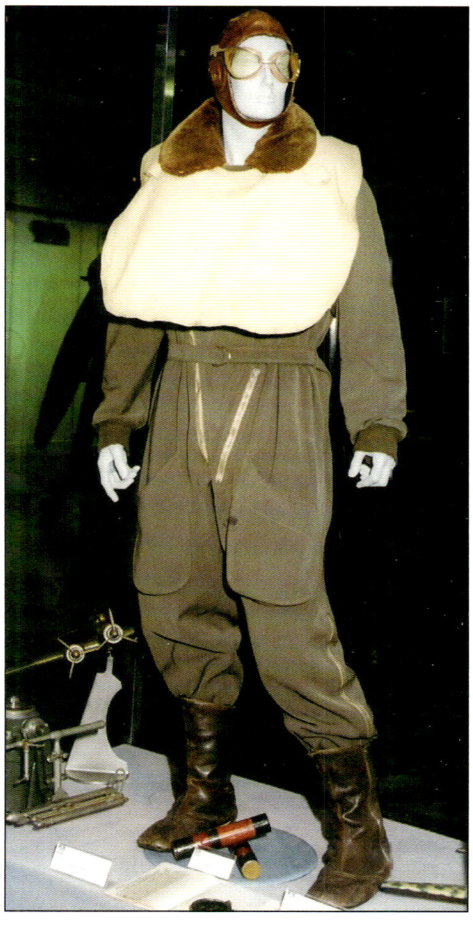

MARUS Model 30 with early type life vest.

Model 30 derivative by Giusti named "AVIO."

Model 30 summer MARUS.

Commercial summer flight suit.

Commercial flight jacket, tailored for an individual. Courtesy Paschi

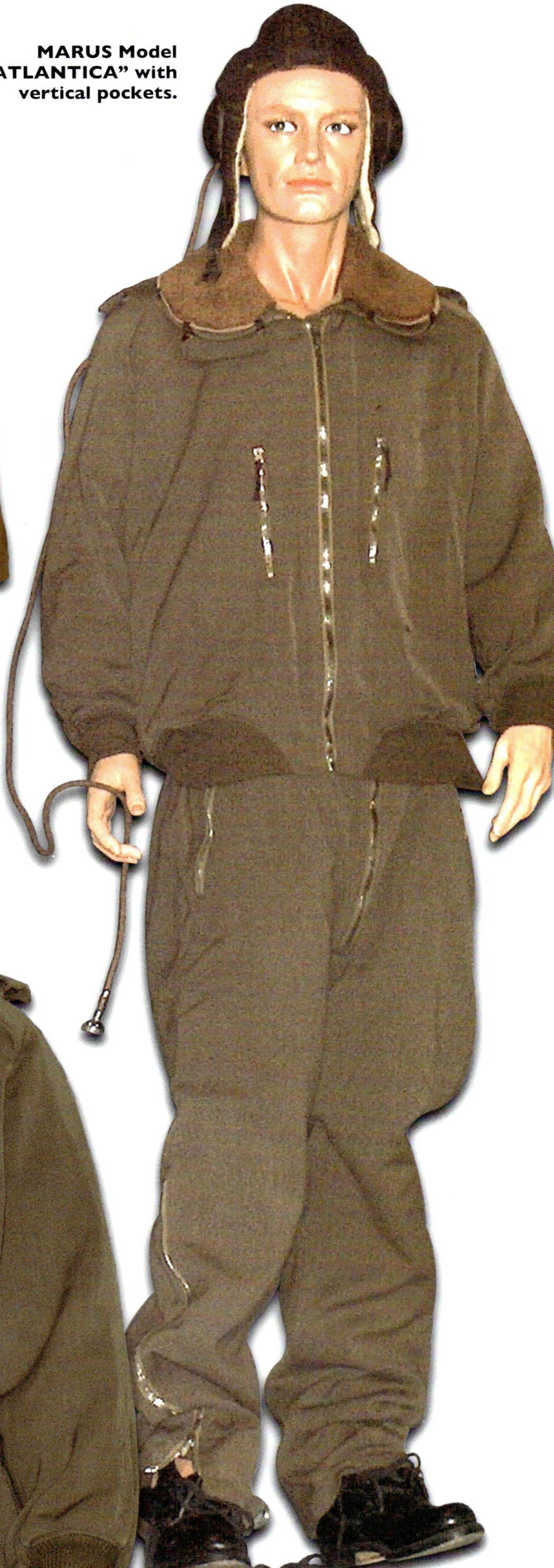

MARUS Model "ATLANTICA" with vertical pockets.

Italo Balbo's flight jacket, part of his own "ATLANTICA" flight suit. Courtesy MUSAM-ITAF

MARUS jacket belonging to a pilot of Balbo's Atlantic crossing formation. Courtesy MUSAM-ITAF

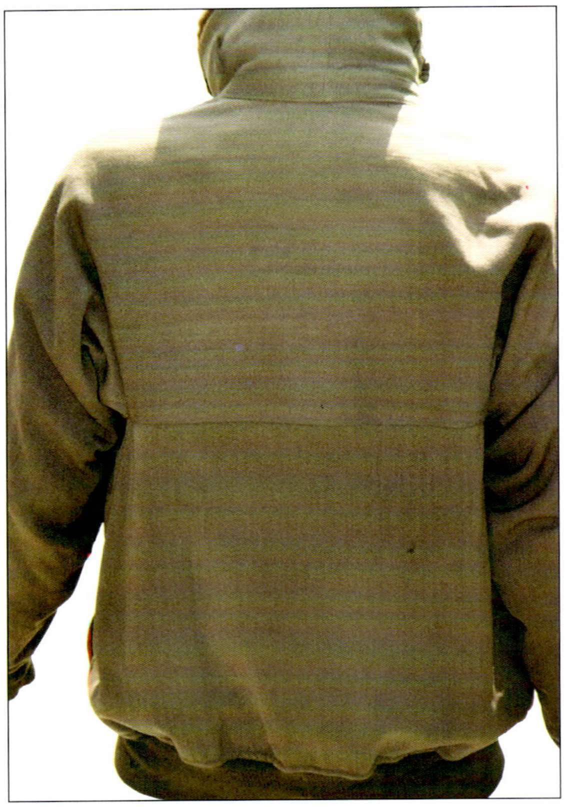

Front and rear view of the winter jacket of the "ATLANTICA" flight suit.

Rare variant of the "ATLANTICA" produced by MARUS. Courtesy Paschi

Jacket and trousers of the Spanish flight suit used during the Spanish Civil War – clearly an Italian MARUS derivative.

Details of the MARUS "ATLANTICA" flight suit.

"ATLANTICA" jacket derivative with liner fitted with buttons by Giusti.

Another variant of the "ATLANTICA" jacket, note the brass rank badges sewn on the sleeves. Courtesy P. Marzetti Archive

Variant of the "ATLANTICA" flight suit. The fitting system is made of silk strings sewn onto the jacket and metal eyelets fitted onto the liner.

Another flight suit derived from the "ATLANTICA" made in moleskin by Giusti. Courtesy MUSAM-ITAF

"ATLANTICA" winter jacket made by Gennerino tailor of Milan. Courtesy MUSAM-ITAF

Only wealthy officers could afford the purchase of this flight suit made by Gennerino of Milan with high-quality tailoring. Courtesy A. Gaiani

Rare summer variant of the "ATLANTICA."

Summer two-piece "ATLANTICA" flight suit.

Summer two-piece flight suit tailored by Vittoria of Milan. Courtesy MUSAM-ITAF

MARUS summer trousers variants.

Colonial variant of the two-piece summer MARUS. Courtesy A. Gaiani

Italo Balbo's summer flight suit. Courtesy MUSAM-ITAF

RA student pilots with the moleskin flight suit.

Often in Africa, the winter Model 40 MARUS jacket was worn over the "SAHARIANA" uniform.

Summer "ATLANTICA" by MARUS. Courtesy A. Gaiani

Lieutenant of the 22nd Fighter Group wearing the Model 40 with the jacket tucked into the trousers, due to the looseness of the jacket waistband.

Winter moleskin Model 40 flight suit made by M.I.T.A. of Genoa.

Model 40 winter flight suit.

Model 40 jacket.

As clearly stated by the RA uniform rules, the flight suit had to be worn over the uniform.

Front and rear view of the Model 40 winter jacket.

Summer Model 40 flight suit. Courtesy F. Burgio

Leather jacket produced by Giusti in the early-1940s. Courtesy MUSAM-ITAF

Summer variant of the Model 40 suit. Courtesy D. Rao

Summer flight jacket. Courtesy MUSAM-ITAF

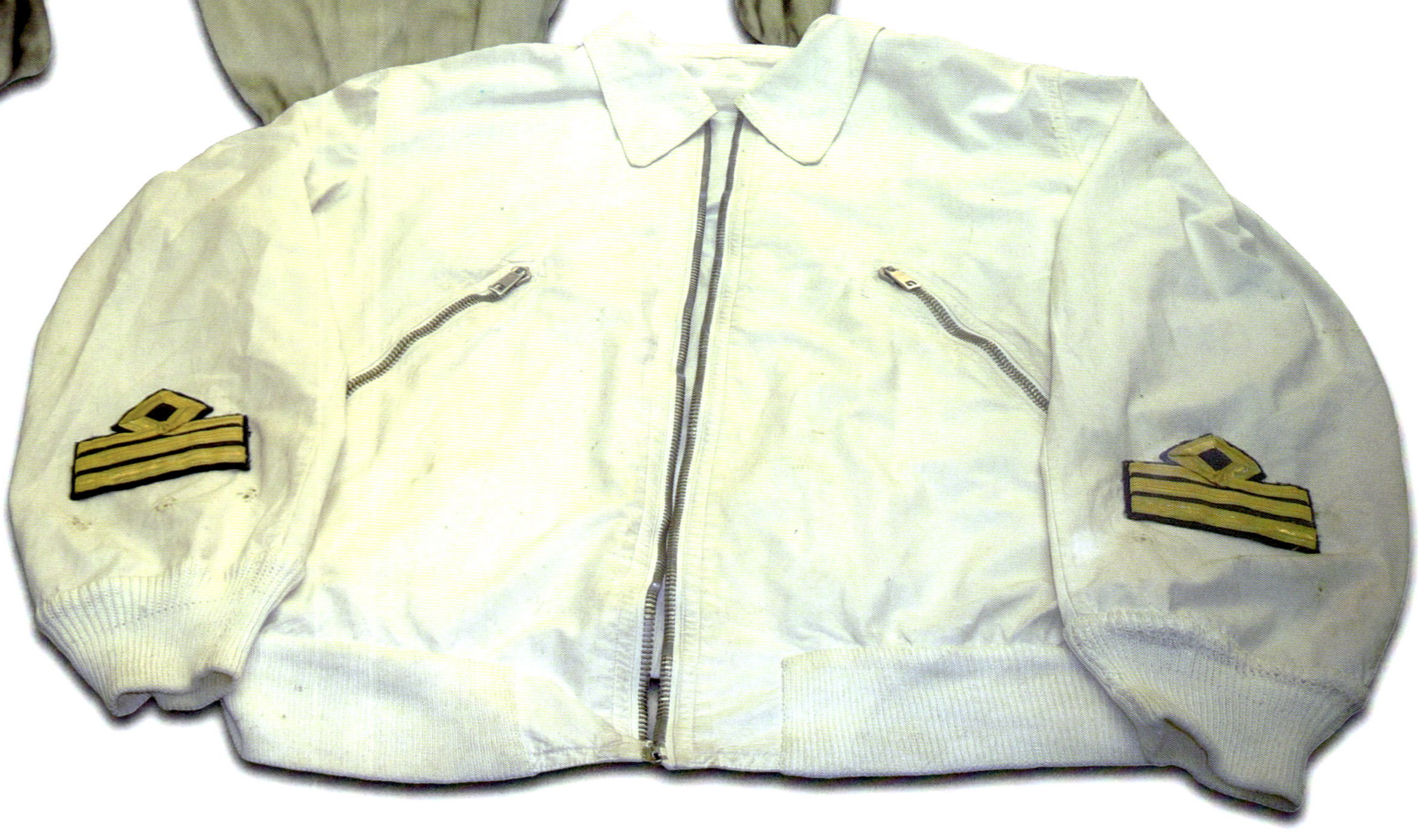

Blue-gray moleskin flight trousers, identical to the Model 40 but without liner.

MARUS Model 40 jacket.

Details of the size and lot stamps of a M.I.T.A. Model 40 suit.

MARUS Model 40 jacket belonging to a 13th Bomber Wing aviator. Courtesy N. Pavan

Trousers Model 40 with electrical heating by M.I.T.A. of Genoa. Courtesy MUSAM-ITAF

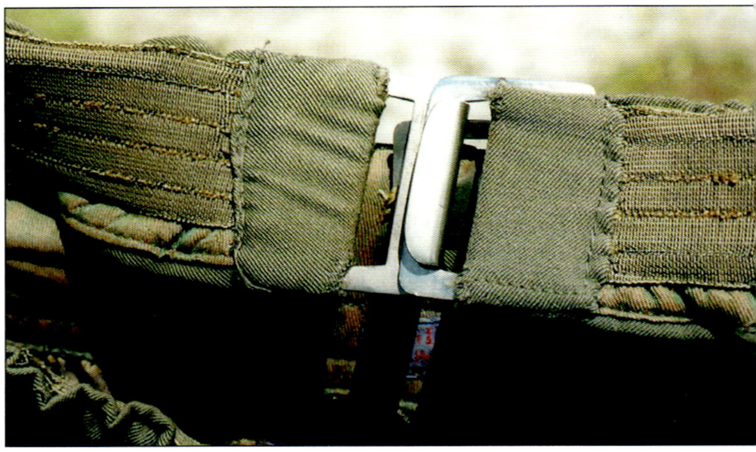

Detail of the trousers elasticated belt hook on a Giusti Model 40 suit.

Inner wiring of the Model 40 MARUS trousers electrical heating system.

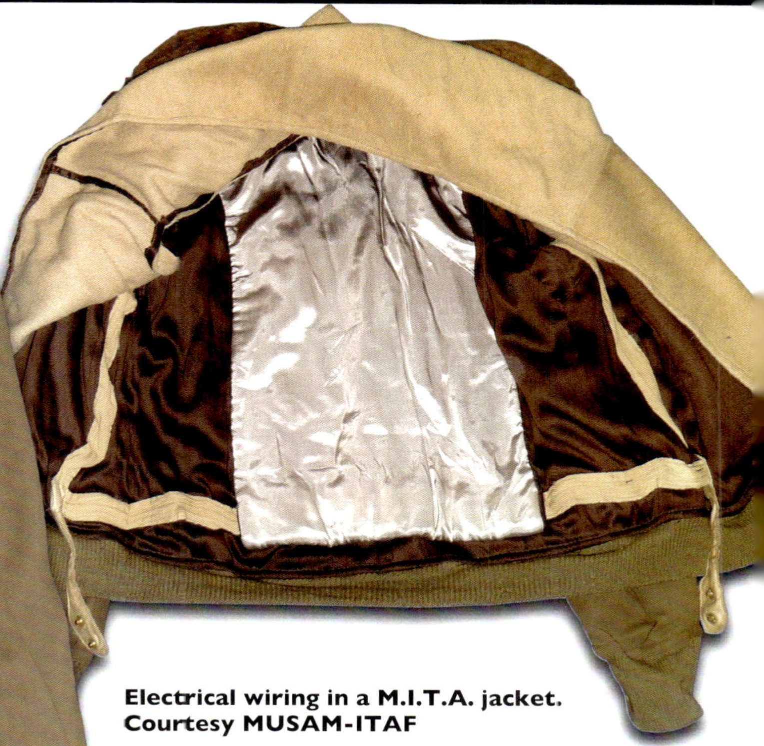

Electrical wiring in a M.I.T.A. jacket. Courtesy MUSAM-ITAF

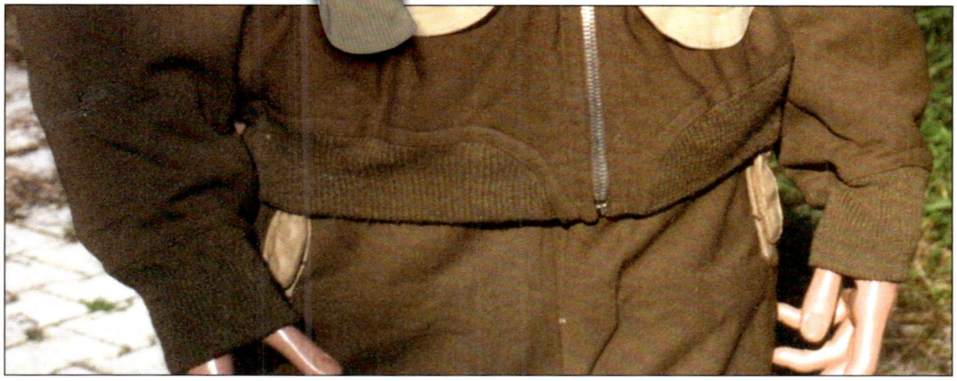

The electrical connection between the jacket and the trousers was provided with metal studs that linked the upper to the lower wiring.

Details of the resistors and wiring for the 24 Volt electrical heating produced by MARUS for all flight suits makers and named "THERMOMAX." Courtesy MUSAM-ITAF

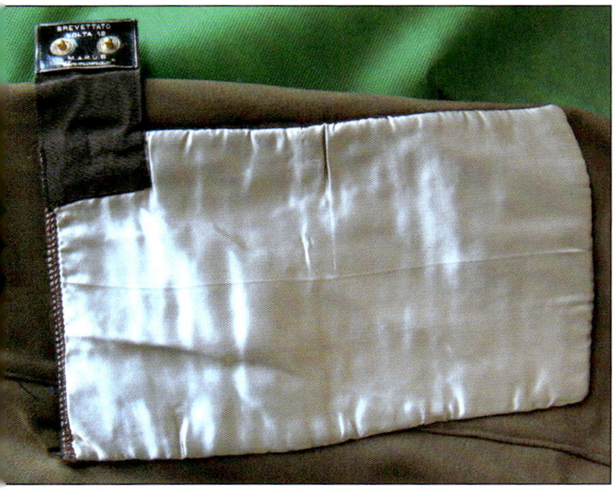

Plugs for the wiring of a M.I.T.A. late-production jacket.

Marus Model 40 trousers with electrical heating.

ANR fighter pilot wearing a RSI MARUS, SAFAR flight helmet and German oxygen mask and life vest. The suit color is greenish; the previous Model 40 suits were in various shades of brown. Circa 1944-1945.

Right
M.I.T.A. jacket produced during the RSI for the ANR airmen.

Left
ANR MARUS flight jacket

ANR flight suit trousers produced by MARUS.

ANR jacket by MARUS. Note the collar closure system with two separate flaps.

German electrically heated flight suit named the "Channel suit," which was used extensively by ANR aviators.

Channel suit variant used by an ANR pilot. Courtesy MUSAM-ITAF

German summer trousers mostly used by RA Bf 109s pilots.

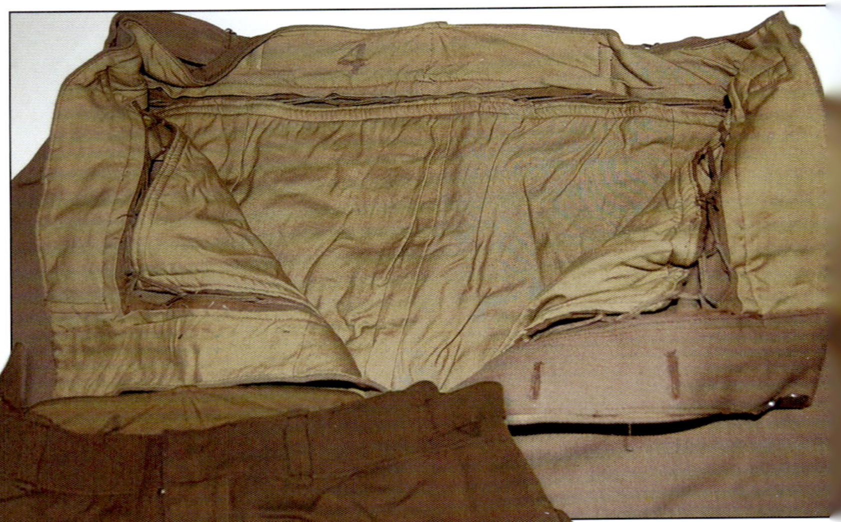

Trousers for the suit used by Cobelligerent Air Forces, mostly by Baltimore Bomber crews since 1944 and used until the early-1950s. Courtesy Paschi

Postwar MARUS suit derivative produced by Giusti from the early-1950s to the early-1960s.

Gennerino tailor label.

Avio-Giusti tailor label.

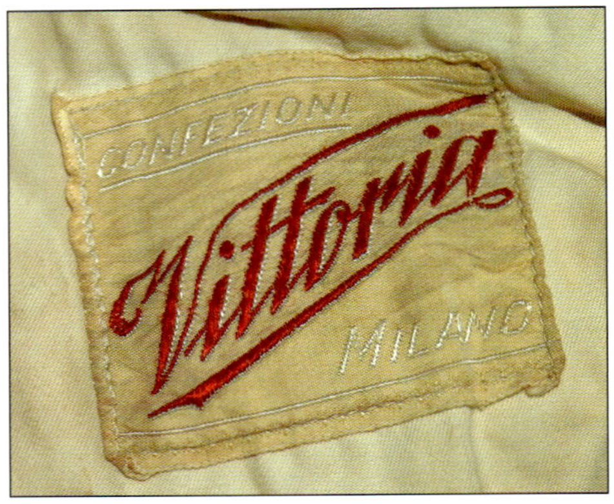

Vittoria tailor label.

M.I.T.A. label attached to a pair of mint flight trousers showing size and contract number.

MARUS Model 30 label.

M.I.T.A. inner wool thermoliner label. Courtesy D.Rao

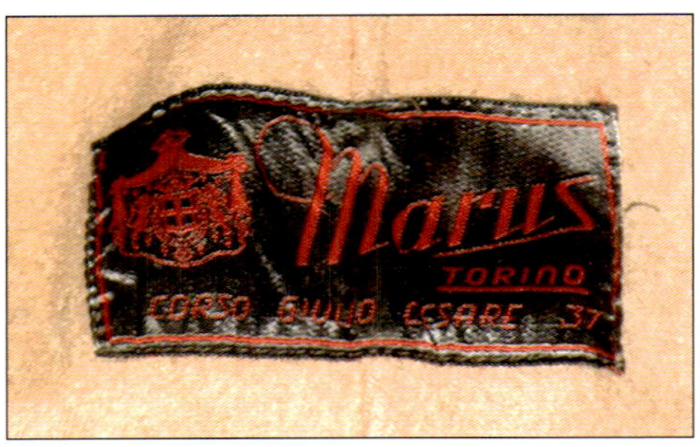

Late-production MARUS Model 40 trousers' label.

Model 40 M.I.T.A. trousers stamp.

Model 40 MARUS label.

ANR M.I.T.A. jacket label.

ANR MARUS jacket label. Note the absence of the Savoia's insignia and the Turin plant mark.

MARUS "ATLANTICA" jacket label of the late-1930s.

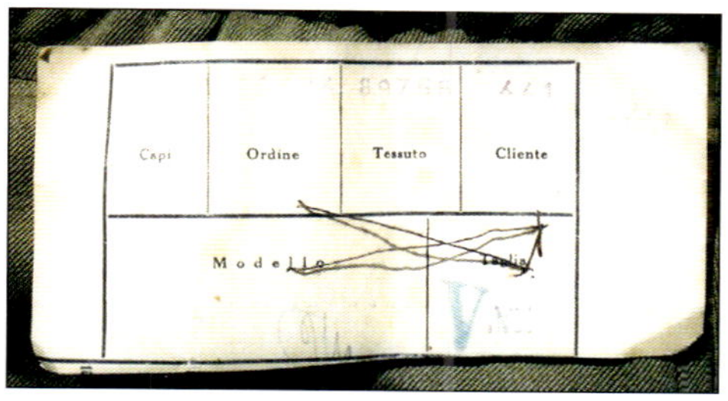

Mint Model 40 MARUS trousers warehouse label shows detail of order.

MARUS Model 40 jacket.

Model 30 suit label.

Model 30 summer suit MARUS label.

Late-production MARUS summer trousers.

Giusti summer trousers.

MARUS "ATLANTICA" flight suit label.

Giusti commercial flight jacket.

Giusti Model 40 jacket.

Giusti Model 40 trousers.

M.I.T.A. Model 40 jacket.

Giusti moleskin " ATLANTICA."

Summer suit, unknown maker.

MARUS summer "ATLANTICA."

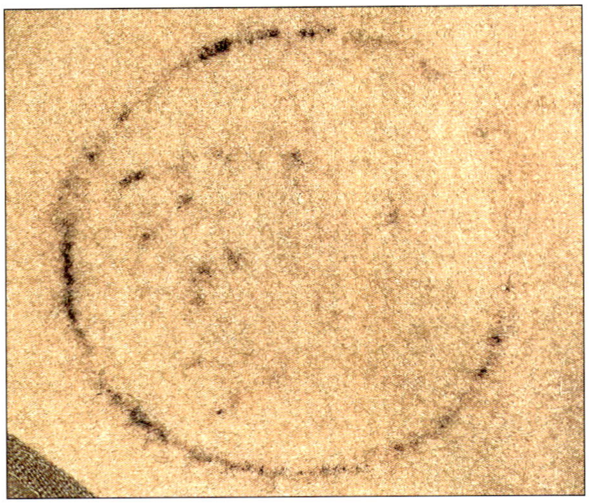

RA approval stamp inside MARUS Model 40 trousers.

Postwar Giusti suit.

ATLANTICA's main zip.

ATLANTICA "riri" make main zip.

ATLANTICA trousers MARUS with "riri" zip.

ATLANTICA early trousers with "Taurus" zip.

Trousers Model 40 "riri."

Model 30 MARUS suit "Rapida."

Commercial suit with "Vici" zip.

Left "riri" zip; right "Taurus" zip.

Avio Giusti suit with "riri."

Model 40 Giusti trousers with Taurus zip.

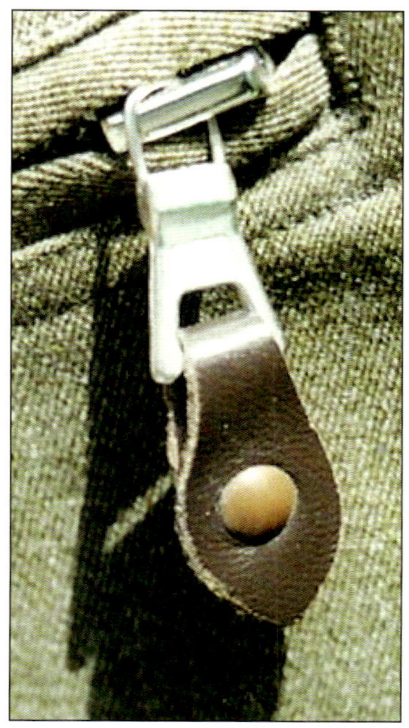

Postwar Giusti suit.

CHAPTER EIGHT

FLIGHT HELMETS

Padded flight helmet and uniform cap of an infantry officer assigned to the "Aviators Batallion" in 1914. Courtesy MUSAM-ITAF

Variants of the Roold flight helmet used during World War I. Courtesy L. Di Gabriele

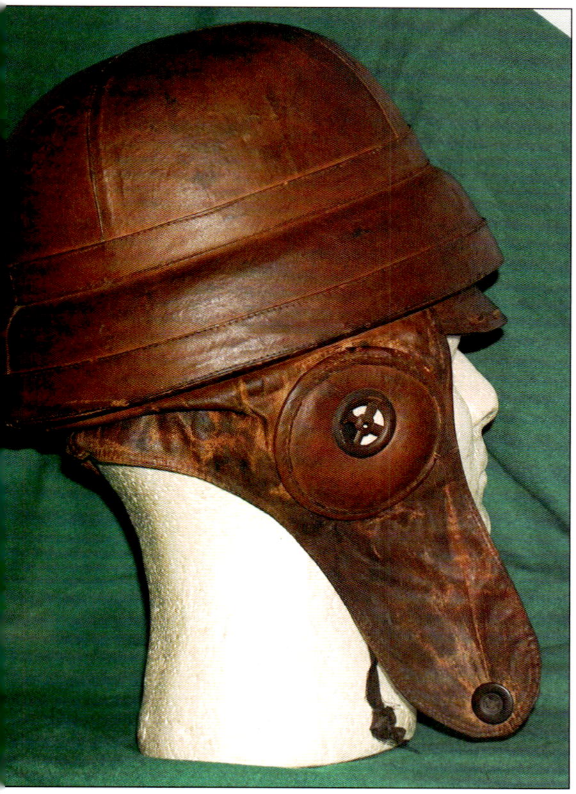

Roold flight helmet.

Italian derivative of the original French Roold flight helmet belonging to an Italian aviator in World War I.

Italian tropical flight helmed made with cork and fabric.

Roold flight helmet with facemask.

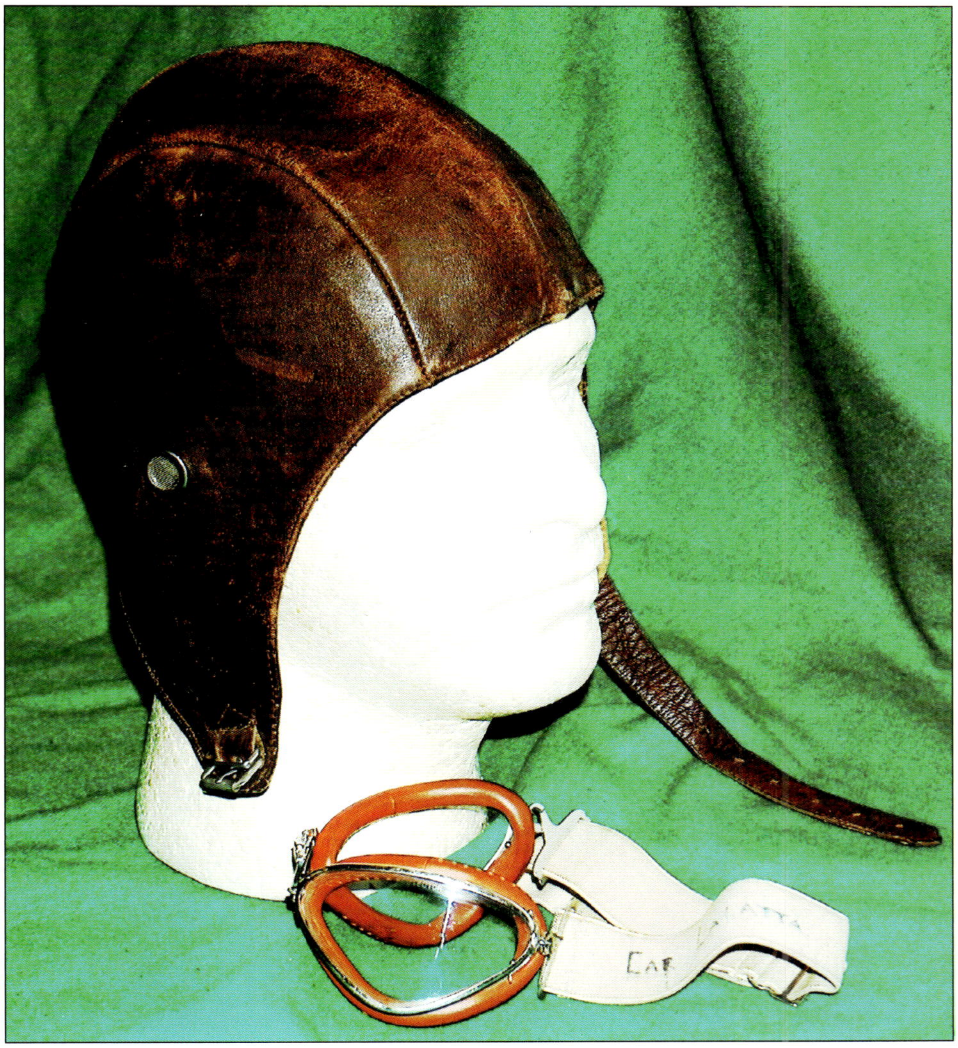

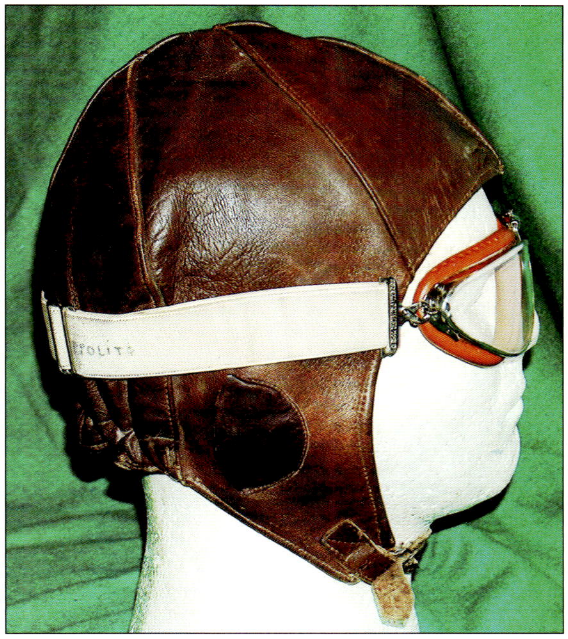

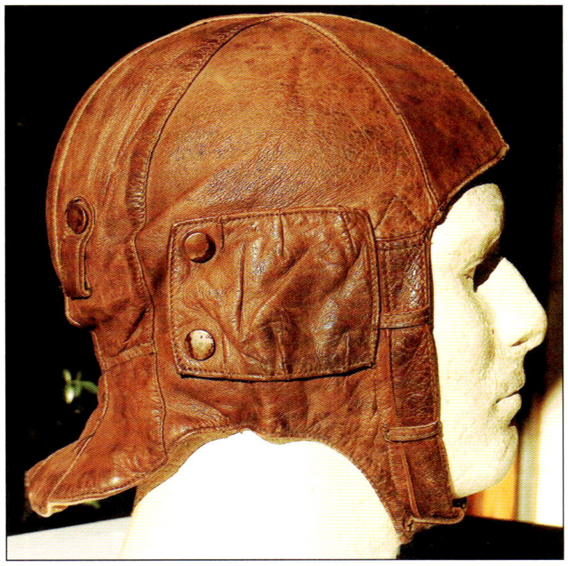

Auto driver helmets used by Italian flyers in the 1920s.

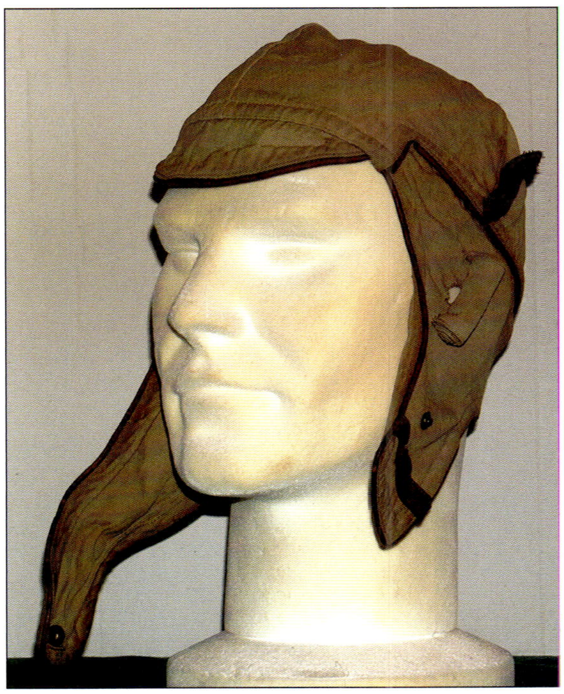

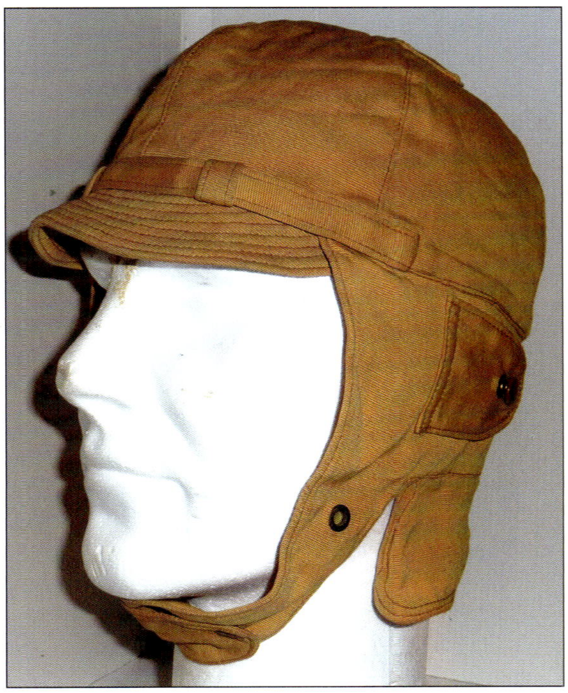

Helmet made with a material named "devil's skin" and produced by Belfe in the 1930s. Courtesy P. Moncalvo

Samples of fabric summer flight helmets with the classic "snail" over the ears like the Giusti's models. Courtesy P. Moncalvo

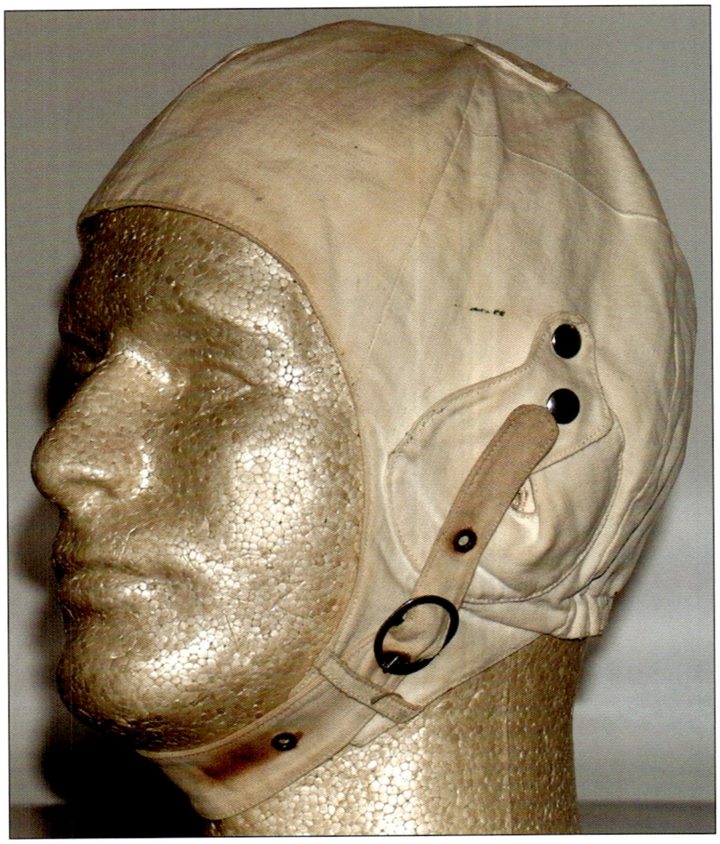

Summer variant produced by the Giampaoli tailor of Rome.

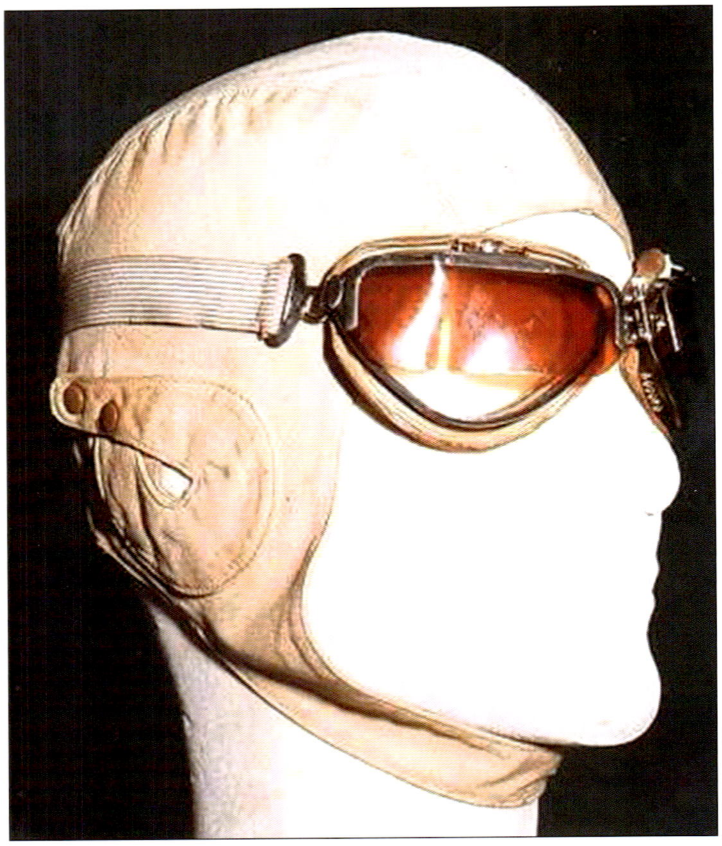

Cotton flight helmet by Giusti with FOPAIS pilot goggles.

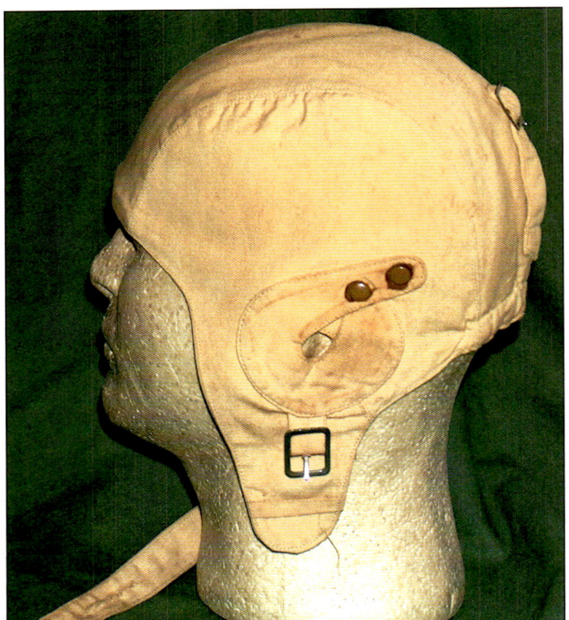

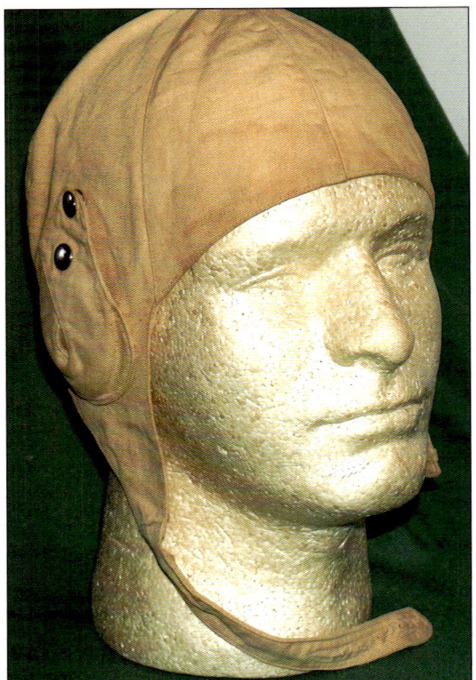

Commercial examples of summer flight helmets used by RA flyers. Note the tab on the helmet top used to take off the helmet by passing a finger under it and pulling it up. This device was present also on some leather flight helmets.

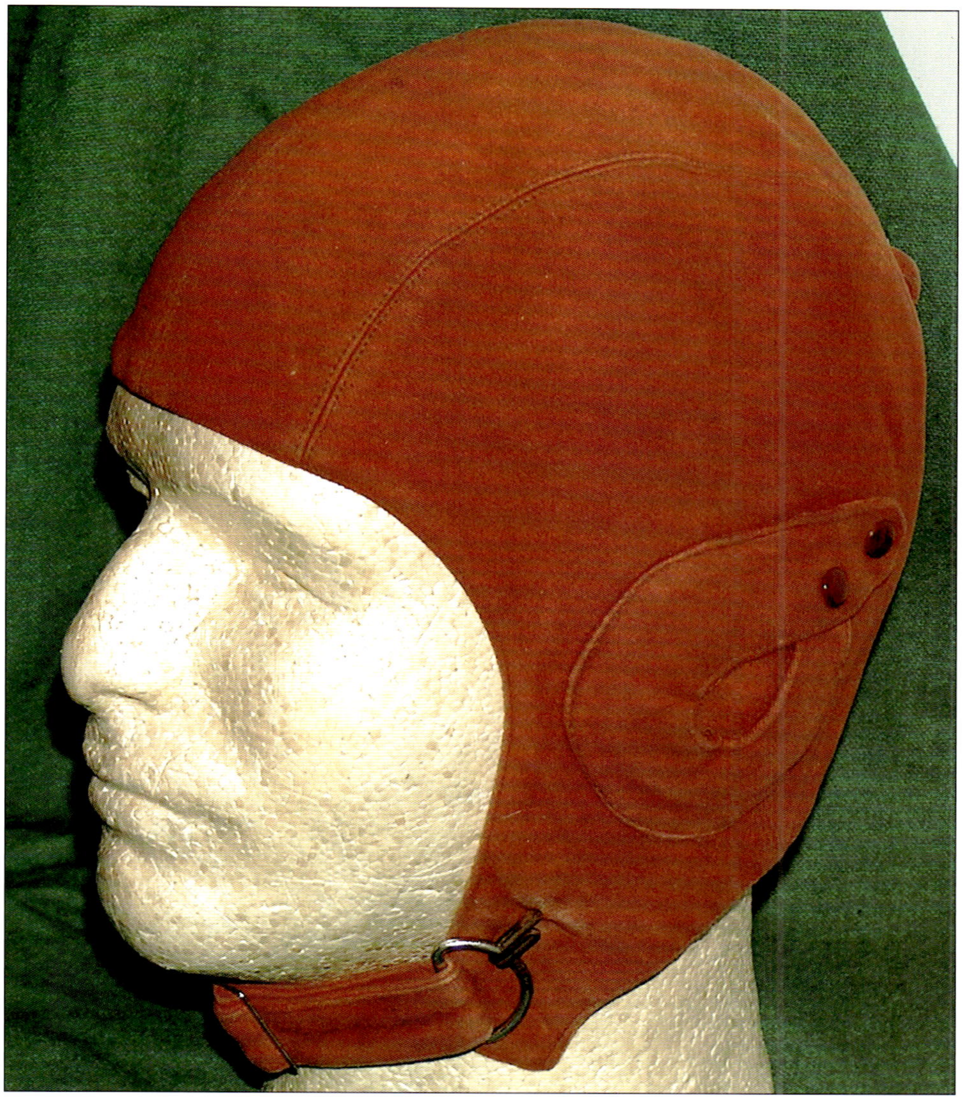

Another example produced by the Donati tailor factory of Udine made with the strong "devil's skin."

Auto driver leather helmet used by an RA flyer.

Cotton summer flight helmet patterned after the standard model by Gennerino factory of Milan. Courtesy A. Gaiani

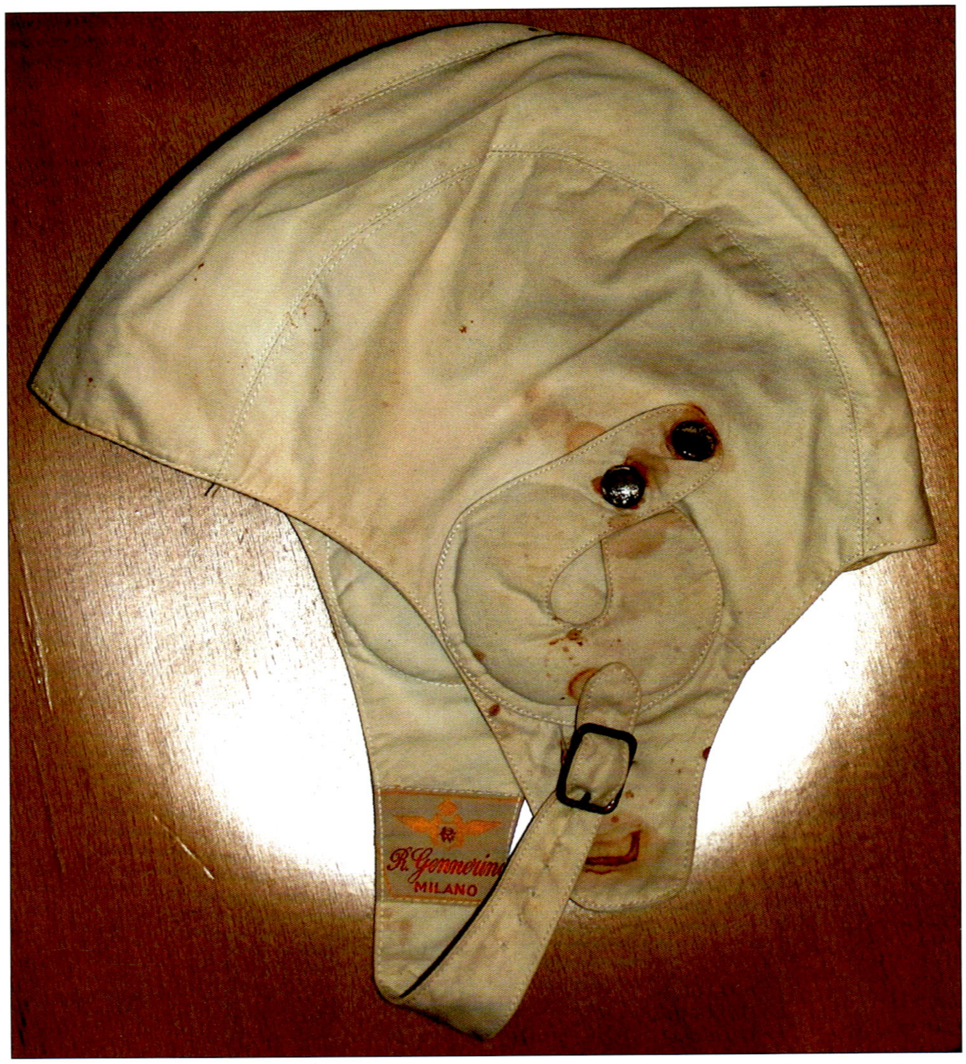

Above: Leather flight helmet belonging to an RA seaplane pilot. *Below*: Giampaoli tailor label.

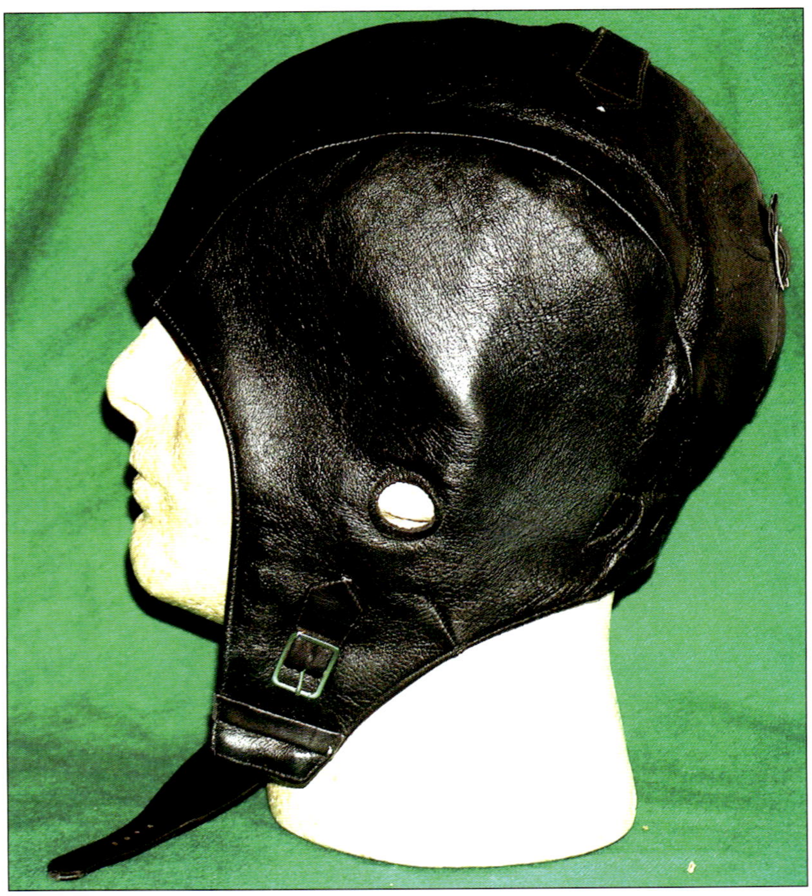

Right: Black leather flight helmet similar to the standard RA brown leather helmet; the main differences are the lack of "snails" over the ears, elasticated nape band, and the quick doffing top tab. It was produced after the war, probably by Giusti of Rome, and rarely used by the ITAF flight schools, and was soon abandoned in favor of RAF/USAAF surplus flight helmets.

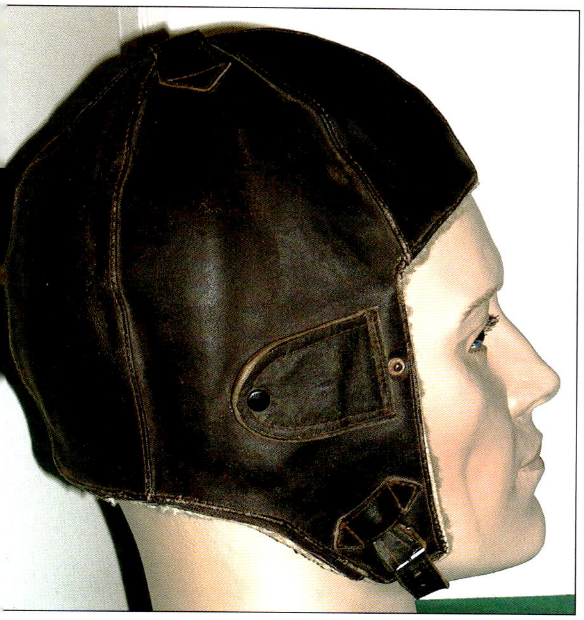

Fur lined commercial flight helmet.

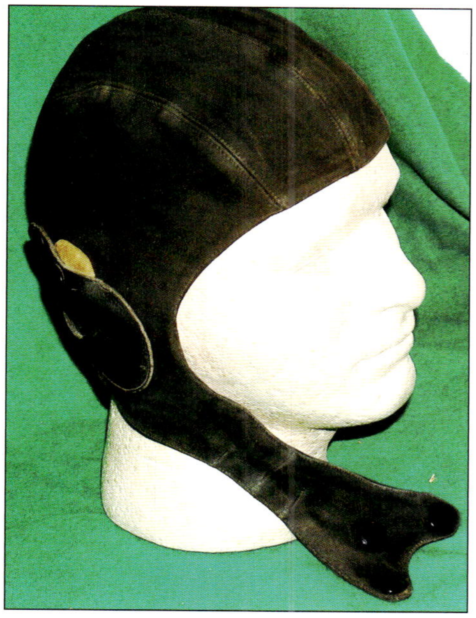

Helmet made with the "devil's skin" by an unknown maker.

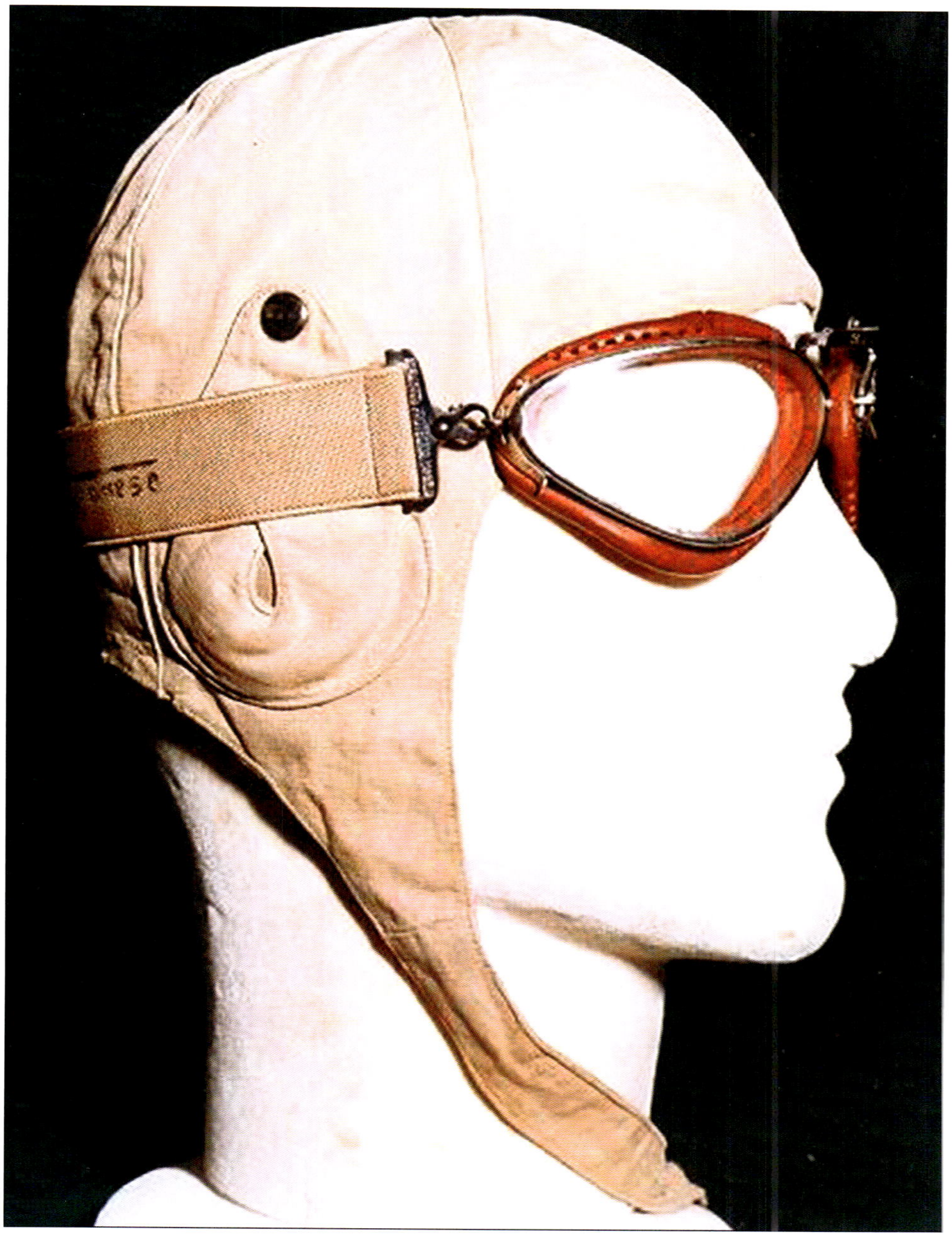

White summer cotton flight helmet belonging to a Ju 87 Stuka RA pilot.

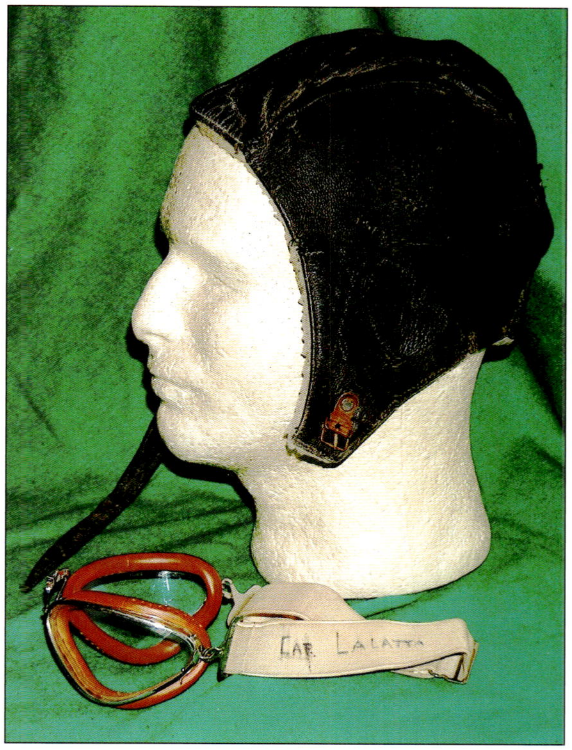

Fur-lined flight helmet belonging to Capt. Ippolito Lalatta in World War II.

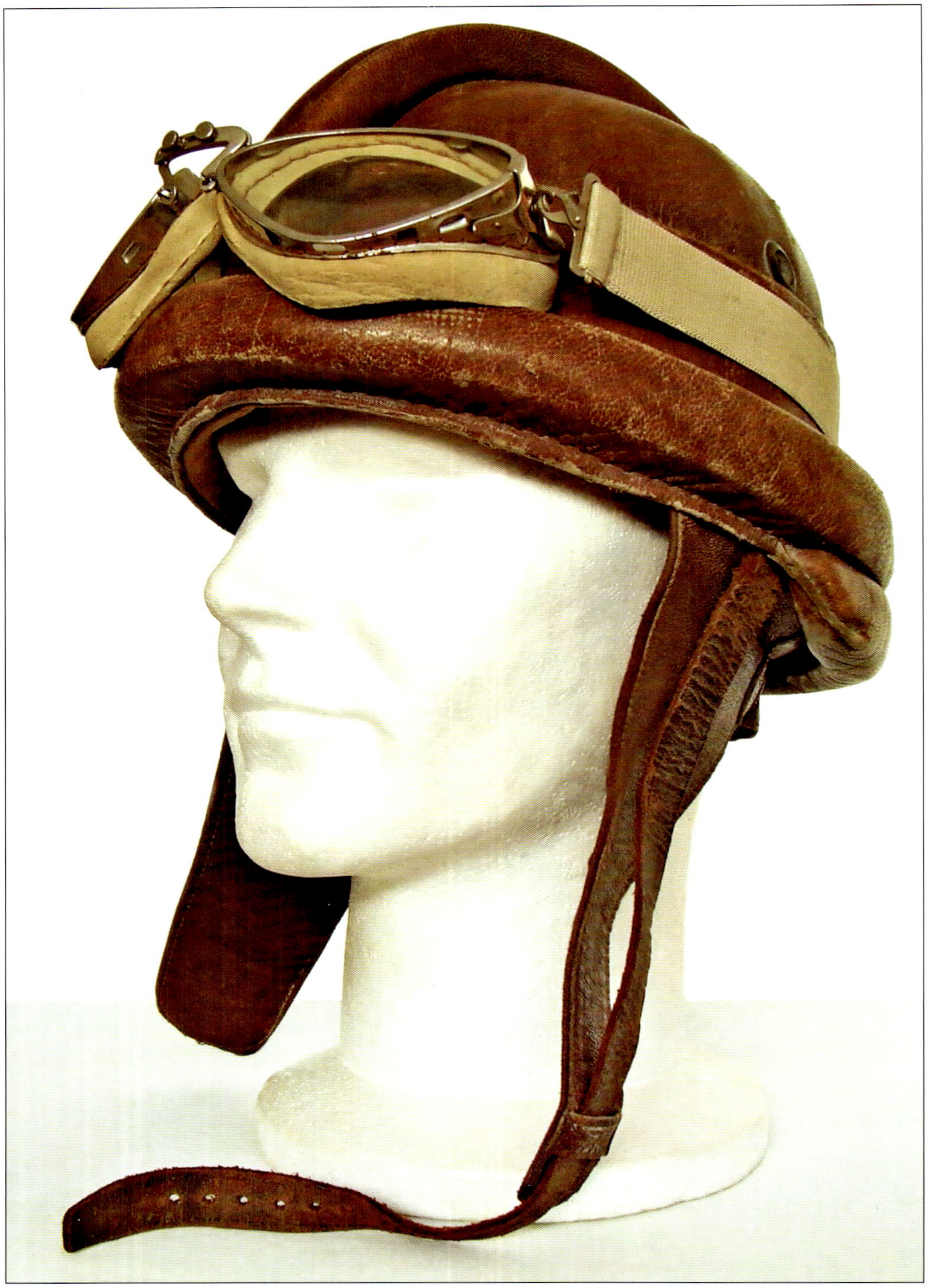

Protective hard helmet used by RA flight schools from the late-1930s, and produced by the Franco factory of Milan. There are also identical helmets produced by the Breda firm. Courtesy P. Moncalvo

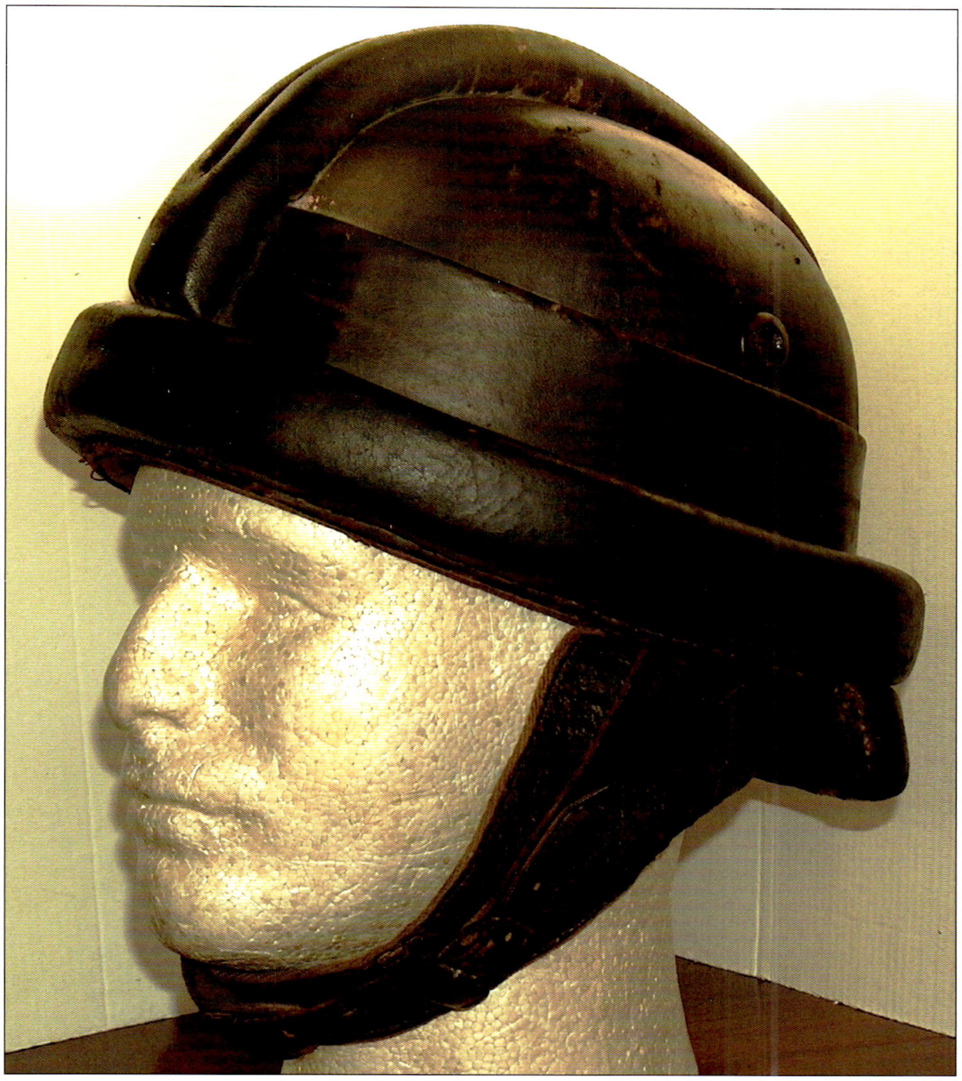

Franco hard helmet in a different color shade.

Franco hard helmet in mint condition.

Official protective hard helmet adopted in 1927 produced under Saratti's licence by the Fumagalli factory of Milan. Superseded by the Franco helmet.

Protective flight helmet of the 1930s.

Integrated protective hard helmet that did not need to be worn over standard flight helmets. Courtesy P. Moncalvo

First version of the Giusti flight helmet of the early-1930s. Note the closure system using a simple hook as on the first summer helmets. Courtesy P. Moncalvo

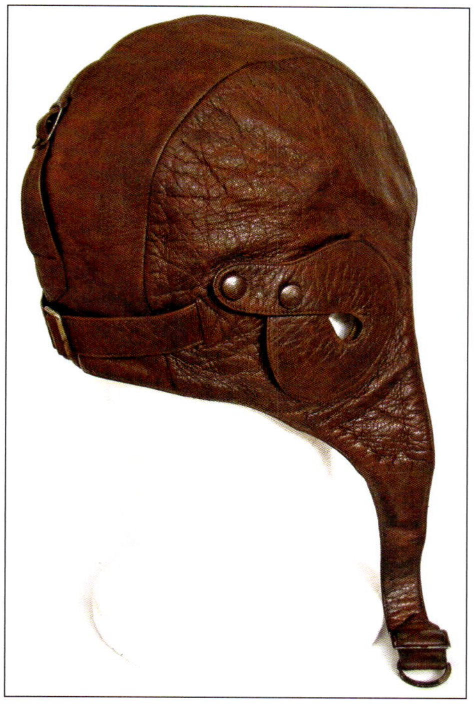

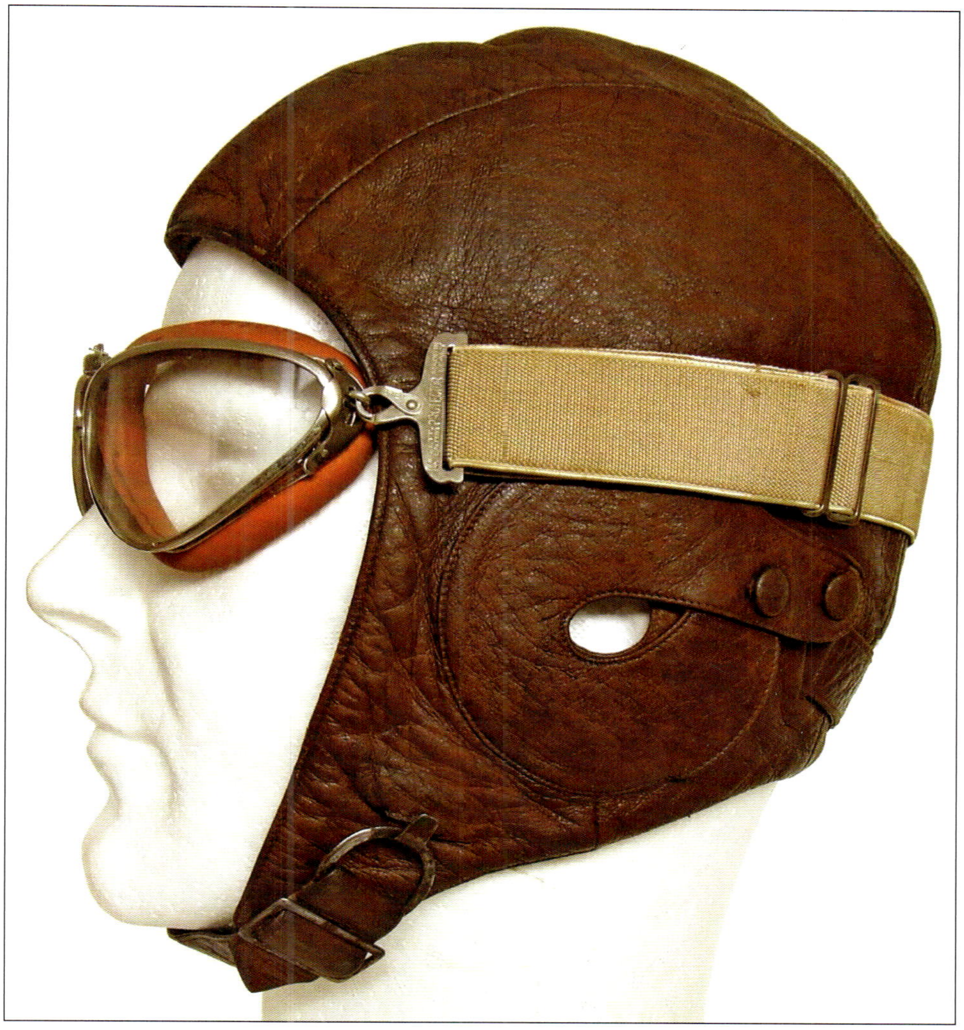

***Below*: Final version of the Giusti leather flight helmet. It was produced in different shades of brown and qualities of leather. Courtesy P. Moncalvo**

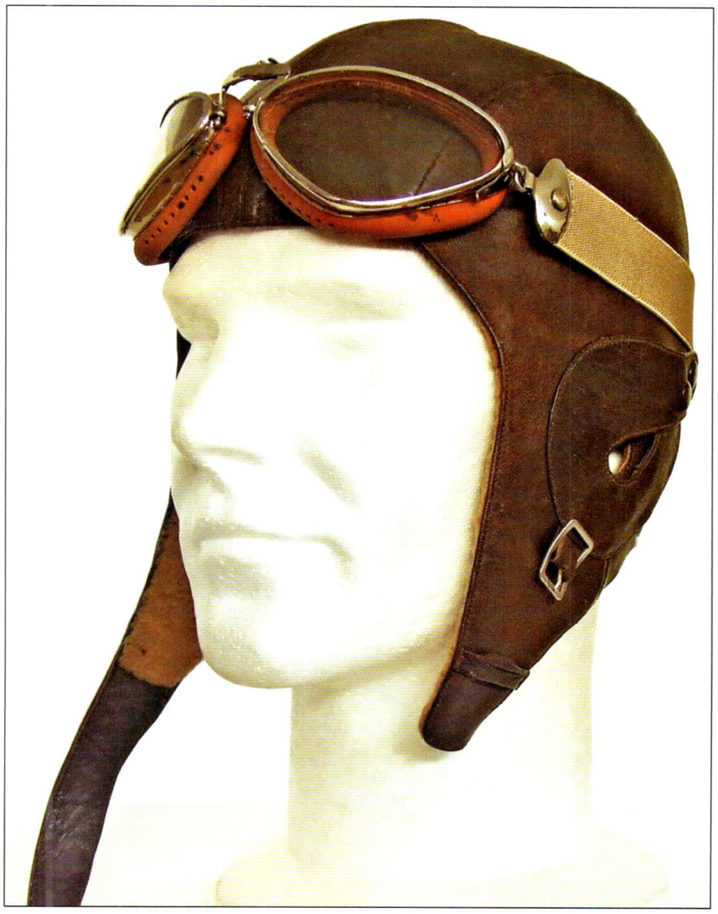

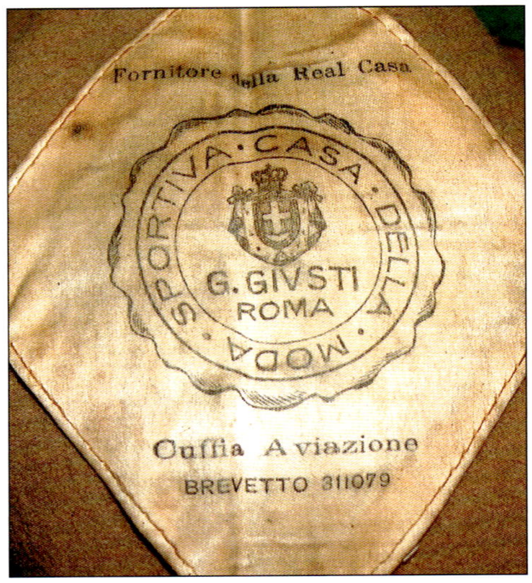

Two different labels with different patent markings of the classic Giusti's flight helmet. In the second photo note the rubber ear disks used to reduce noise levels.

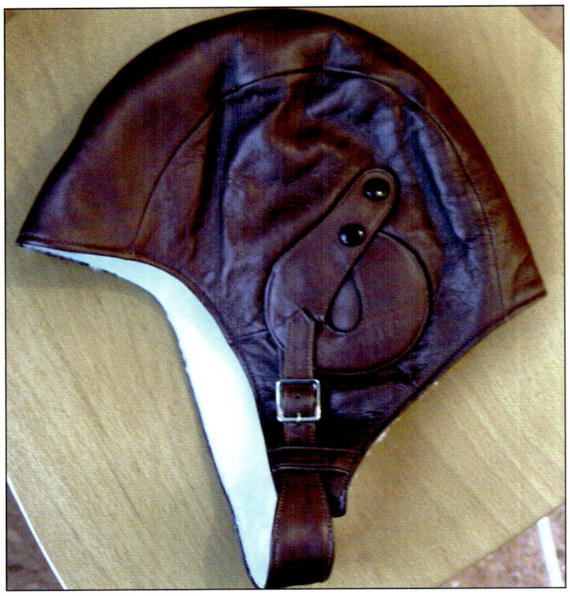

Unusual Giusti flight helmet with lamb's wool lining instead of the usual light brown wool. Courtesy A. Gaiani

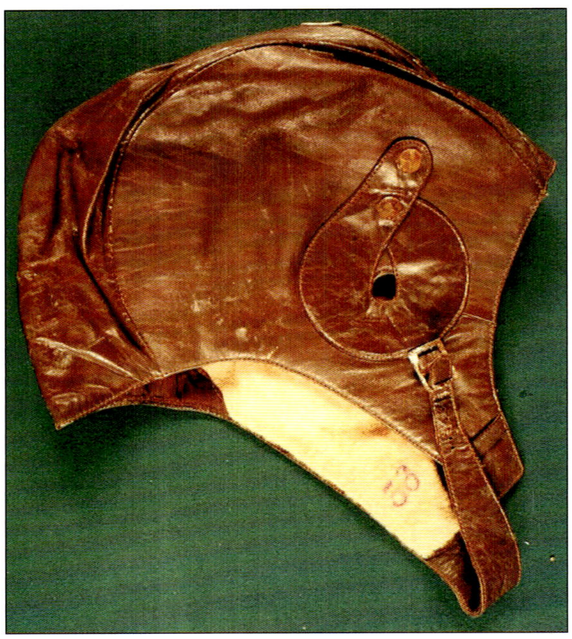

Leather flight helmet belonging to Lt.Gen. Bernardini showing an unusual size stamp, quite uncommon during the war and typical of the postwar years.

Giusti flight helmet for seaplane pilots. Courtesy P. Moncalvo

Variant of the previous flight helmet. Courtesy MUSAM-ITAF

SAFAR flight helmet with provision for use of a radio headset.

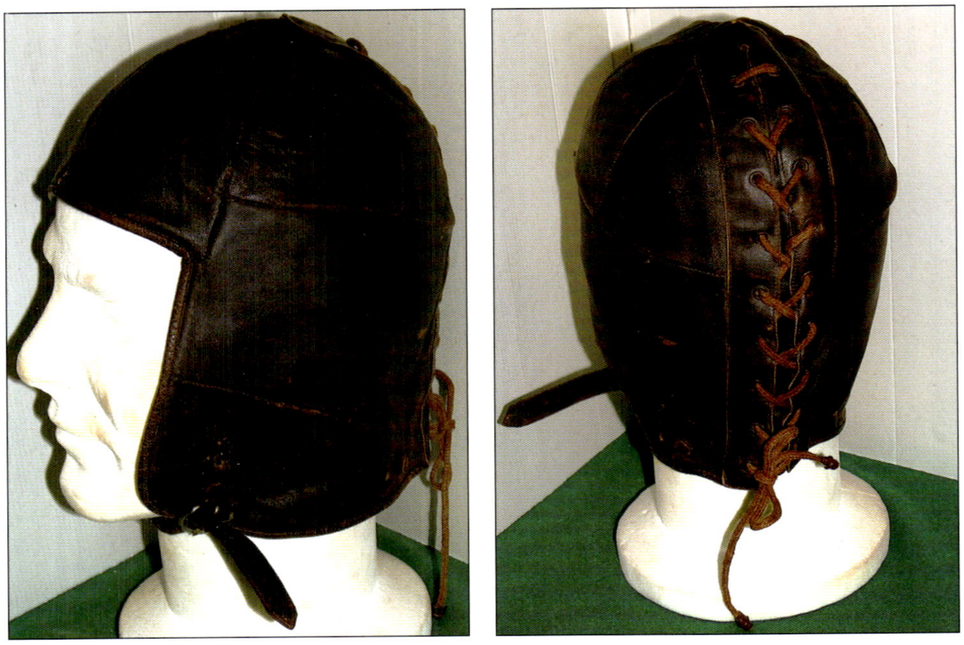

Flight helmet of the early-1930s with silk lining, and probably intended for seaplanes.

The classical Giusti helmet could hold two earphones instead of the noise attenuating rubber disks. If the radio had also a transmitter, a LESA throat mic was used. Courtesy P. Moncalvo.

Detailed views of the SAFAR helmet shown earlier. It was used by both pilots and radiomen. Courtesy P. Moncalvo

Unusual flight helmet with earphones. It was delivered with the onboard radio equipment. Courtesy R. Zizzo

Summer version of the flight helmet with external radio headset.

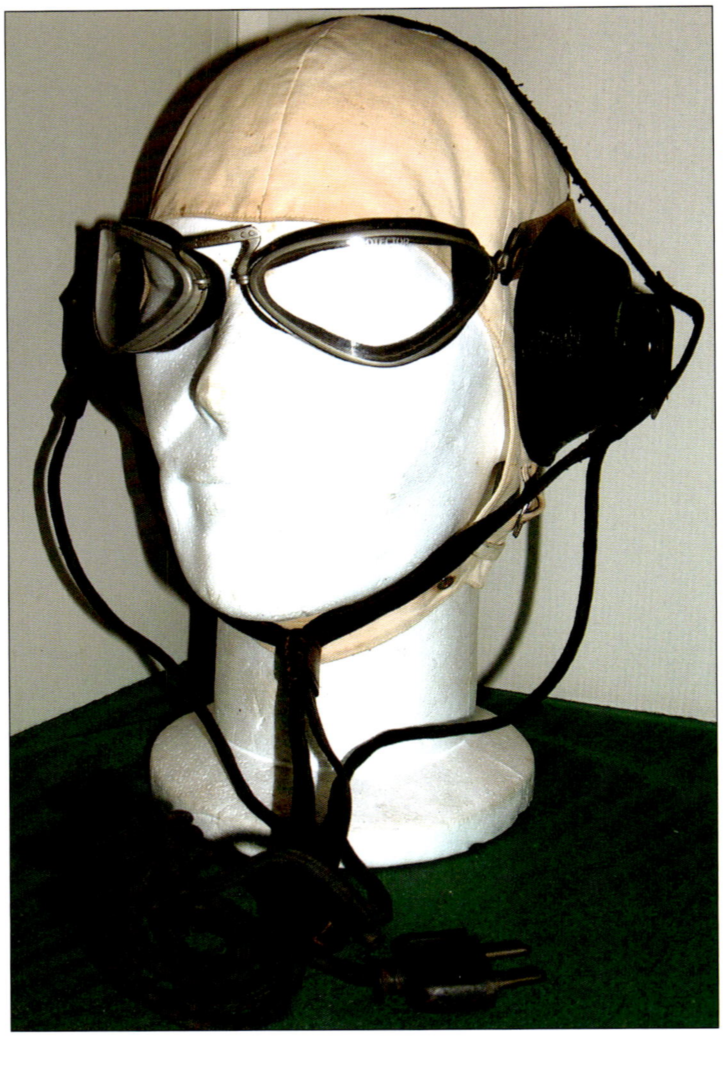

Summer flight helmet with external Marelli radio headset.

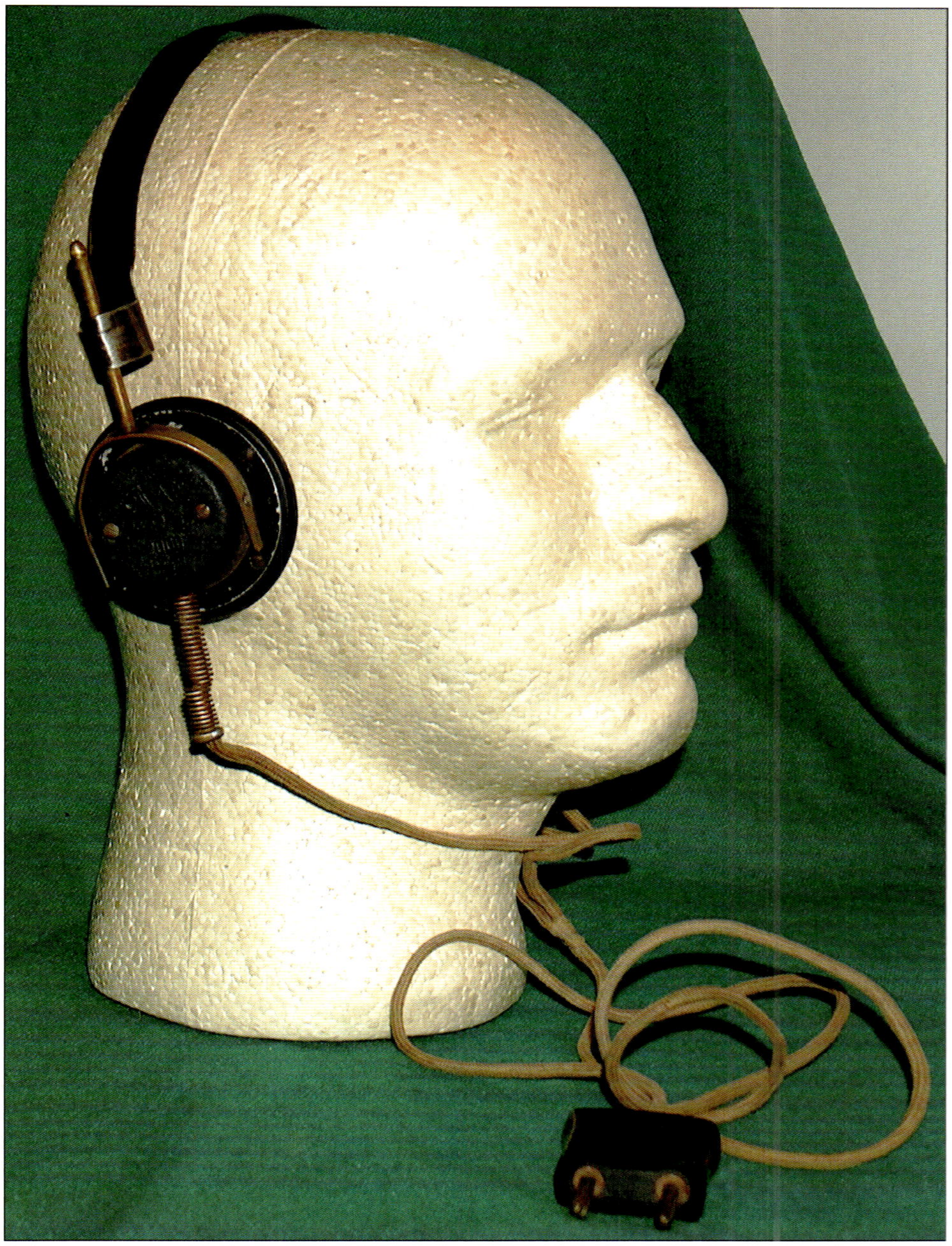

SAFAR headset with receivers intended for flight and ground service. *Above*: Details of the SAFAR earphone capsule.

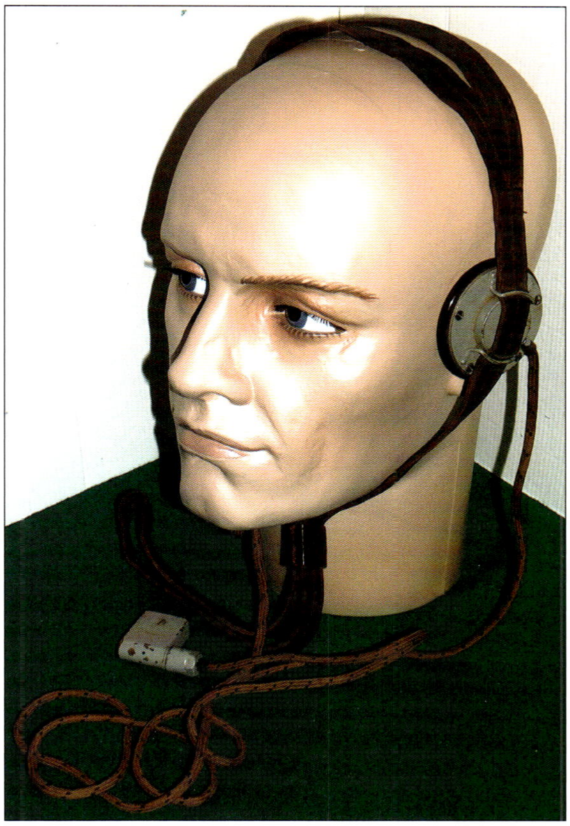

SAFAR receiving headset used by the RA crews.

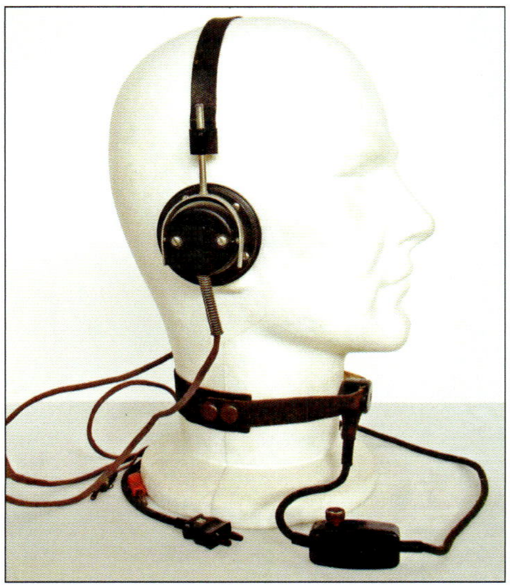

SAFAR headset with receivers used with a LESA magnetic throat microphone.

SAFNAT receiving headset with carbon type throat microphone.

Same model as previous with rubber earpads and double carbon throat microphone.

Right and below: **Early models of the integrated radio-telephonic flight helmet issued in the late-1930s by Italian Siemens and used until the end of World War II. It was a common practice among the fighter units to paint the pilot's name and rank over the helmet earphones.**

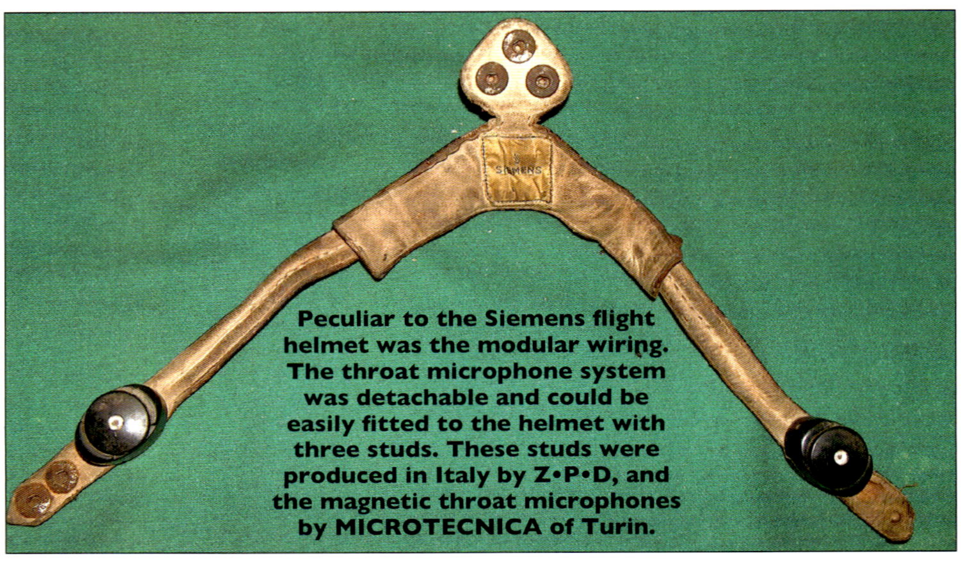

Peculiar to the Siemens flight helmet was the modular wiring. The throat microphone system was detachable and could be easily fitted to the helmet with three studs. These studs were produced in Italy by Z•P•D, and the magnetic throat microphones by MICROTECNICA of Turin.

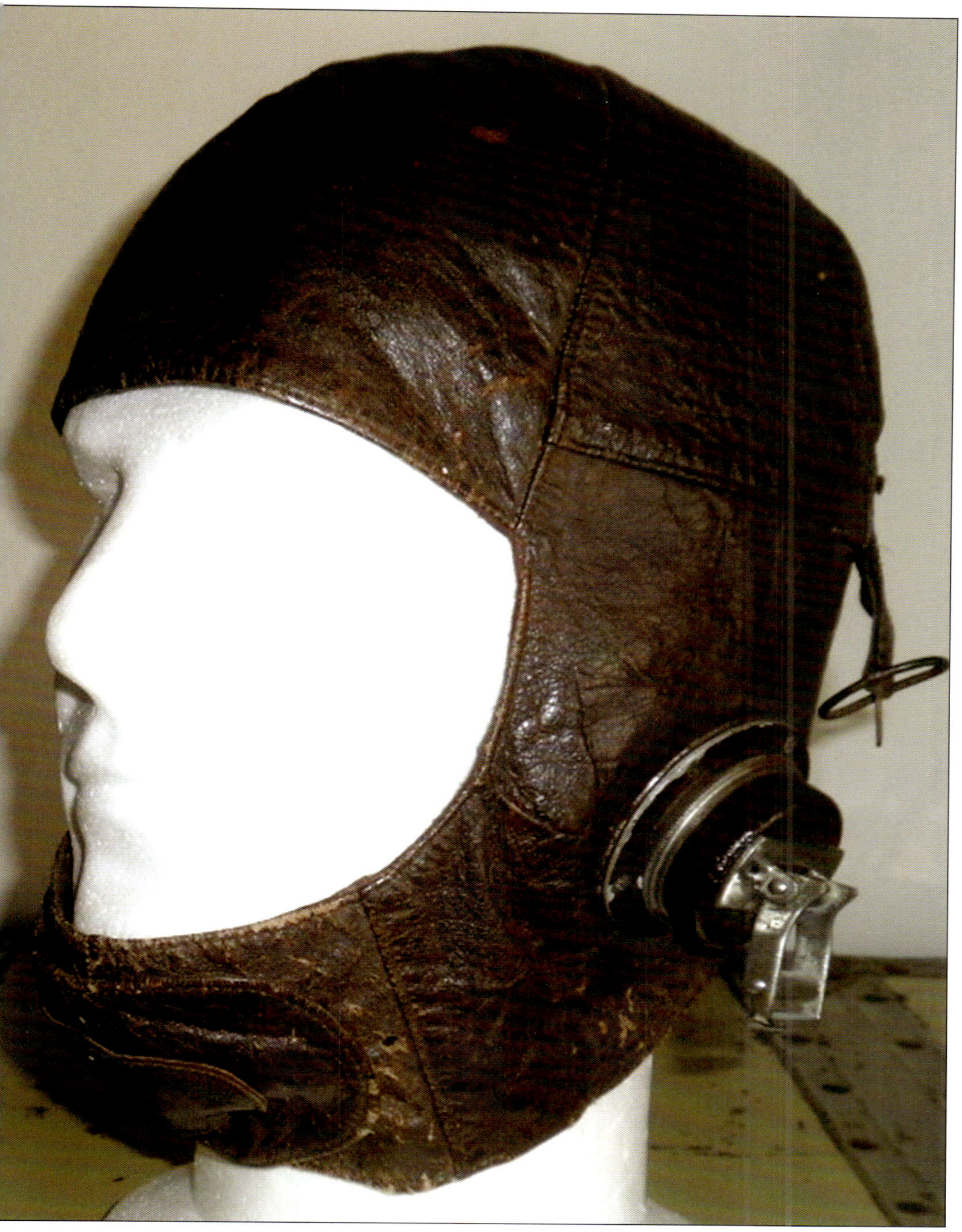

Radio-telephonic helmet with receivers issued in the 1930s for radiomen. This example is missing the crossing belt that held the earphones. Courtesy F. Burgio

Radio-telephonic helmet with earphones and throat microphone produced by LESA and named Model "TC." Courtesy MUSAM-ITAF

Radio-telephonic helmet produced by LESA and identical to the SAFAR.

Radio-telephonic helmet type Siemens produced by MICROTECNICA of the early production batch. Note the factory bakelite logo glued to the metallic earphone shell.

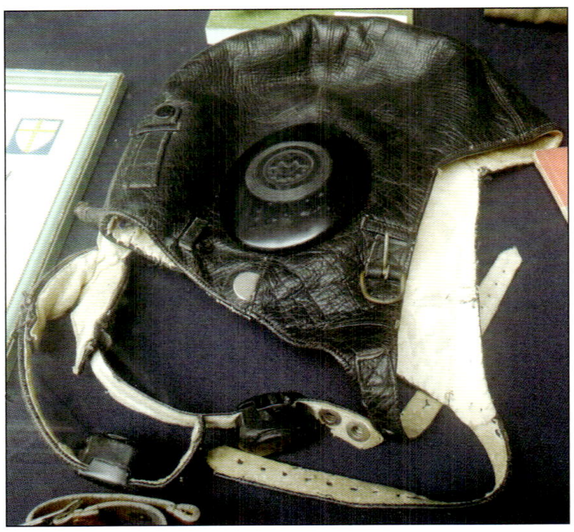

Flight helmet made by MICROTECNICA in 1941 named "Modello Siemens." Courtesy MUSAM-ITAF

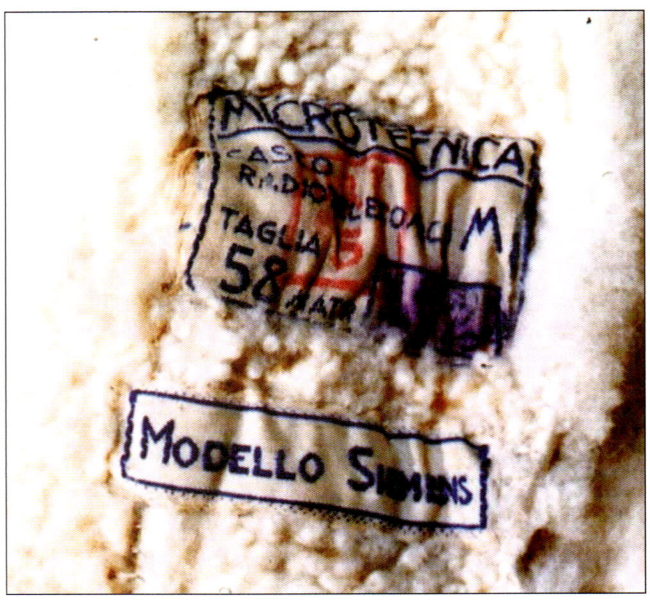

Label from the type Siemens flight helmet depicted earlier.

LESA TC model flight helmet.
Courtesy MUSAM-ITAF

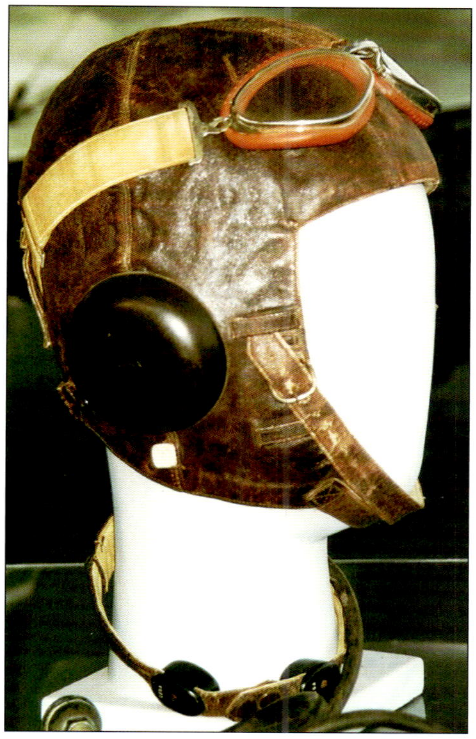

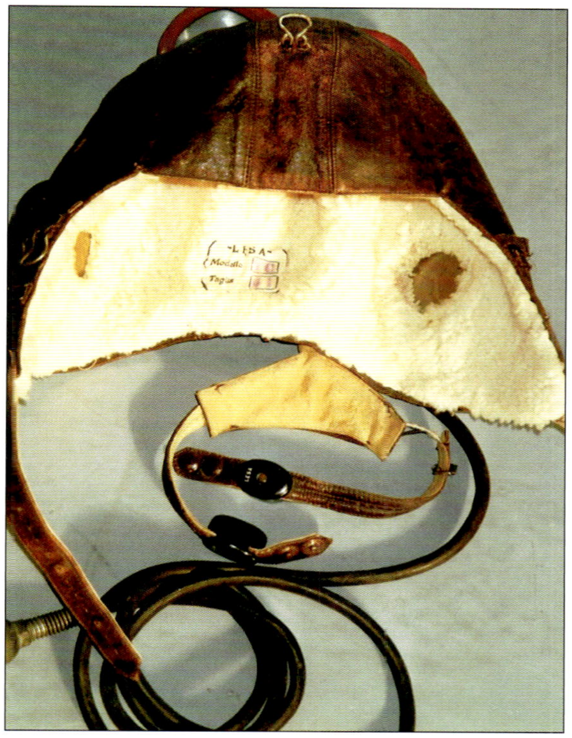

Radio-telephonic helmet model PDT produced by MICROTECNICA in 1944. This example is the summer version of the Siemens model. Some years ago it was an easy task to find these helmets in mint condition at militaria fairs. Supposedly, broad stocks remained stored and there are few evidences of operational use by the ANR during the RSI period. Courtesy P. Moncalvo

Siemens helmet showing the "IRON LEG" insignia of the ANR 2nd Fighter Group. Courtesy P. Moncalvo

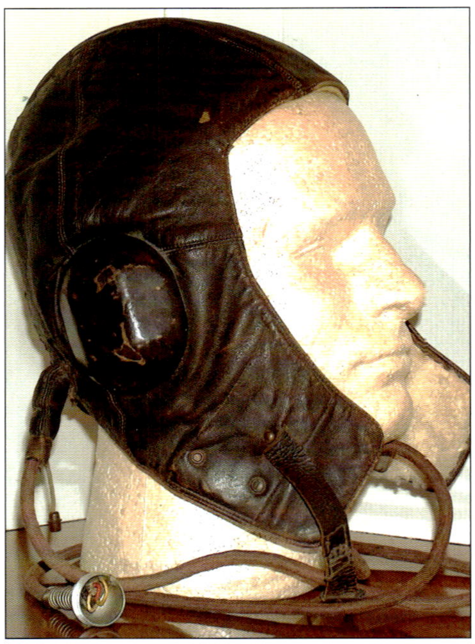

SAFAR winter leather flight helmet, Model 7938, belonging to the first production batch and featuring a leather neckstrap. The cable on the rear right side is missing the two rear studs to hold the goggles band and the mask band and is typical of late production examples. Being of the earlier batch, this helmet is also missing the hooks to fit German oxygen masks.

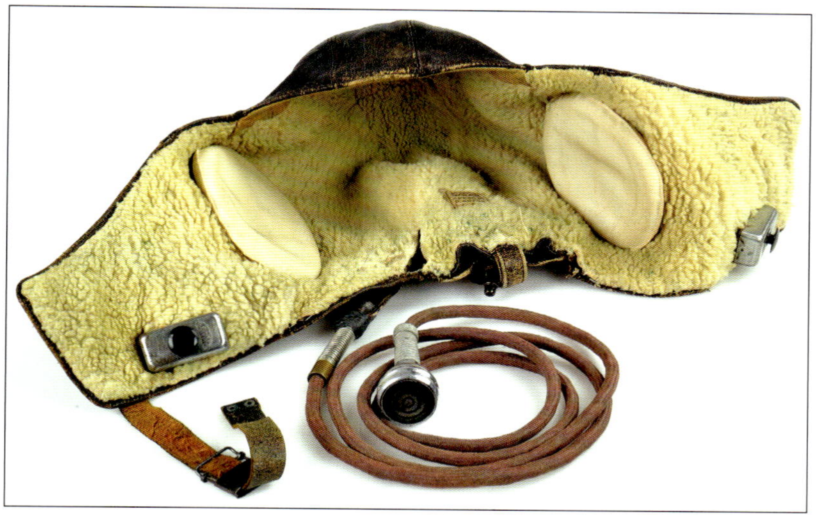

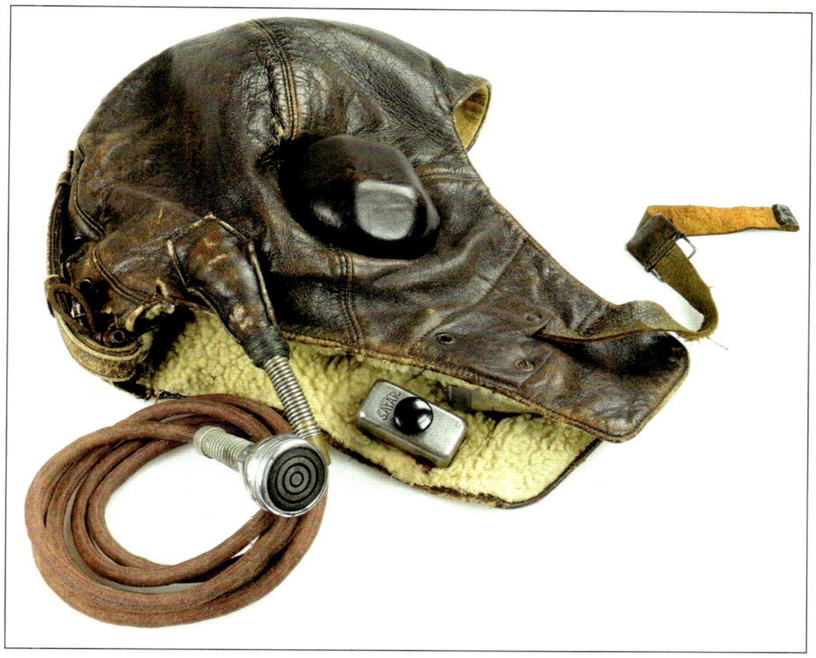

Another sample of the SAFAR winter helmet type APP-8035, identical to the APP-7938. Courtesy Castellani

Late-production SAFAR flight helmet Model APP 8035, as noted on the inner label. With reference to the previous production batches, it features a canvas chinstrap, two leather straps with lower snaps to hold the goggles band. The cable is located on the left rear side and this helmet is provided with the hooks to don a German AUER oxygen mask with two or three fitting hooks. The oxygen mask shown here is a German Model 10-67. Courtesy P. Moncalvo

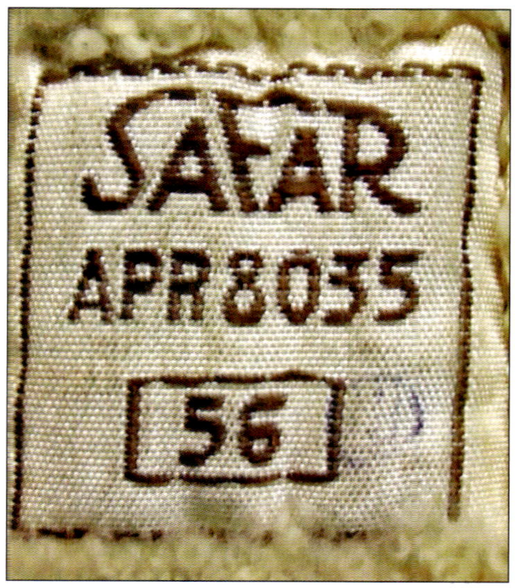

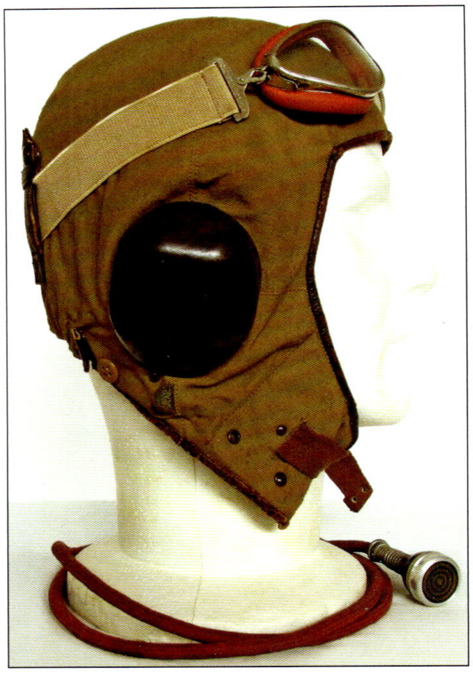

Summer variant of the SAFAR flight helmet Model 8120. Same as in the winter variant, there are the typical metal cast throat microphones, and metal earphone cups covered with imitation leather, and canvas chinstrap. Courtesy P. Moncalvo

SAFAR flight helmet belonging to Captain Merlo of 169th Squadron. This helmet was worn by Merlo the day he was wounded and downed in 1942. Noteworthy are the two aluminium pivots to fit the Italian oxygen mask and the unusual position of the riveted holes on the sides to allow for better ventilation. This helmet shows bloodstains from the wounded pilot who bailed out safely from his stricken Reggiane RE.2002 fighter-bomber.

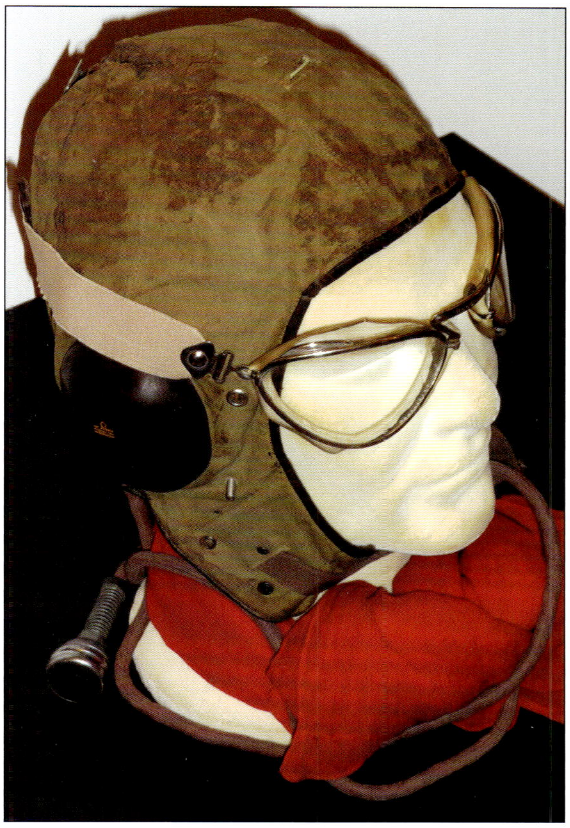

SAFAR Model 8120 flight helmet showing the German oxygen mask hooks and the different position of the ventilation holes.

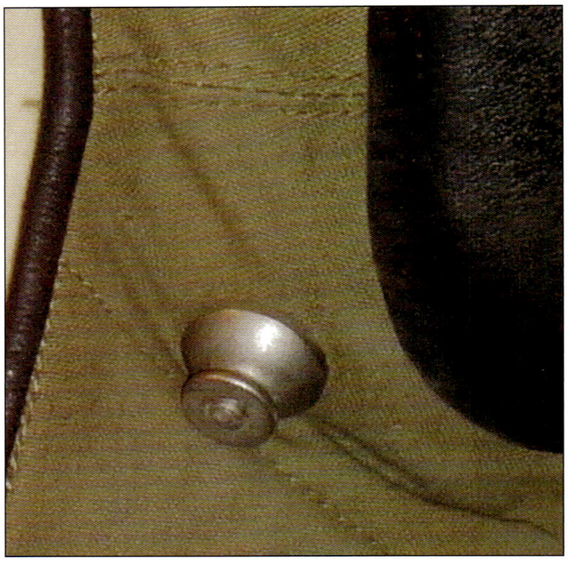

Detail of the fitting pivot of the previous Model 8348 flight helmet.

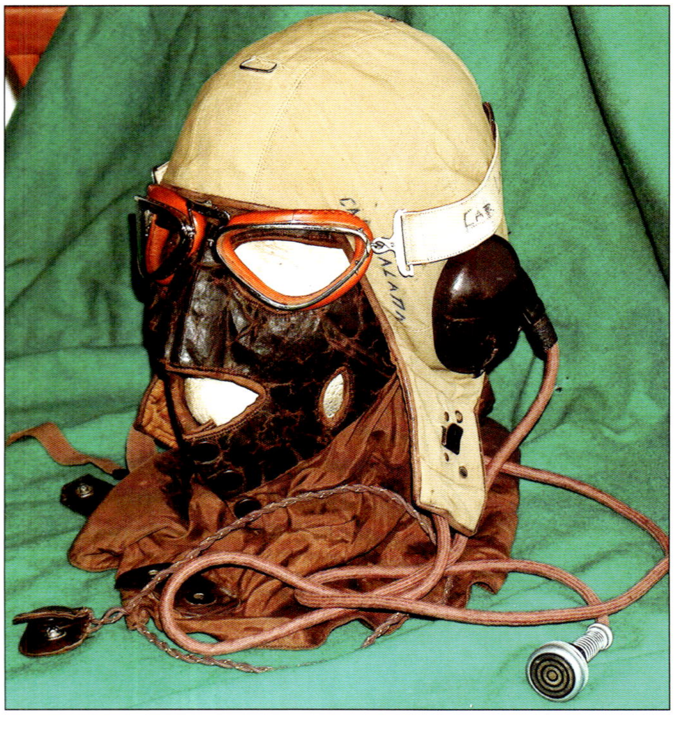

SAFAR Model 8120 flight helmet with Protector flight goggles and electrically heated protective face mask Model "CEBE," taken by Captain Lalatta as a French war prize.

***Above*: Detail of the throat microphone fitted on the SAFAR flight helmets.**

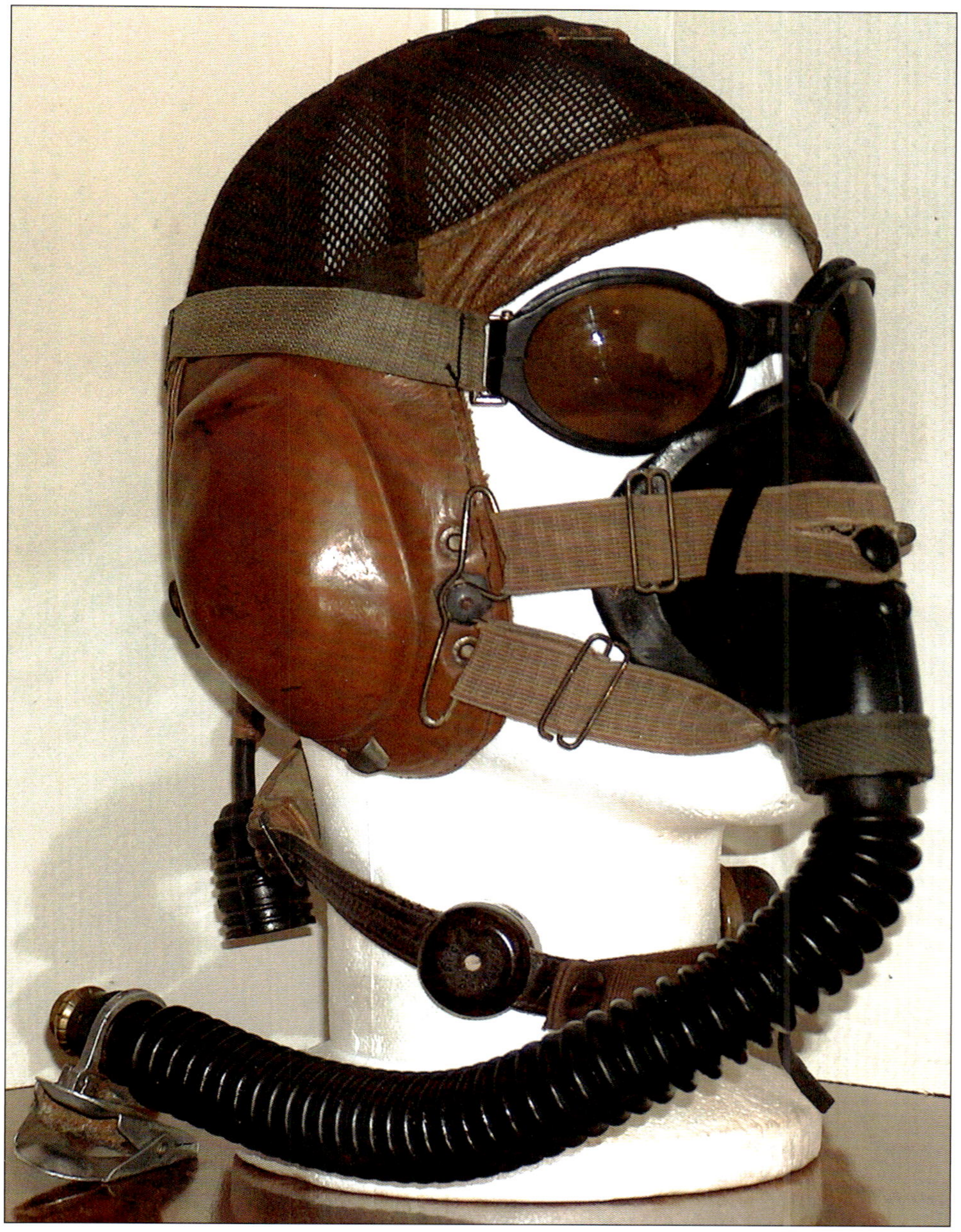

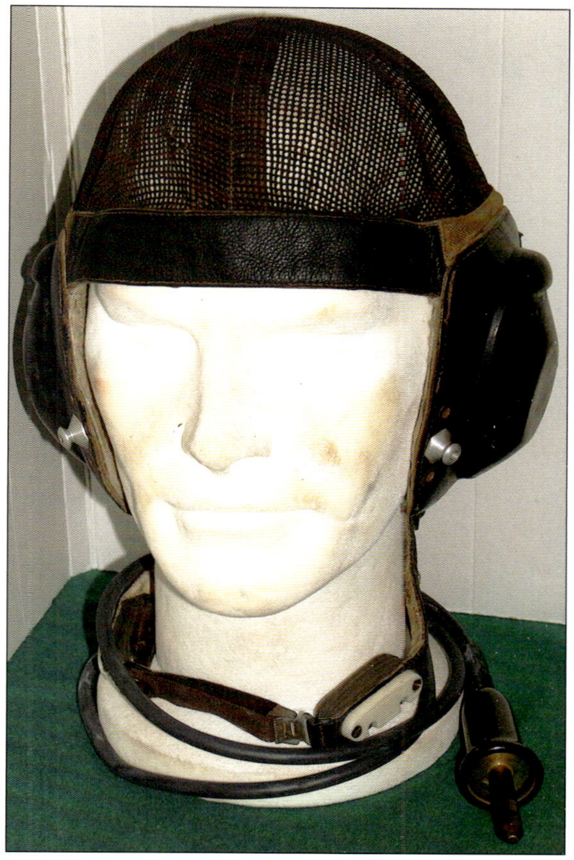

LKpN 101 flight helmet modified with RAF wiring and used by Italian pilots in the early postwar years when flying British aircraft.

***Above*: German LKpN 101 with type 10-6701 oxygen mask and 2nd type Gunther & Nitzsche goggles. These headgear items were used by both the RA and ANR.**

***Left*: Another example of mixed flight gear used in the late-war period by the Cobelligerent Air Force and in the early postwar years by the ITAF: RAF type "E" mesh flight helmet with Protector flight goggles. Courtesy P. Moncalvo**

***Right*: Modified LKpN 101 with Microtecnica throat microphone and FEME plug. This field modification was quite common in the ANR. Courtesy P. Marzetti Archive**

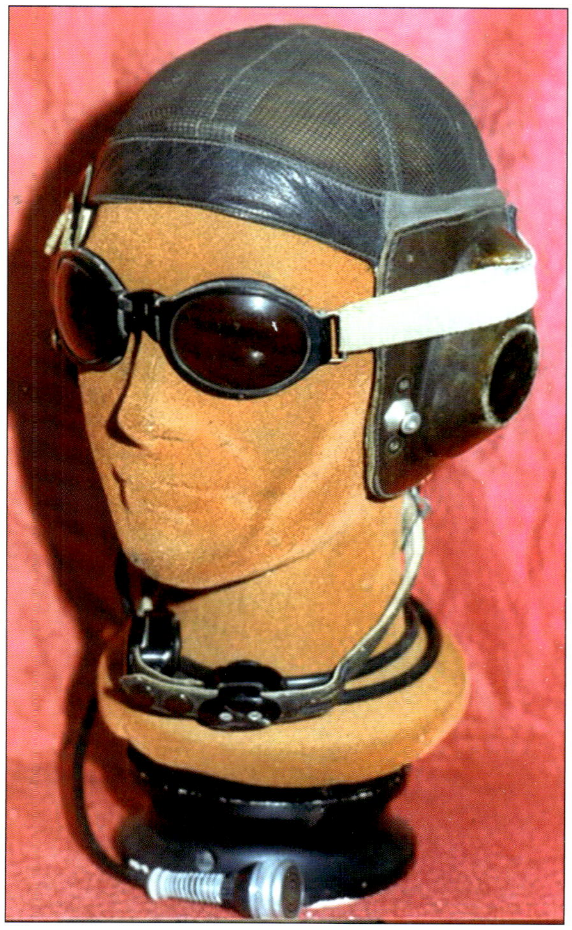

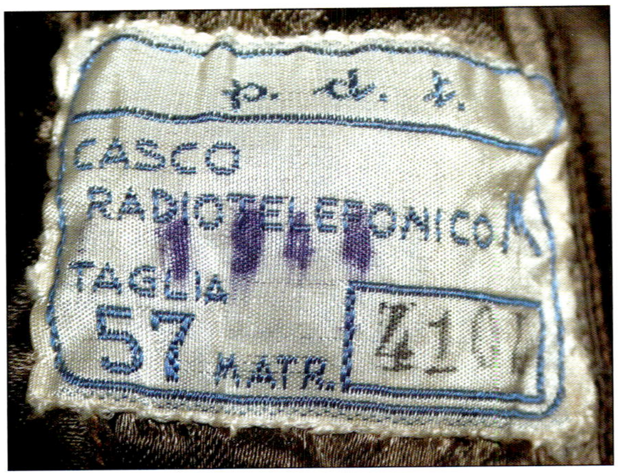

Label on the "M" type flight helmet produced by Microtecnica of Turin. Note that during the late-war period, to avoid targeting of the production factories, there existed a three-letter code to identify the manufacturer, same as in Germany.

SAFAR winter helmet label. The "G" probably stands for "size large," and 61 is the head size. The meaning of "APP" (gear?) and "P" (production?) is still unknown.

Detail of the rather basic label of the Siemens winter flight helmet from the late-1930s.

Detail of the oxygen mask hook on SAFAR helmets with the markings of the manufacturer. Usually these flight helmets were provided with various oxygen mask hooks.

Label of the SAFAR Model 8348 flight helmet made of green fabric and differs from the Model 8120 for the additional oxygen mask hooks.

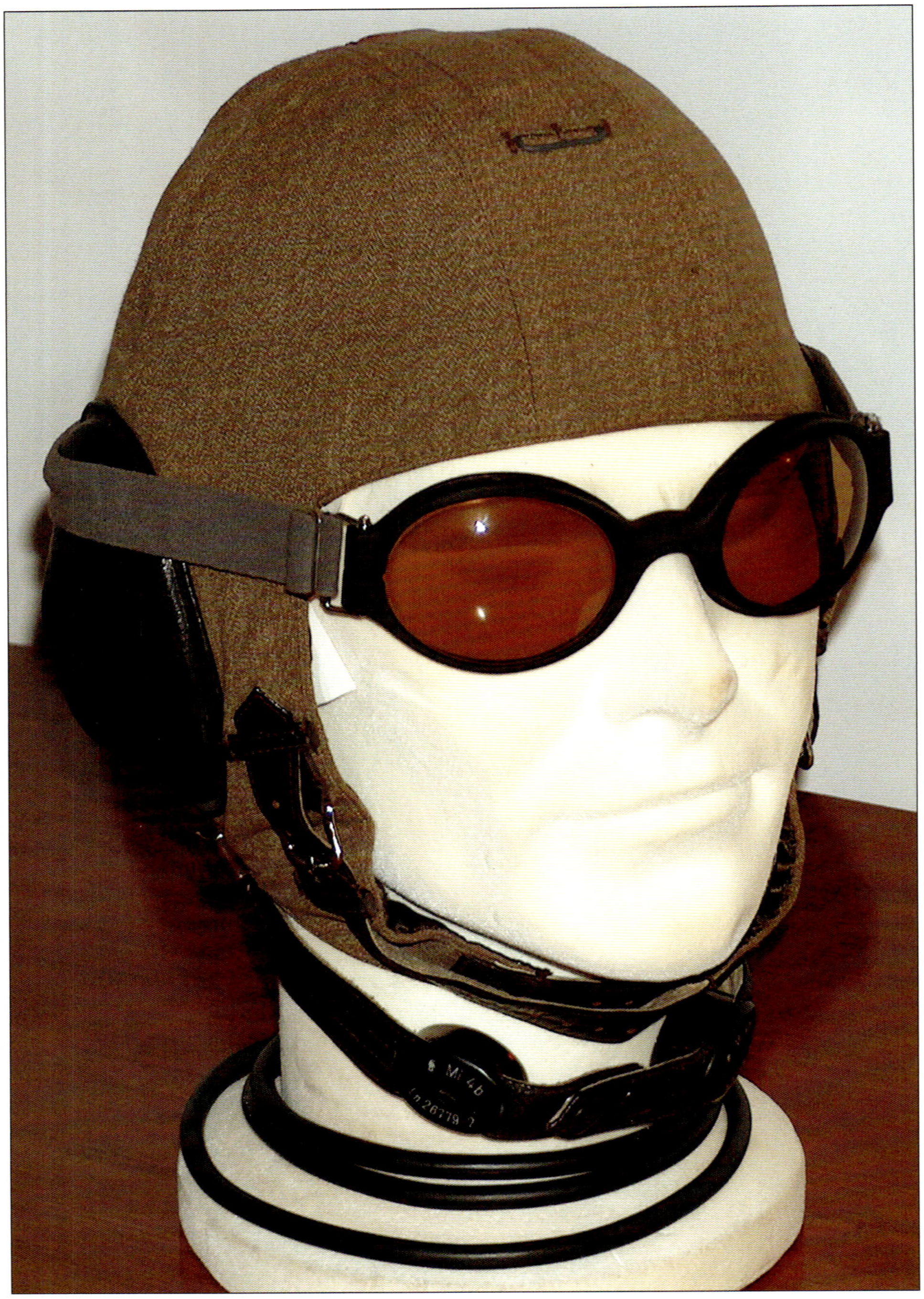

German LKpS 101 summer flight helmet mostly used by the RA Ju 87 Stukas crews were nicknamed in Italy " Picchiatelli" due to their dive-bombing technique (dive = picchiata).

The RAF Model "D" tropical flight helmet was used by the Cobelligerent Air Force in the late-World War II years and by the ITAF in the early postwar years. Courtesy P. Moncalvo

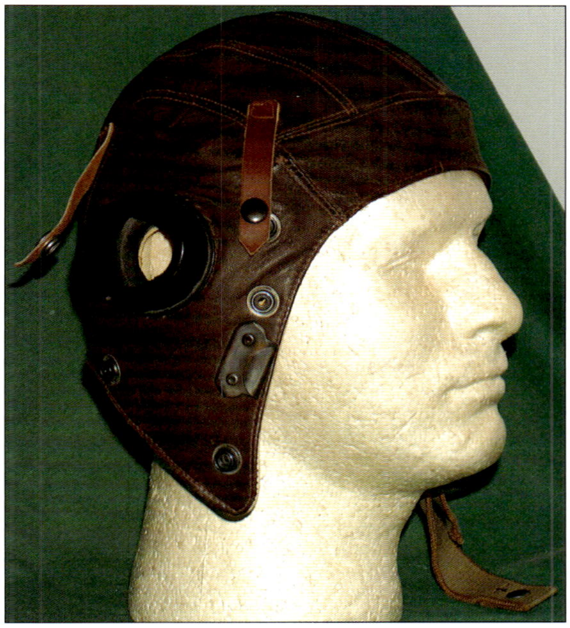

Italian made type "C" leather flight helmet patterned after the original RAF helmet with several differences. It was used when flying ITAF Spitfires and Vampires in the late-1940s and early-1950s.

The USAAF A-11 leather flight helmet together with the ANH-15 summer flight helmet were part of the large American supplies of the late-war/early-postwar years. These flight helmets were used until 1951, mostly to fly the P-38s, P-47s and P-51s delivered to the ITAF.

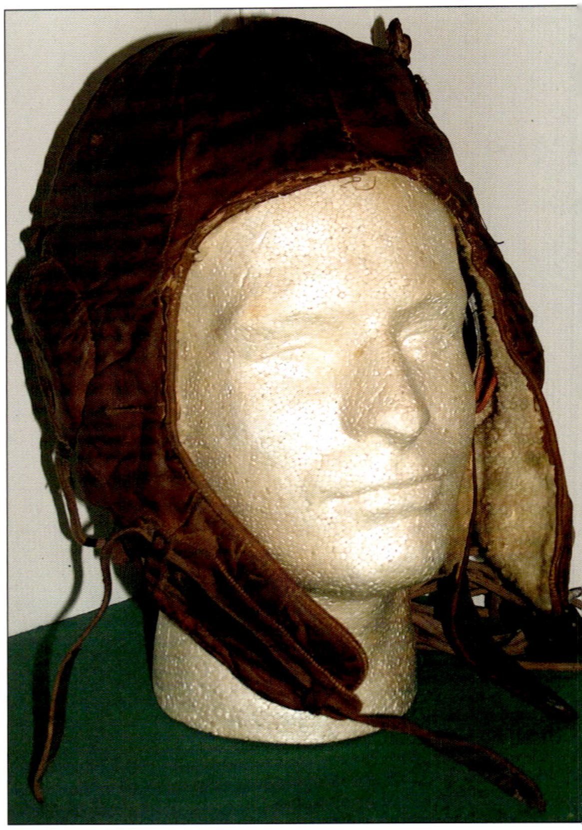

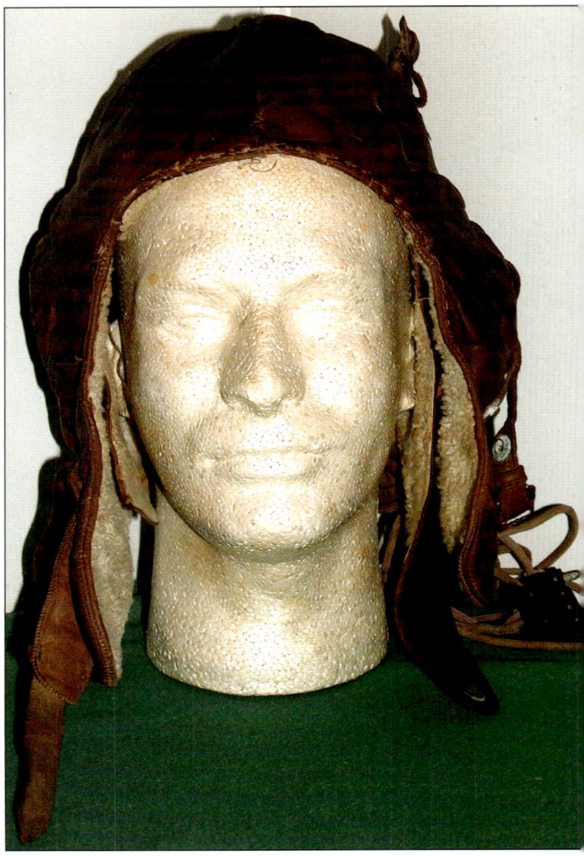

SAFAR radiotelephonic flight helmet for radiomen of the late-1920s.

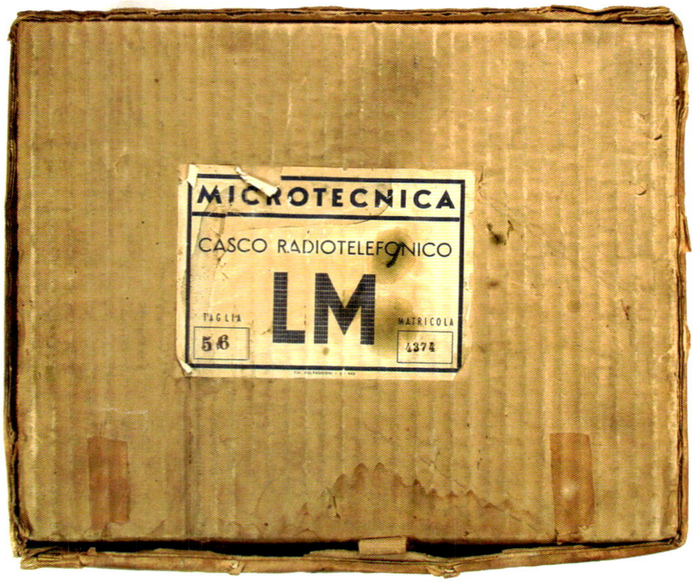

Original issue box for the "Microtecnica" summer flight helmet.
Courtesy Collector's Guild via P. Whamond

CHAPTER NINE

GOGGLES

***Left*: Flight goggles with the "stork" marking of the Ratti factory, and used during World War I. The manufacturer's initials "GR" are engraved on the elasticated band fittings.**

***Below*: Italian made goggles of the pioneers' age.**

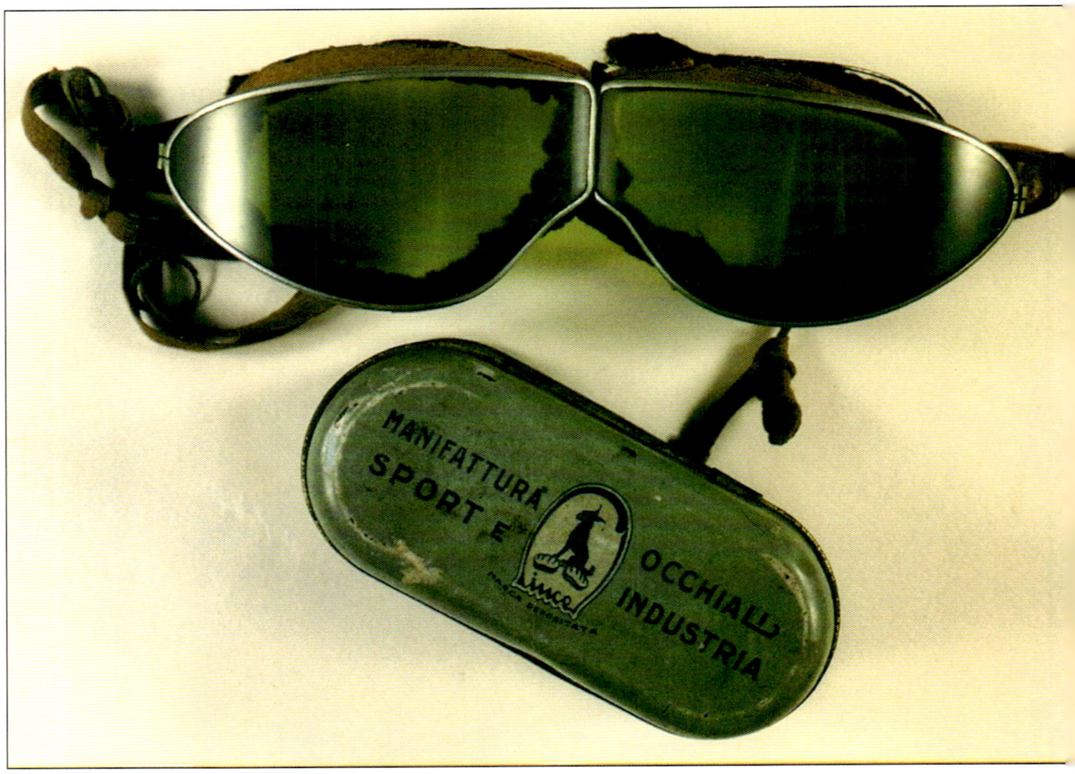

Commercial "LINCE" (lynx) goggles with metal issue case, and used from 1915 to 1930.

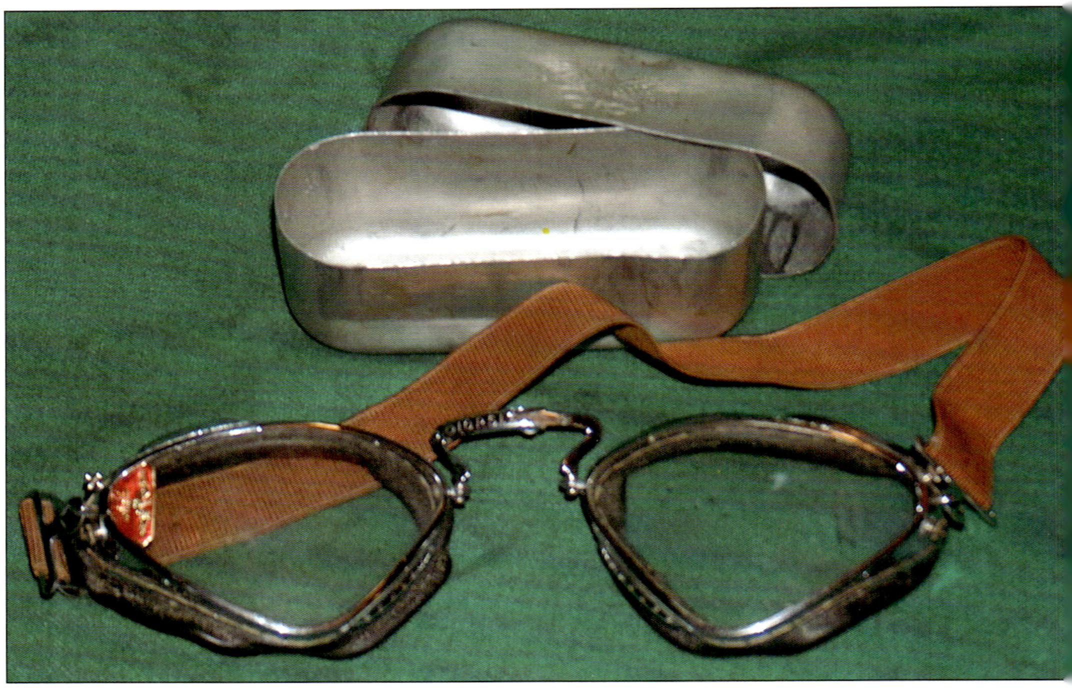

Commercial goggles for used in autos and planes.

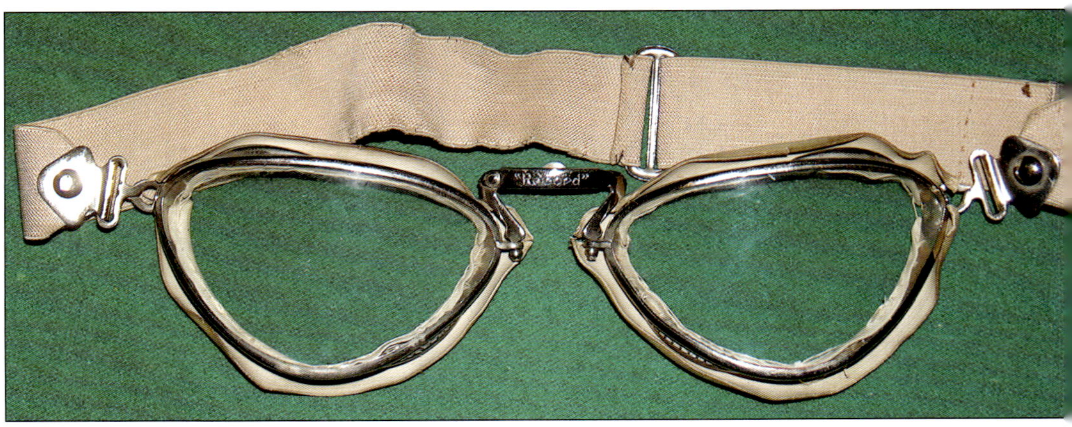

Goggles with protective leather mask, produced by FOPAIS, Model TRISVEL with stratified lenses. Courtesy S. Santucci

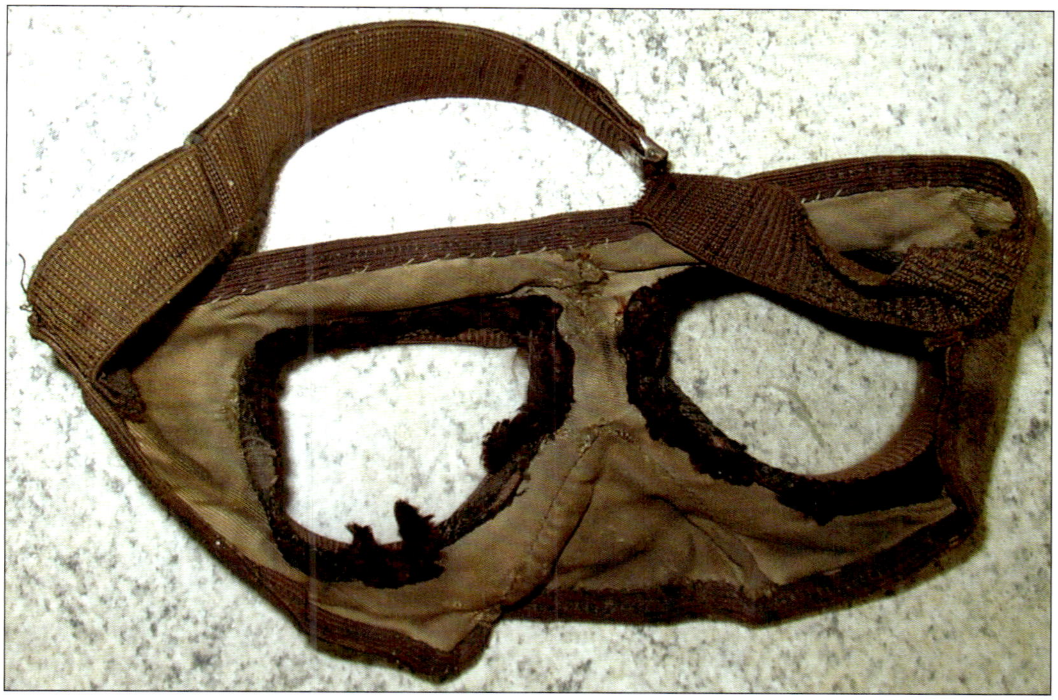

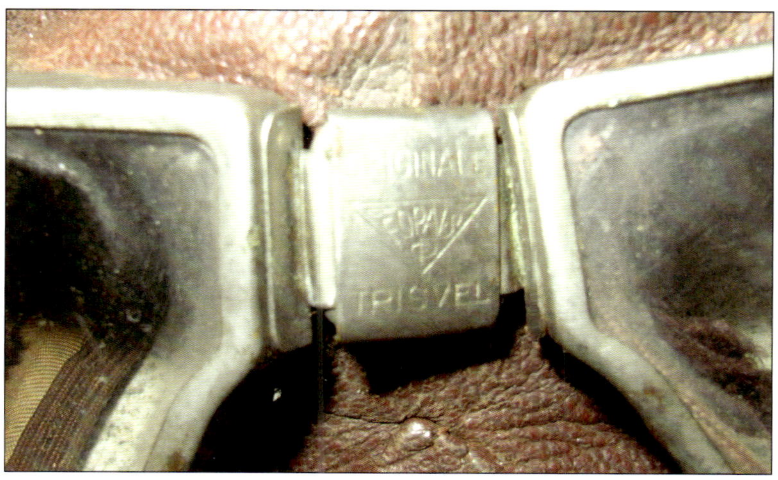

Celluloid eyeshields, sunshield and fire resistant device produced by Ratti as the Model 51. An example is displayed at NASM in Washington, D.C. in the RA gallery.

Commercial model of the early-1930s with the typical adjusting bridge.

Similar to the preceding example, these goggles, produced by FOPAIS, have a provision for the fitting of celluloid dark lenses over the clear.

Two like models by Ratti, suitable for auto drivers and aviators.

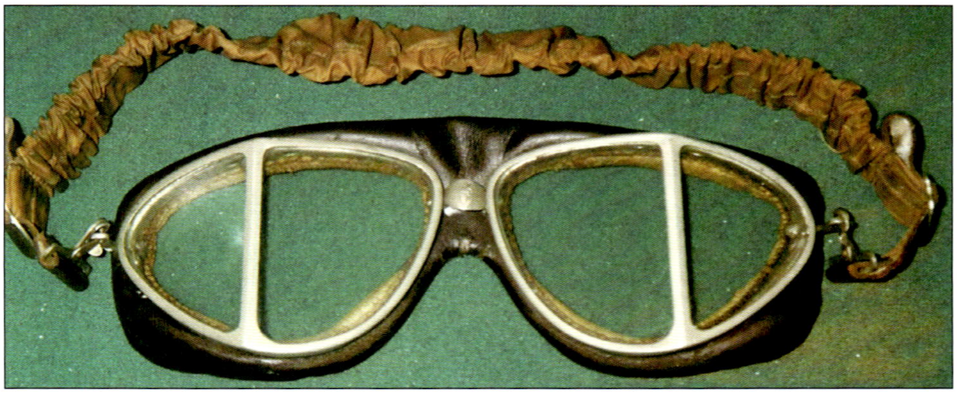

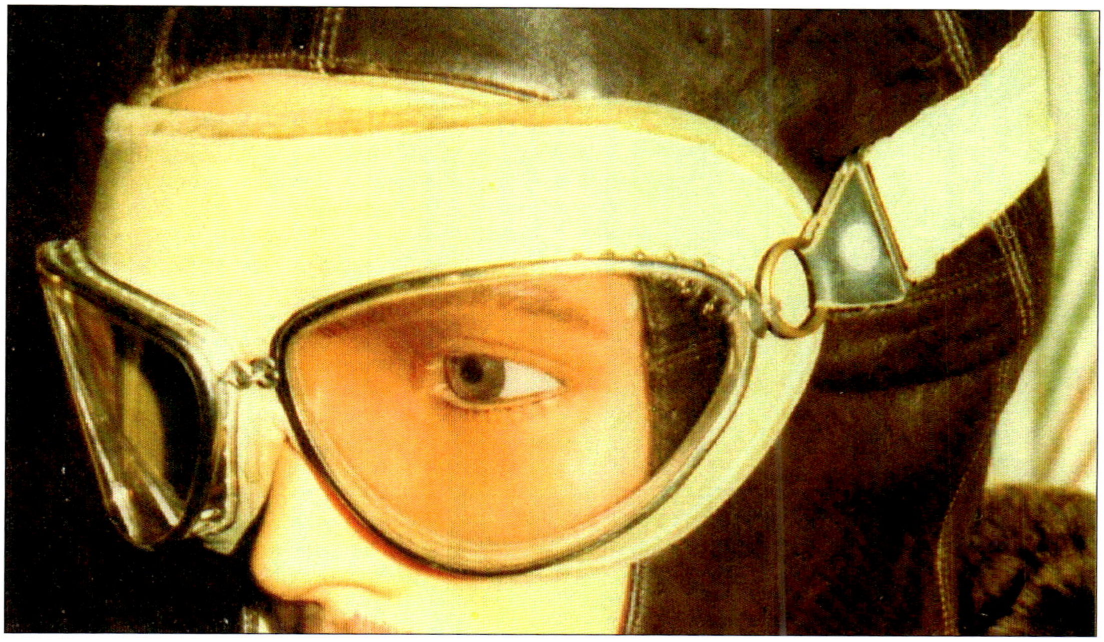

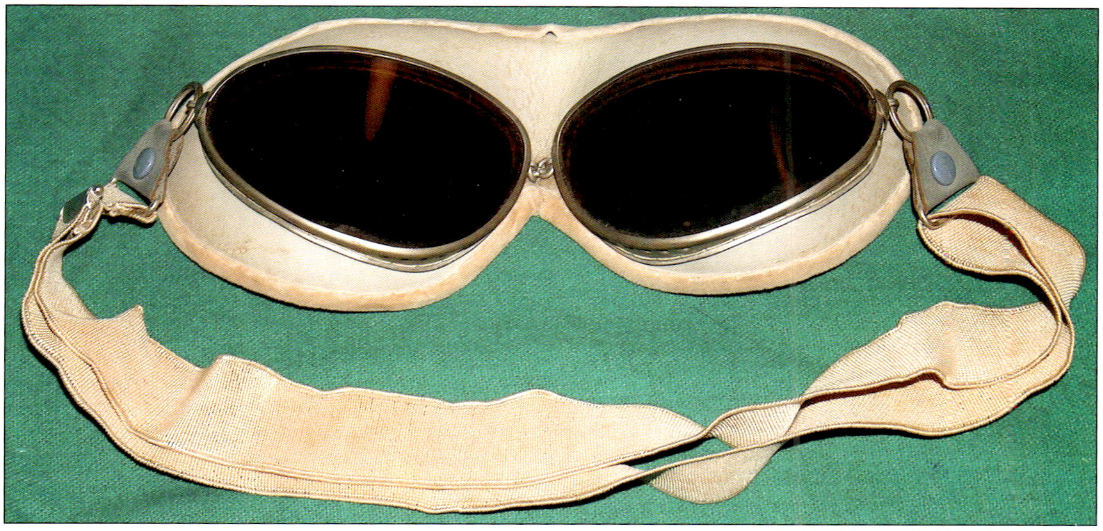

German goggles with large rubber cushions and velvet lining, used by RA bomber crews during the early months of World War II.

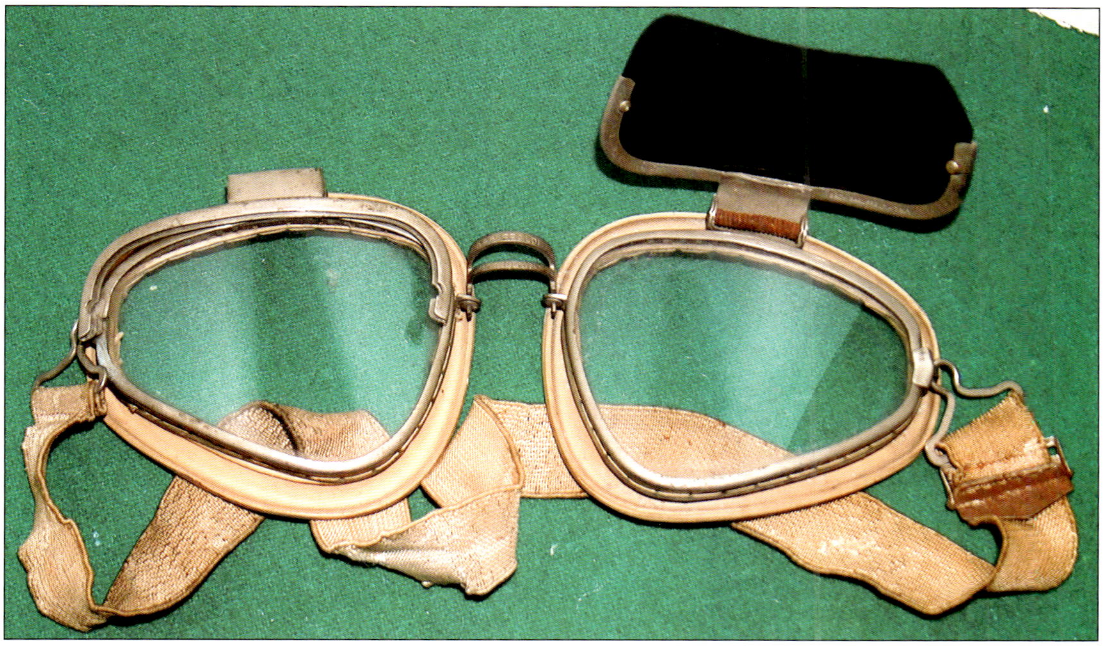

Commercial goggles by Baruffaldi with movable sunshields.

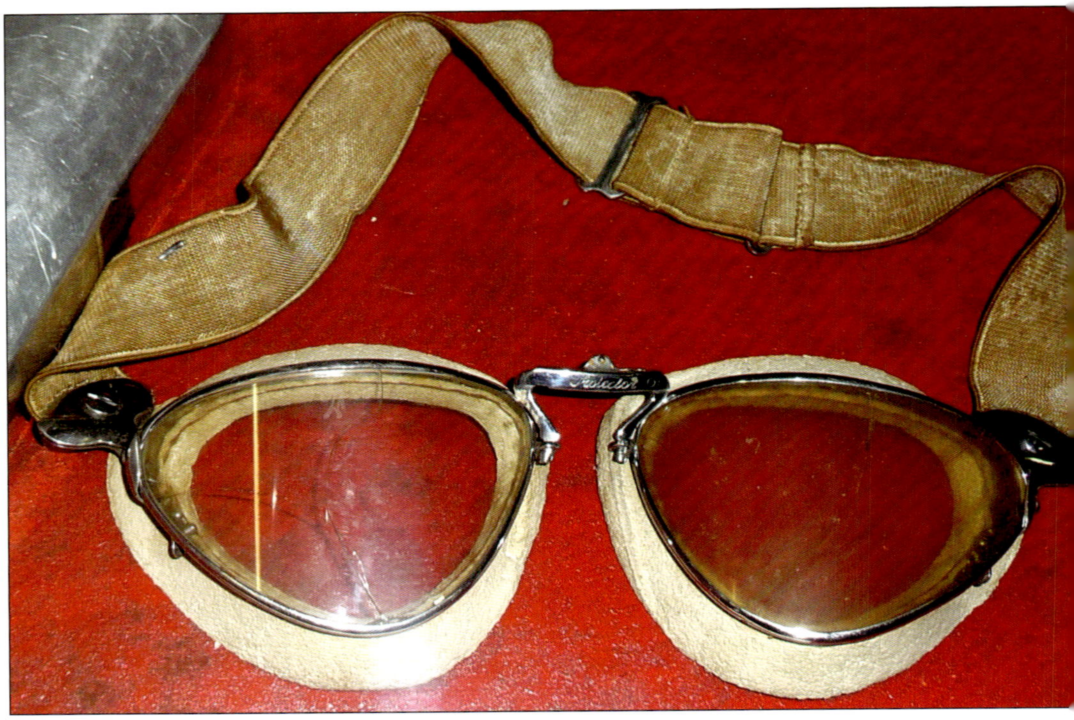

Super Protector 50 by Ratti of Turin.

Goggles by FOPAIS with flat lenses, foam rubber cushions and waterproof elasticated band.

Mint condition VELTRIS goggles by FOPAIS in their cardboard case. Note that the factory sticker as still present on the left lens.

Aluminiun case of the FRANCOR models by FOPAIS.

VELTRIS goggles by **FOPAIS** similar to the previous example with fixed bridge.

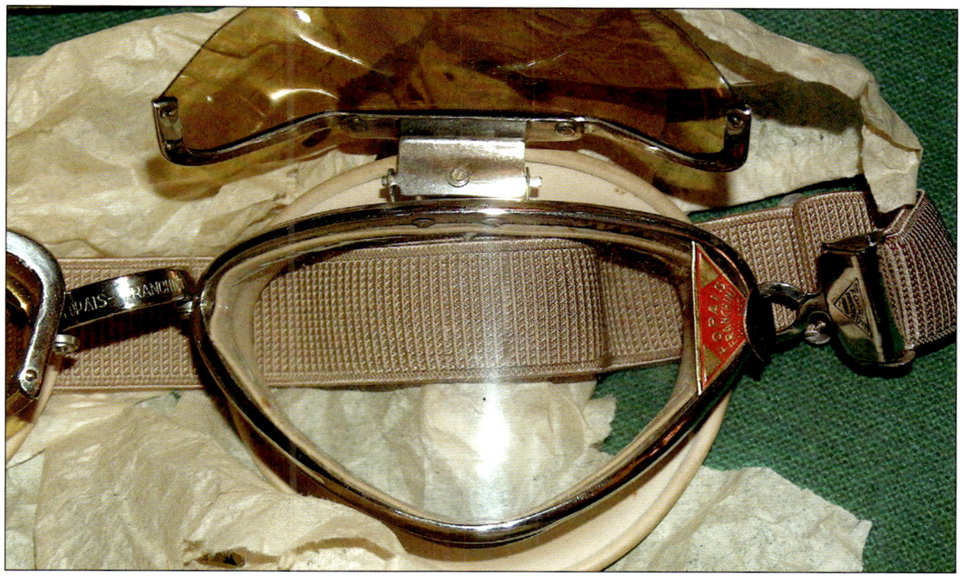

Protector Model 27 goggles of the early production batch with their aluminiun case. The adjusting bridge travel is horizontal.

Protector Model 27 goggles worn over a standard issue leather flying helmet

Protector Model 27 goggles worn over a standard Giusti flight helmet.

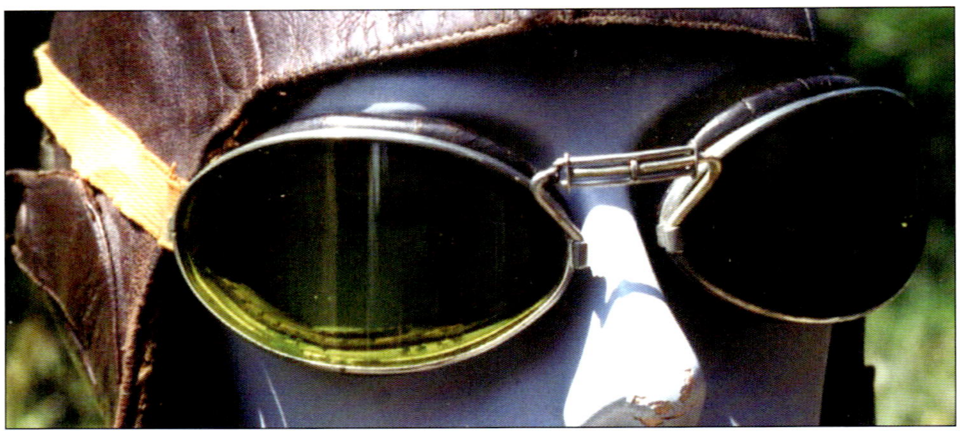

Model 27 Protector with curved lenses. Courtesy MUSAM-ITAF

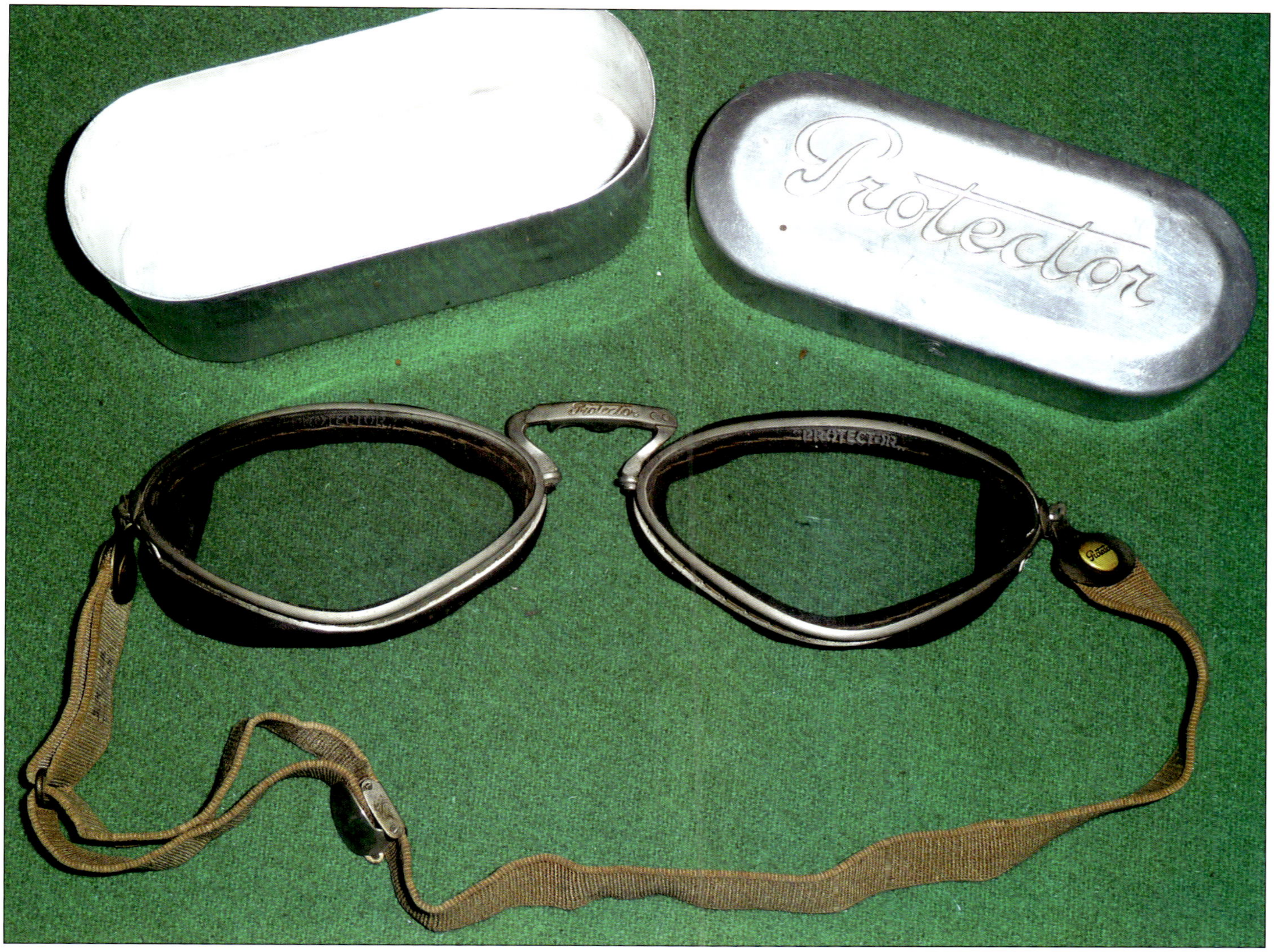

Other samples of the Protector 27 goggles, with cases. Note the details of the adjusting bridge and the manufacturer marks on the elasticated band.

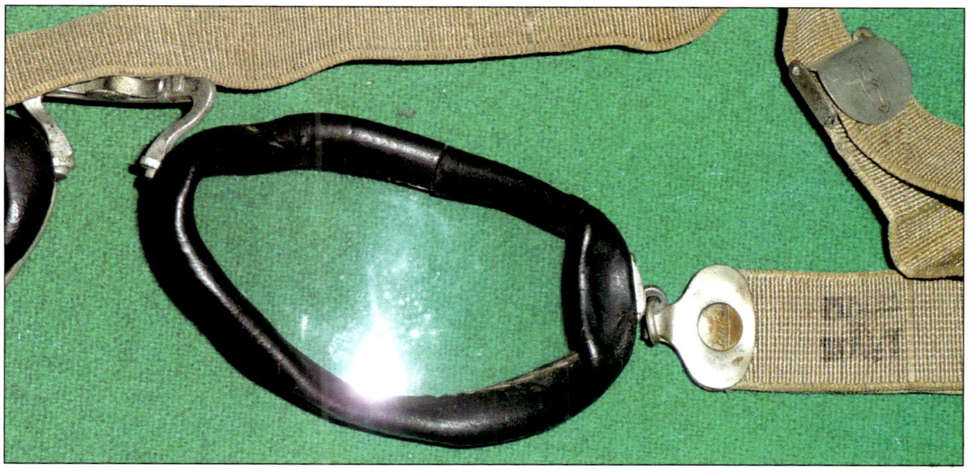

Superprotector Model 50.

Superprotector Model 30 with flat lenses.

Model 340 by Ratti. The "Protector" series frames were made of nickel-plated brass. The lenses were made with single curved glass and tubular rubber cushions. The leather case was offered as an option to the standard aluminiun version.

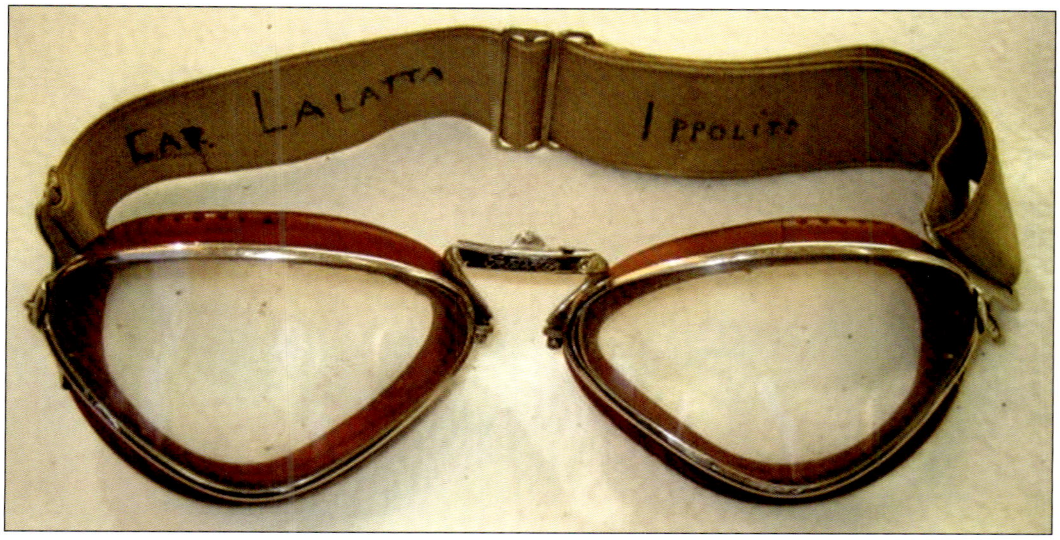

Protector 27 belonging to the then Captain Lalatta.

General view of the main Ratti models. Courtesy R. Zizzo

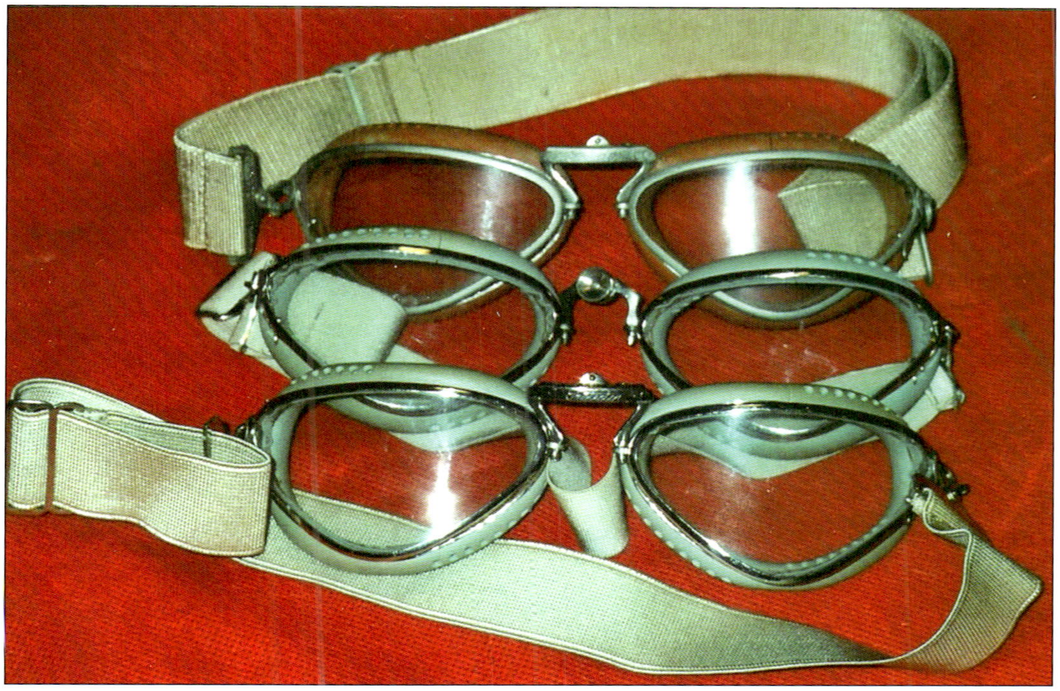

***Below*: VELTRIS goggles by FOPAIS.**

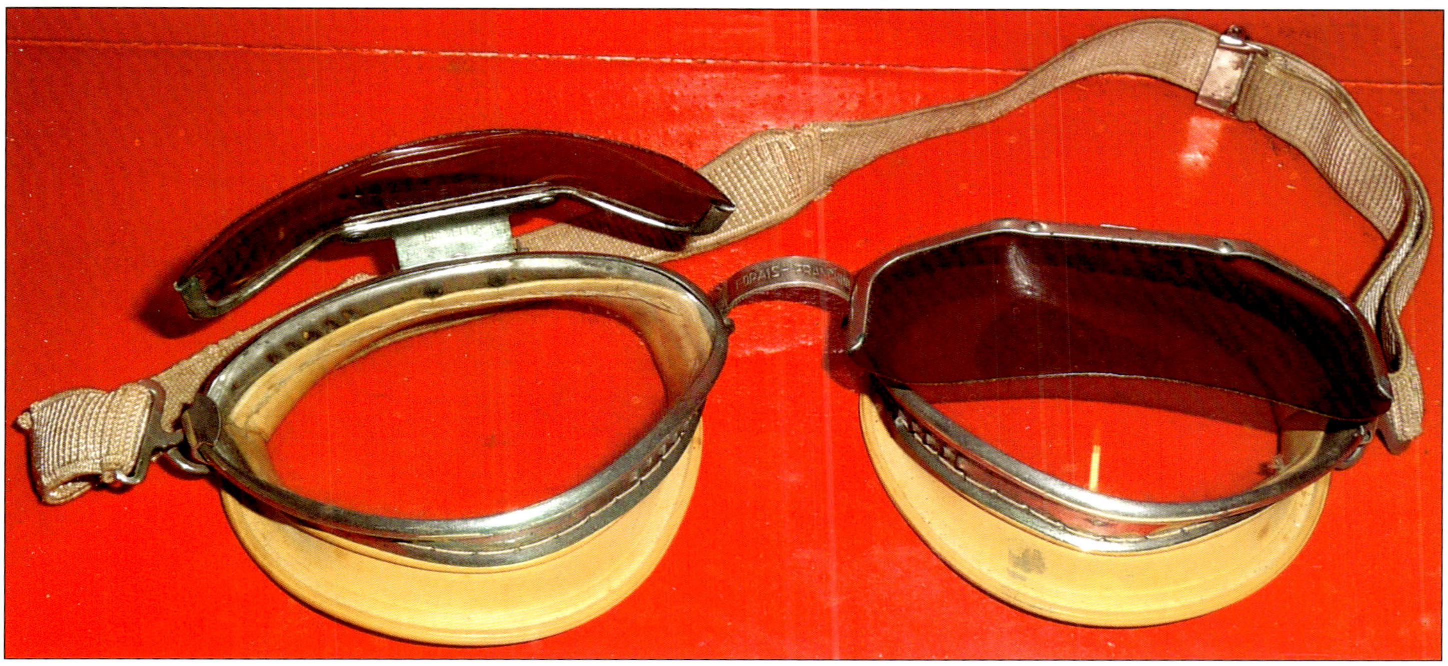

FRANCOR pilot goggles by **FOPAIS.** Note the anti-fog, adjustable ports. Detail of the adjusting bridge on the earlier batch of Protector goggles.

VELTRIS GOGGLES by **FOPAIS** with metal case.

Model 337 **DICTATOR** goggles with sunshields and cardboard case.

Variants of the FOPAIS goggles of "FRANCOR" series, with rectangular lenses with copper or aluminiun frames.

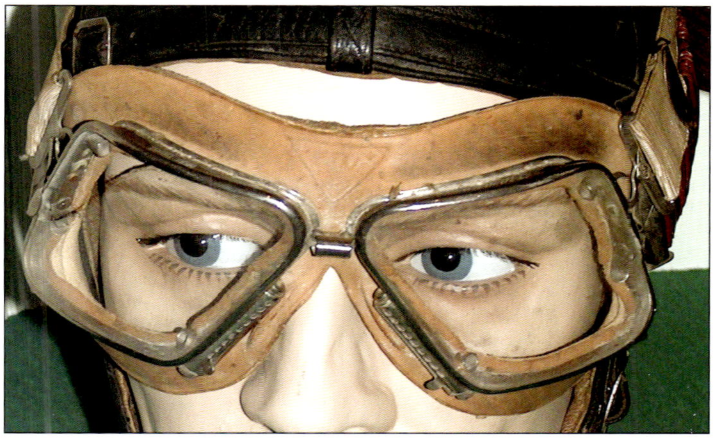

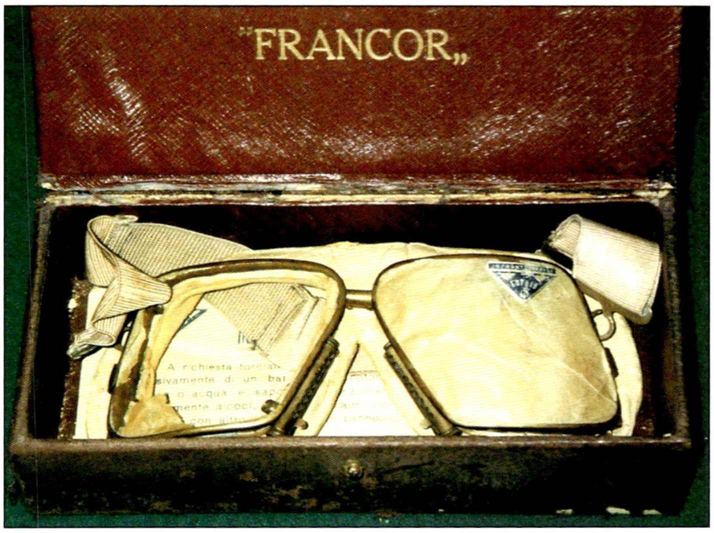

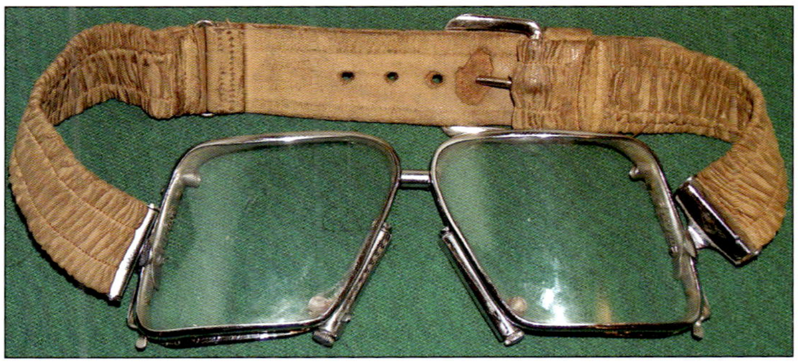

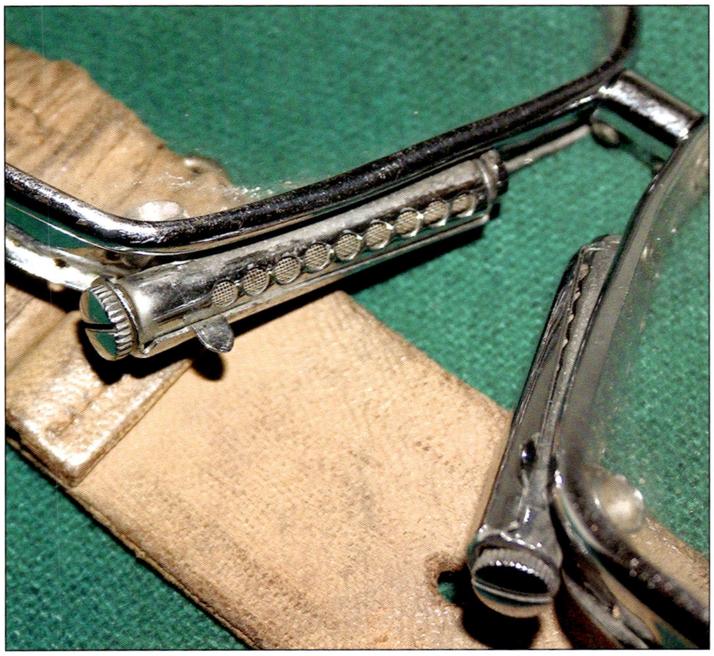

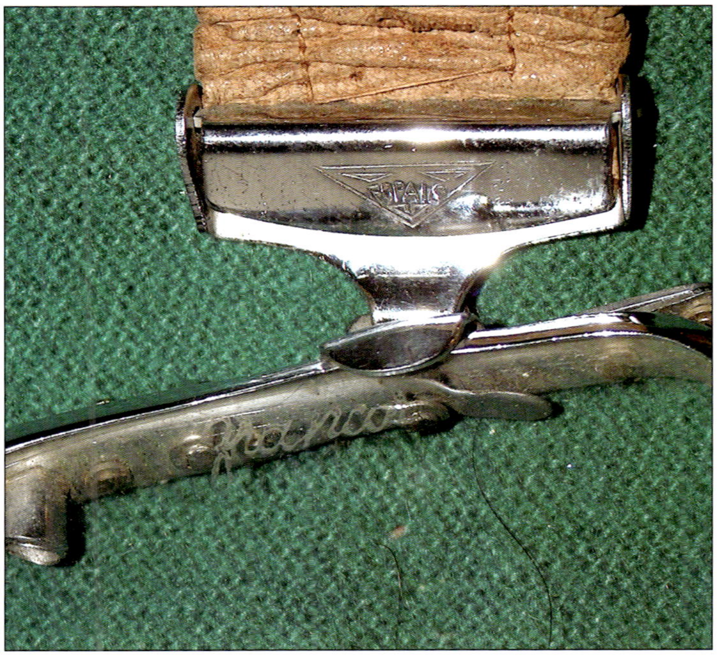

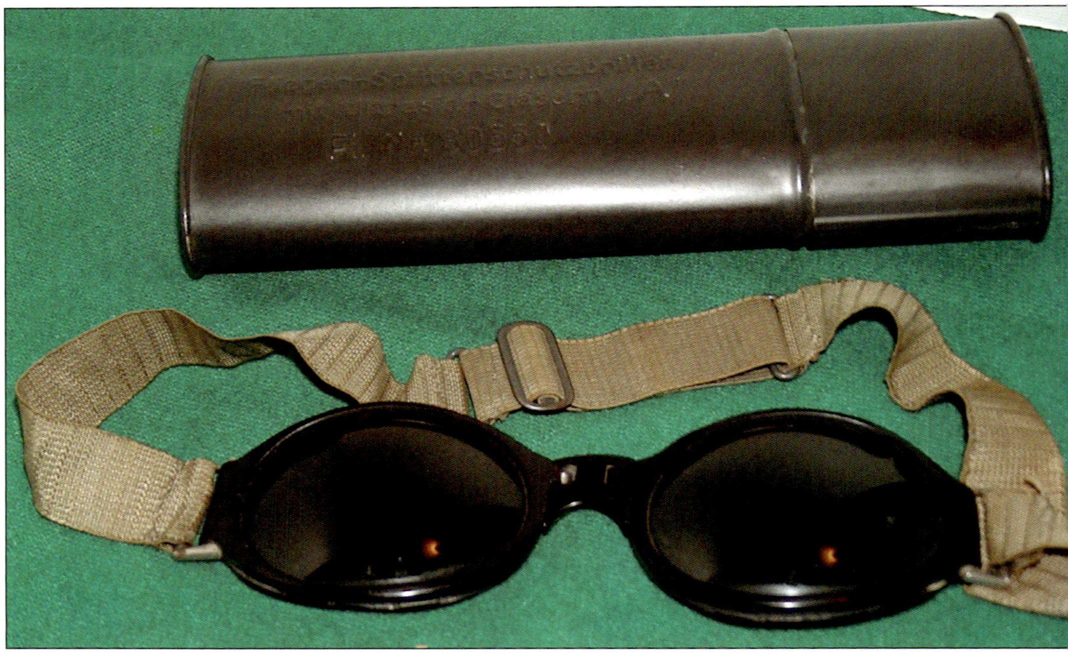

German Splitterschutzbrillen by Nietsche & Gunther used by an Italian pilot of 4th Fighter Wing.

DICTATOR Model 27 with case.

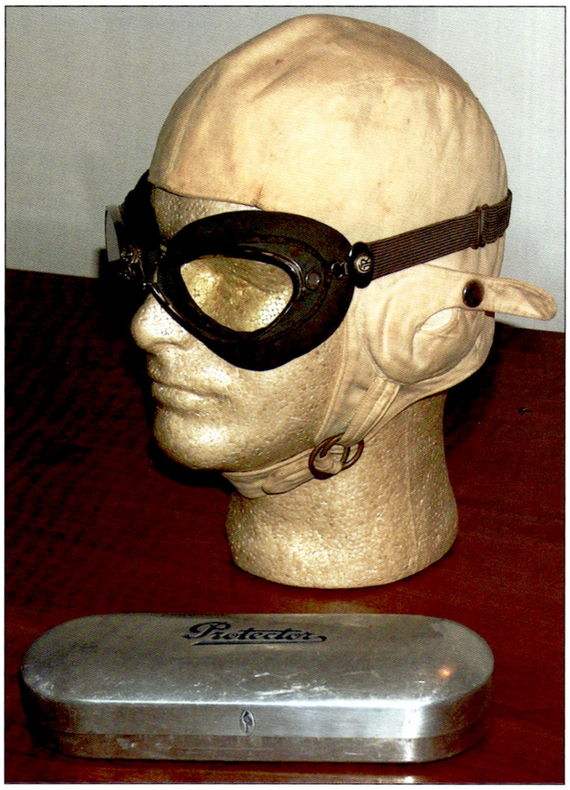

SUPER 512 Model by Ratti, with flat safety lenses, leather sides, adjusting bridge, and foam rubber cushions.

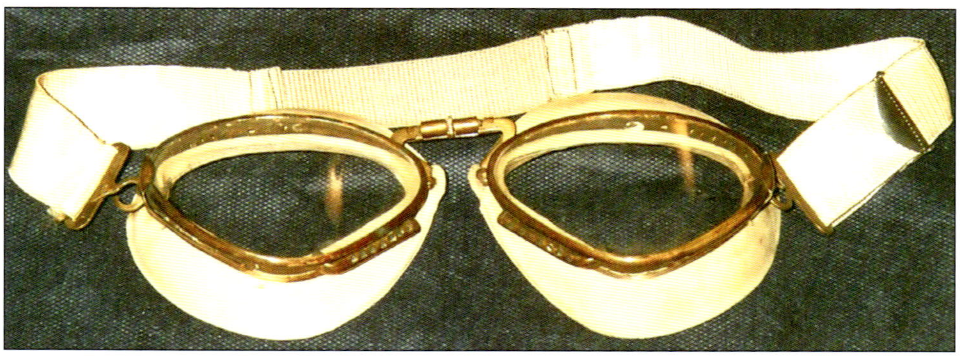

Another pair of FOPAIS aviator goggles.

Two different French made CEBE goggles – war prizes used by the Italians. The former is quite similar to some American commercial models, and the latter has electrical heating.

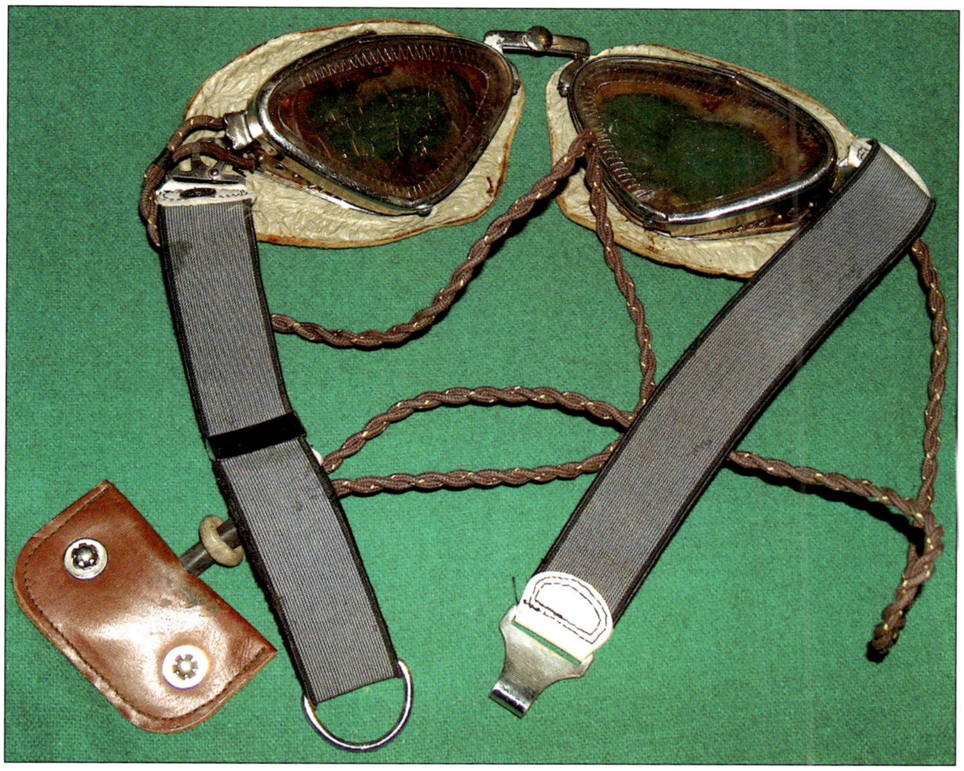

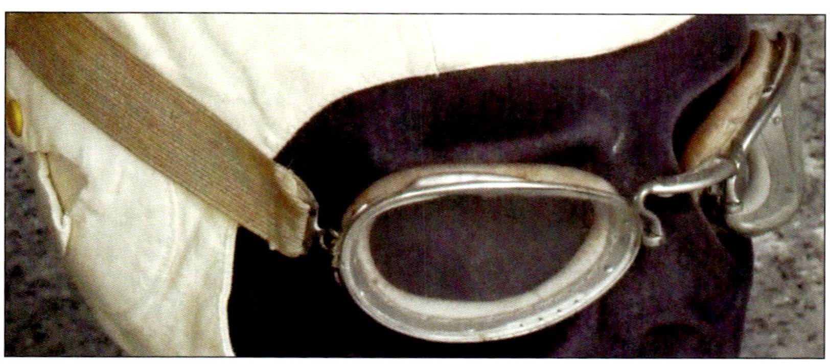

Type B-6 Meyrowitz goggles belonging to an Italian pilot. Courtesy D. Rao

Fopais goggles with flat lenses.

CHAPTER TEN

PARACHUTES

SALVATOR type B parachute. Courtesy P. Marzetti Archive

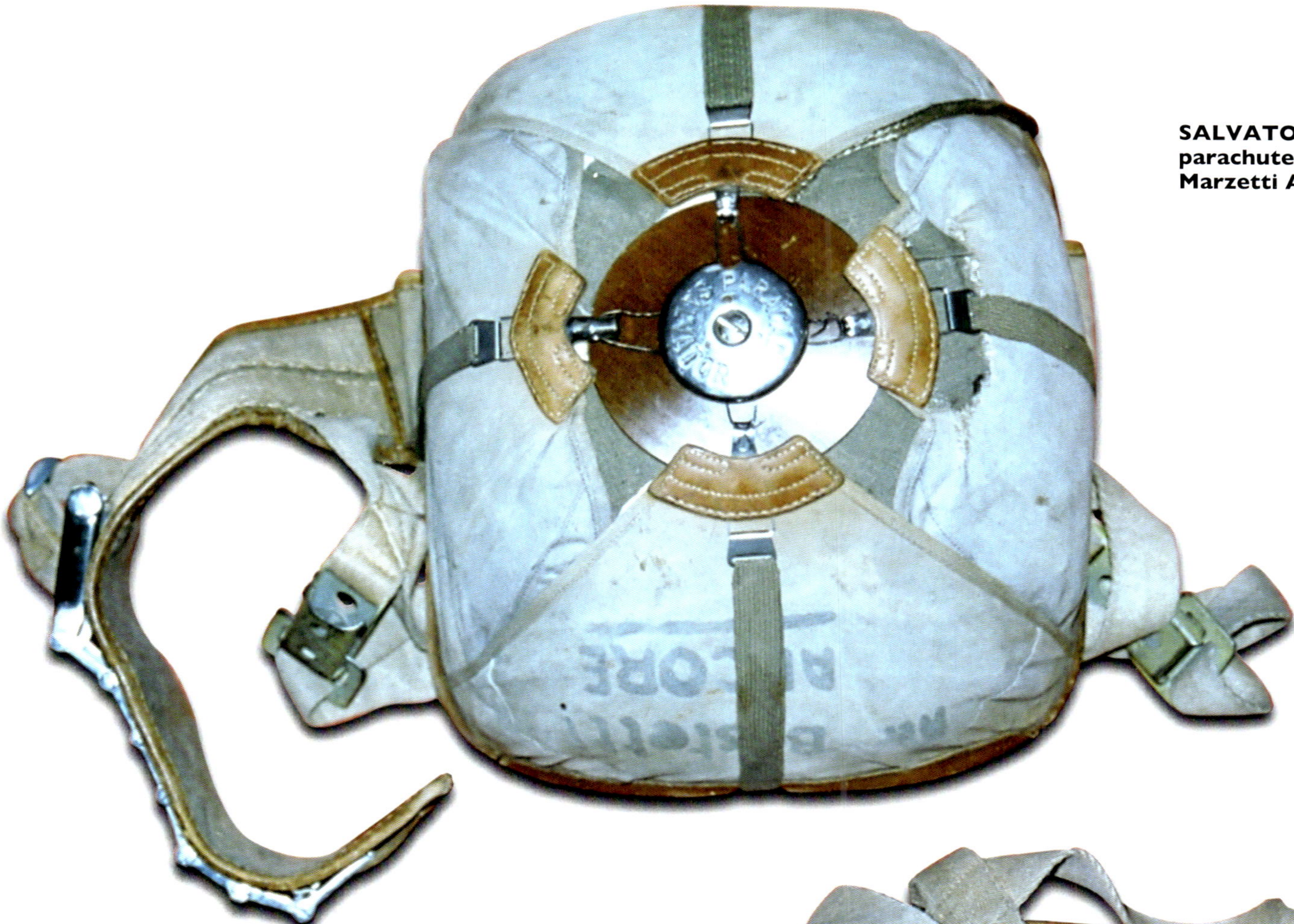

SALVATOR type D-30 parachute. Courtesy P. Marzetti Archive

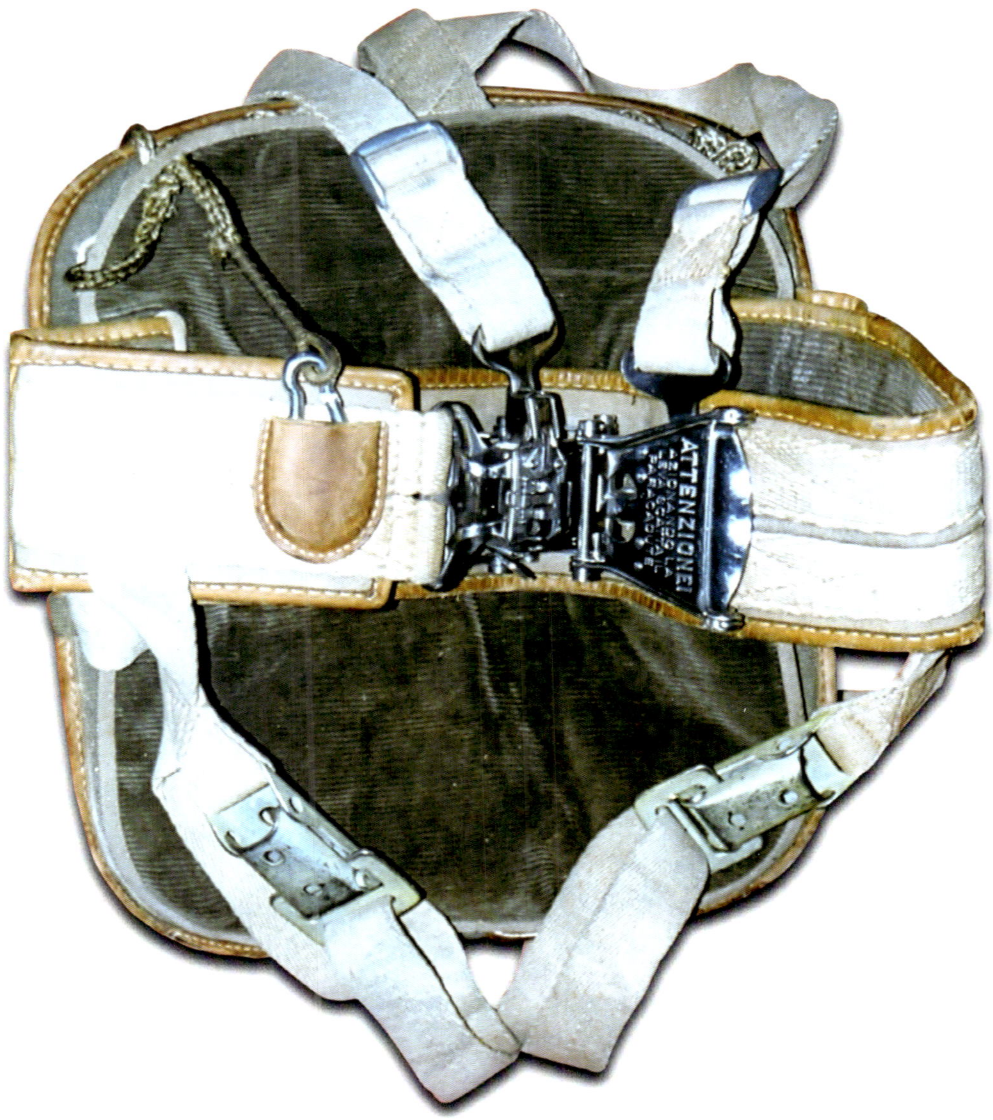

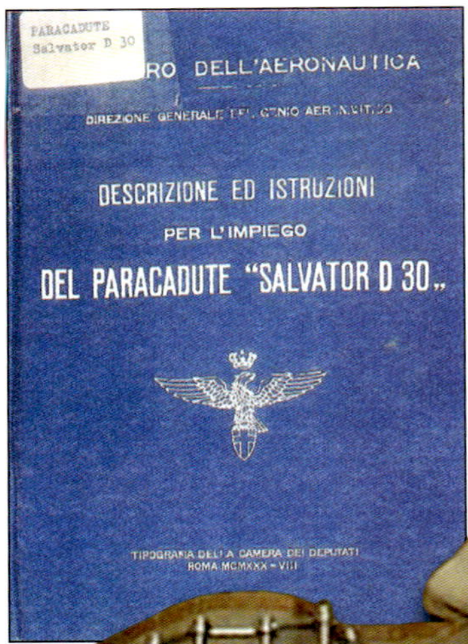

Instruction booklet for the SALVATOR D-30 parachute.

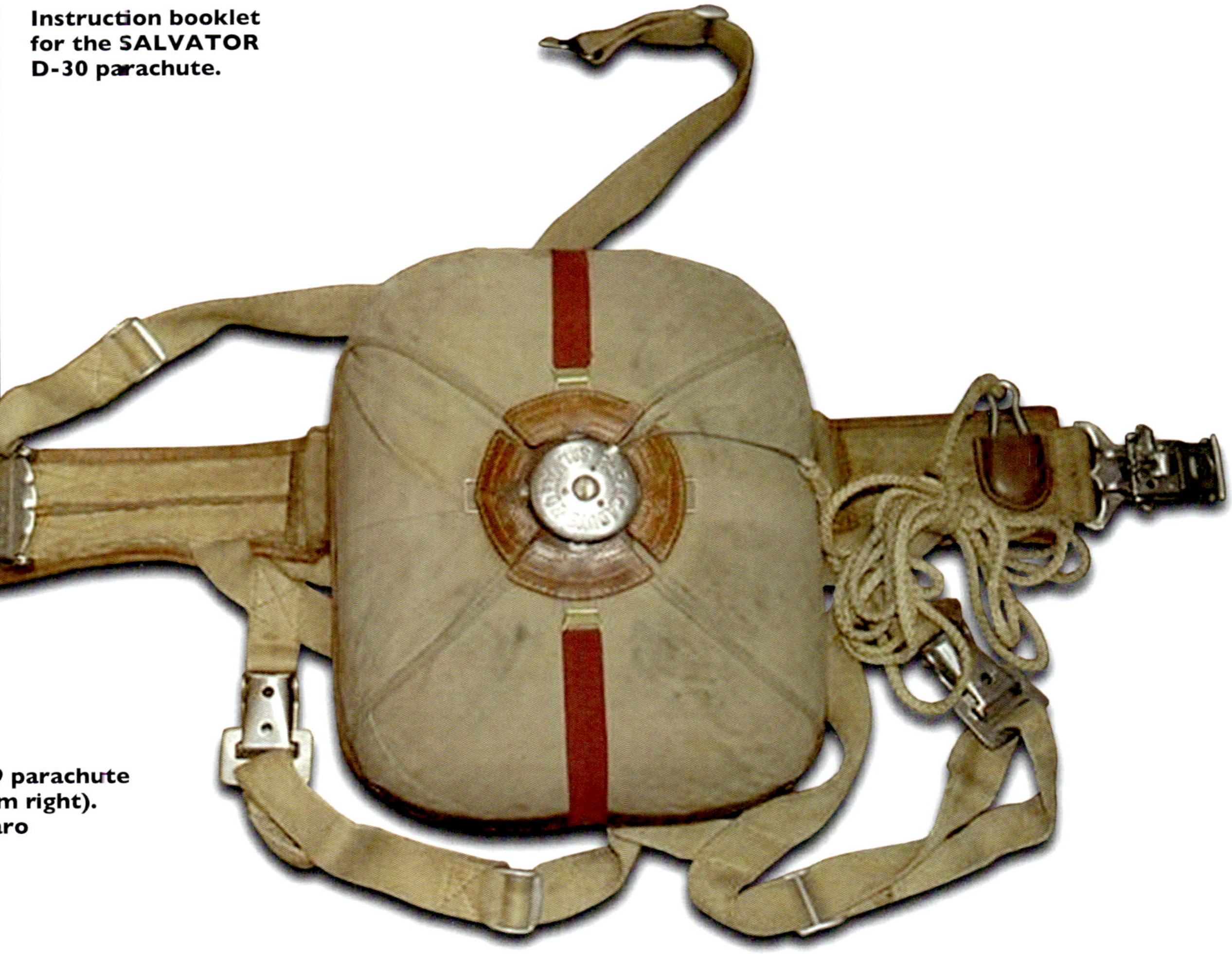

SALVATOR D-39 parachute with pack (bottom right). Courtesy L. Ongaro

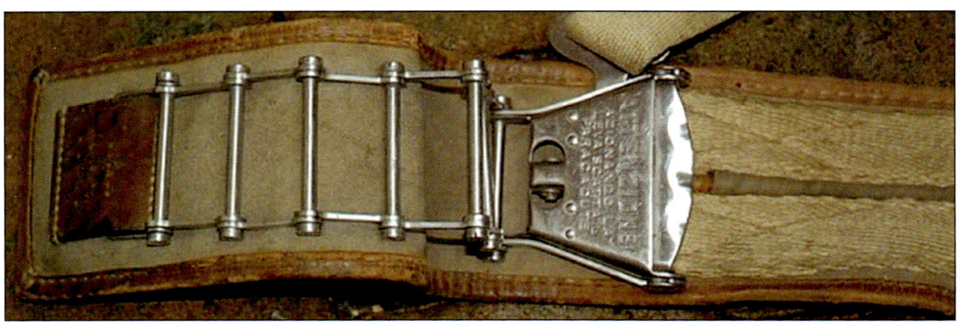

Instruction booklet for the SALVATOR D-39 parachute.

A fighter pilot donning his SALVATOR D-39 parachute. Courtesy MUSAM-ITAF

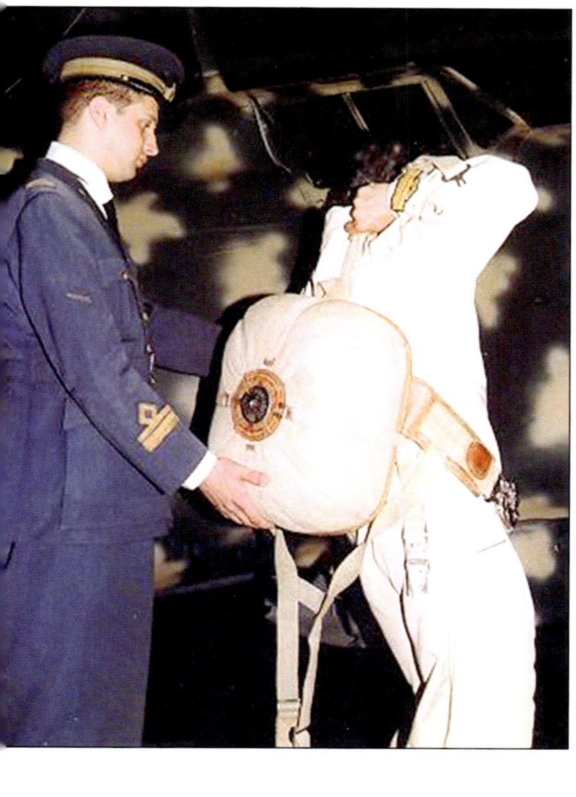

Detail views of the SALVATOR D-39 N. Courtesy MUSAM-ITAF

SALVATOR parachute worn over the life vest.

Hard carrying bag for the SALVATOR parachute.

The German backpack parachute was also used in some RA units. Courtesy P. Marzetti Archive

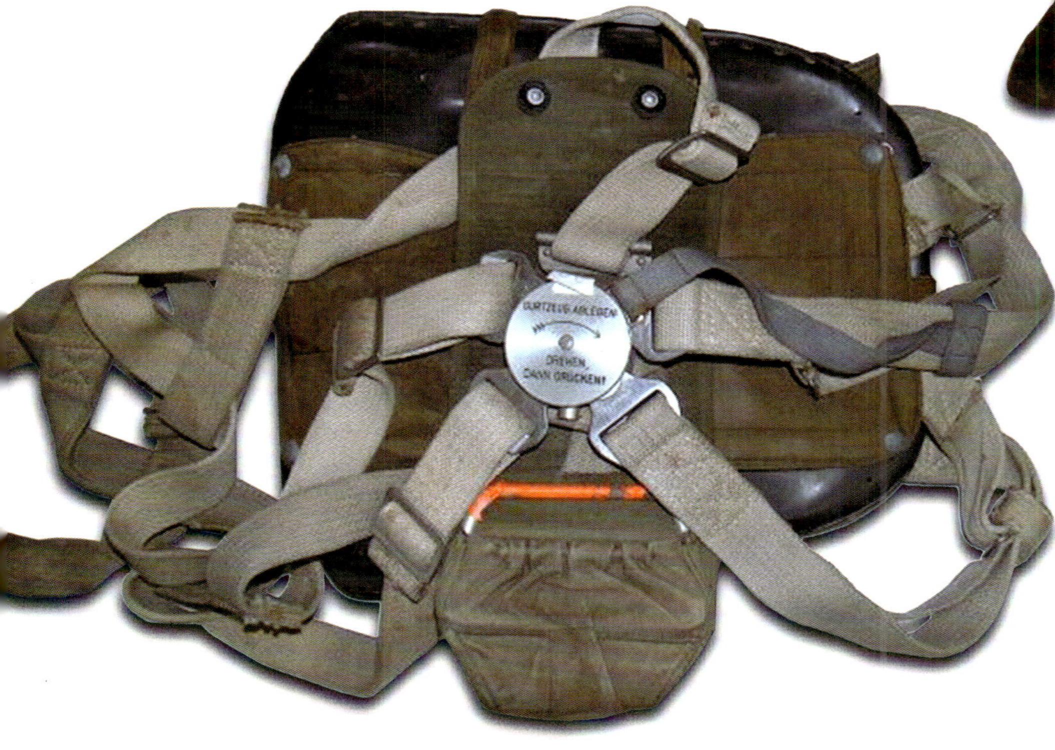

Details of the A 50N parachute harness used in multi-engined aircraft. It was issued in the 1950s and used up into the mid-1970s. The close similarity to war-era types is evident.

CHAPTER ELEVEN

LIFE VESTS

Pneumatic collar type life preserver produced by Pirelli. This model, along with its variants, was the type mostly used by Italian crews in World War II. It had to be inflated orally using the front rubber tube.

Variant of the previous life preserver, still a Pirelli model as stated by the factory logo molded on the rubber of the inflation tube. Note the wooden cap to close the inflation tube.

Detail of the Pirelli collar type life preserver with the wooden cap on the inflation tube.

Typical Pirelli life preserver used by the RA This type has a safer harness with three straps on the right side and a longer one that goes from the back to the lower front passing between the wearer's legs. All of the straps are locked by metal buckles. Another feature of this model is the rear upper section intended to keep the wearer's head above water, and in a correct floating position. (From the magazine "Nei cieli di guerra," 1943).

This page and opposite
The Pirelli life preserver shown earlier in detail. As stated by the inner stamp, it was produced by the Pirelli plant of Tivoli, near Rome. Courtesy G. Tugliani

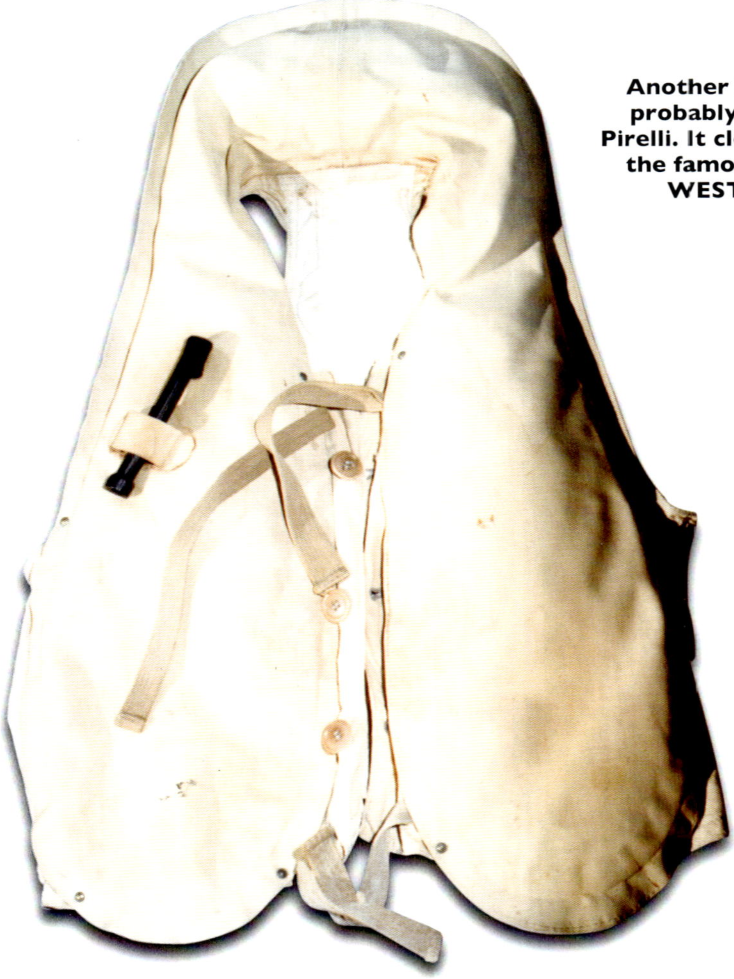

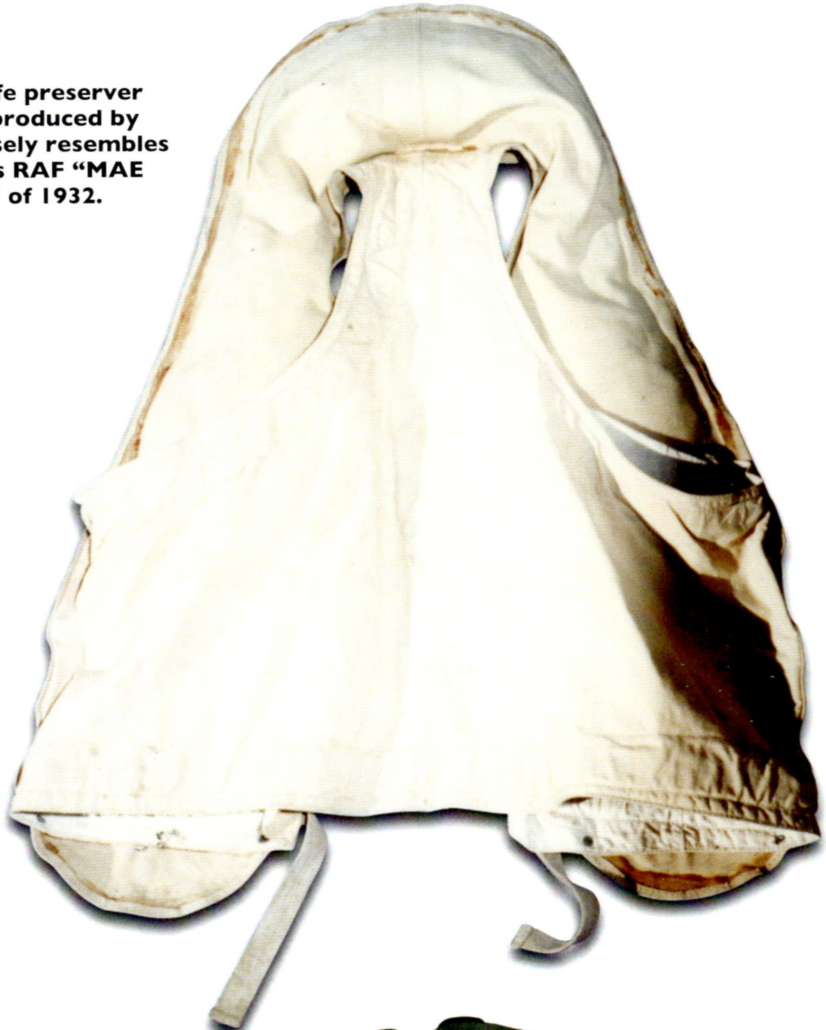

Another life preserver probably produced by Pirelli. It closely resembles the famous RAF "MAE WEST" of 1932.

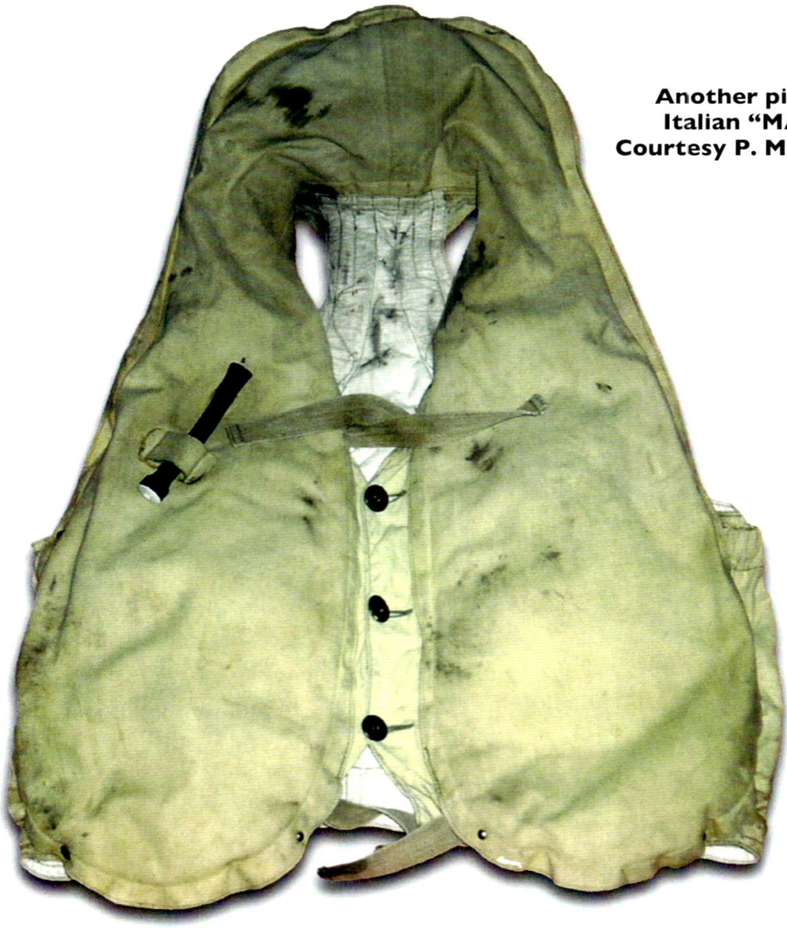

Another picture of the Italian "MAE WEST." Courtesy P. Marzetti Archive

"MAE WEST" worn over a Model 40 flight suit. The suit is the type with electrical heating produced by M.I.T.A.

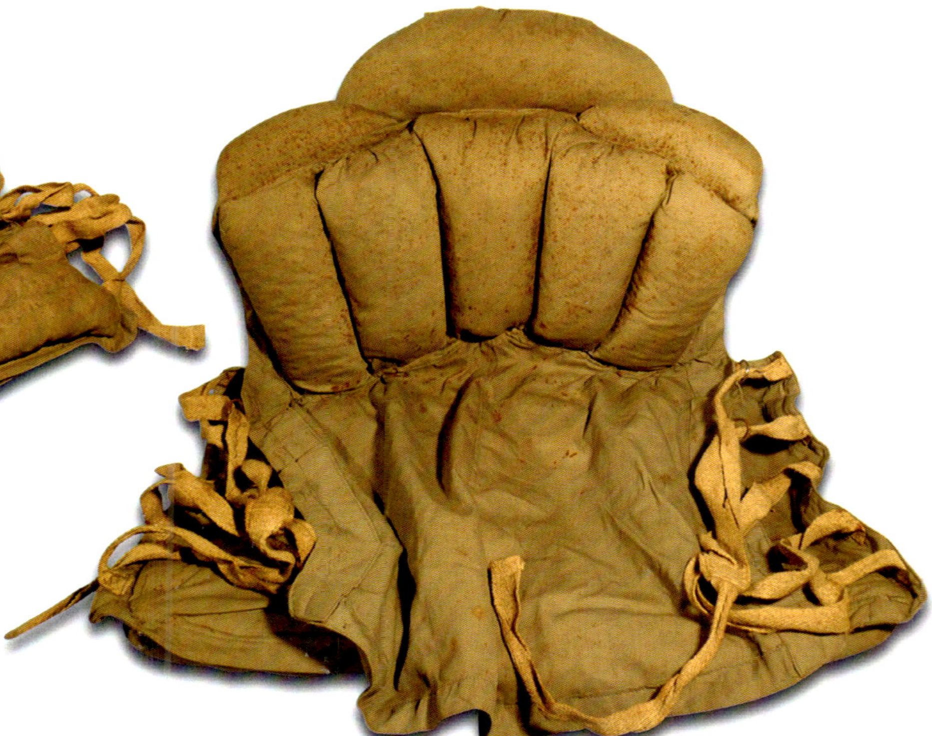

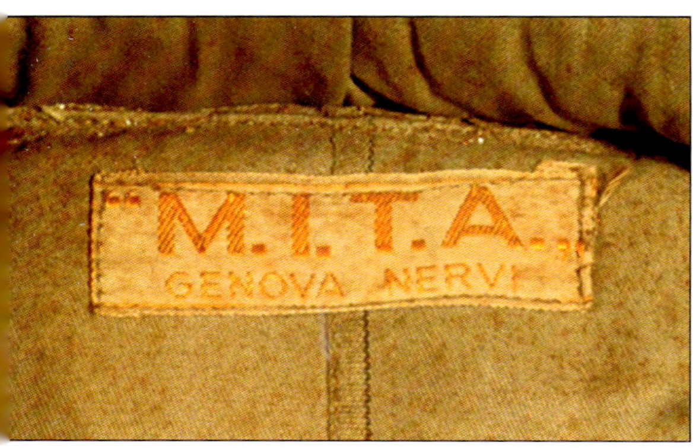

One of the most widespread models without air bladders was this type produced by M.I.T.A. It was made of strong, waterproof fabric, and included "sausage" shaped flotation material like kapok or cork shavings. As shown in the photo, the life preserver is shaped in order to be worn under the parachute whose central main harness passed between two front floating "sausages." The harness was made of strong canvas straps. Courtesy Ivano Rossi Museo della Guerra Castel del Rio

Left
The most advanced RA life preserver was the "SICURSALVA" model, although it was not provided with compressed gas bottles for the automatic inflation. This life preserver is provided with an inflation tube and a safety outflow valve that allowed dumping of the residual air contained in the bladders to avoid improper inflation at high altitude. On the upper side there are red and white reflective devices.

Below
The SALVATOR D-39 parachute could be worn over the SICURSALVA life preserver.

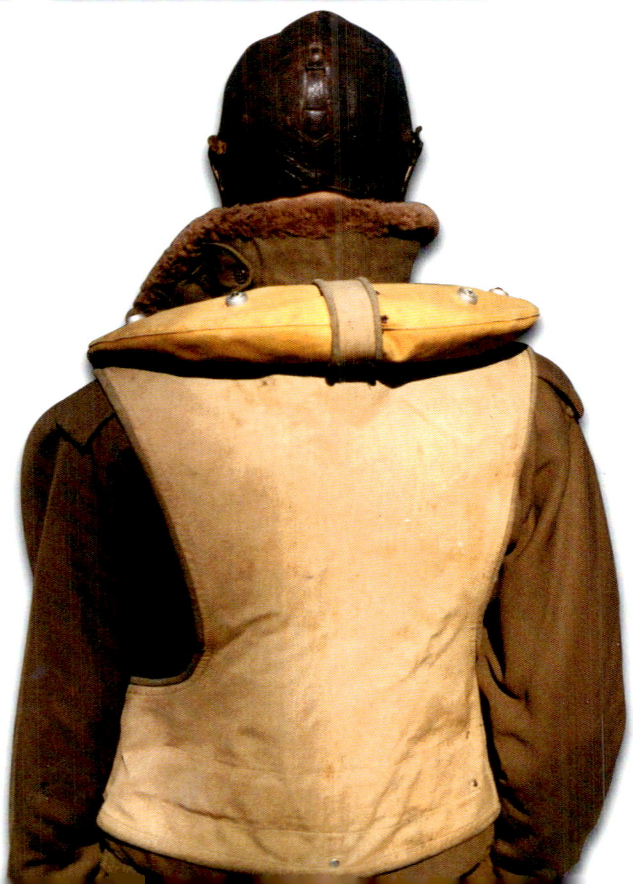

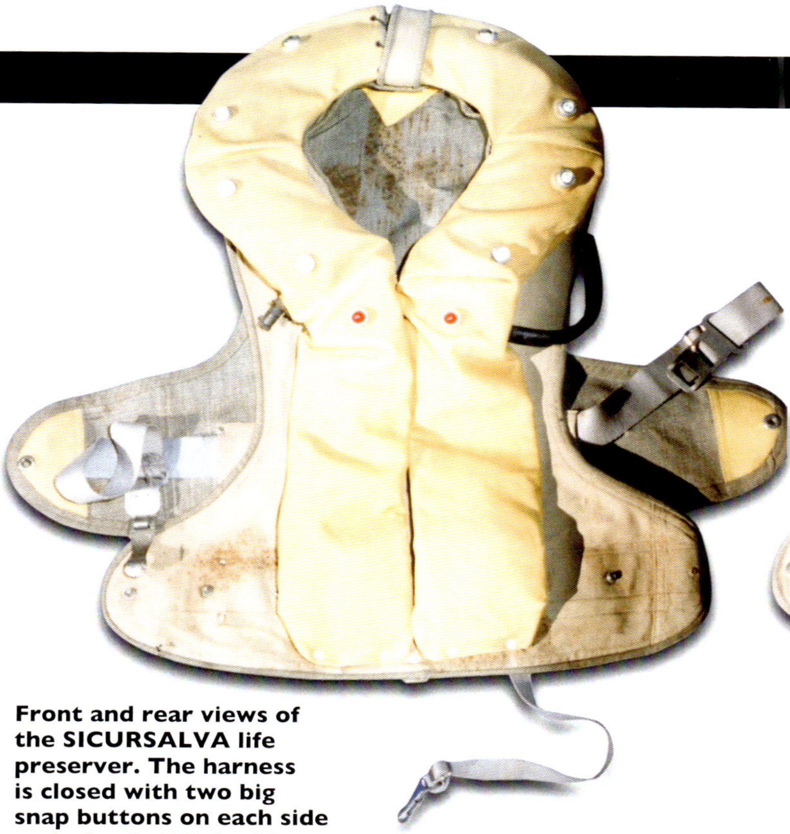

Front and rear views of the SICURSALVA life preserver. The harness is closed with two big snap buttons on each side and a lap belt linked to another crotch belt.

This SICURSALVA life preserver belonged to Lt. Giovanni Barcaro of 4th Fighter Wing who was wearing it when he was hit in his left shoulder flying his MC.202 in a dogfight over North Africa in May 1943. The life preserver clearly shows the bullet holes.

These two Italians show the different equipment combinations in RA units. The aircrewman on the left wears the Model 40 MARUS flight suit, while the other wears an unidentified jacket coupled with German winter flight trousers type CHANNEL SUIT or KANALHOSE. Both are wearing the German SCHWIMMWESTE 10-30 B2. The second aircrewman also has an inflatable life raft. (Nei Cieli di Guerra Magazine, 1943)

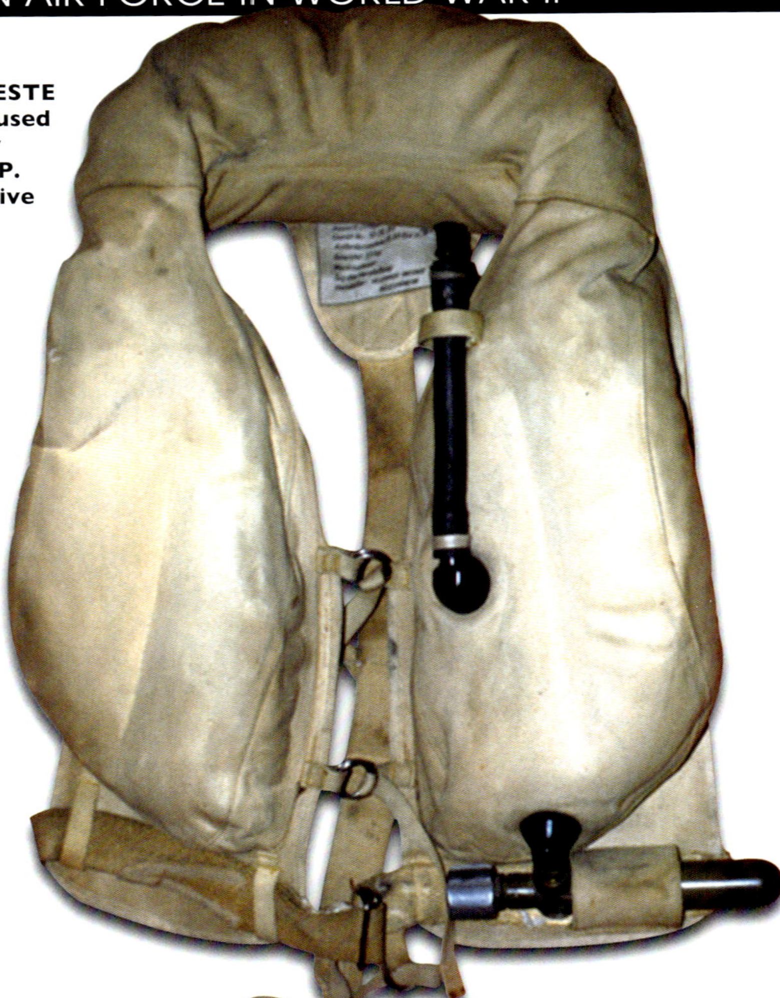

The German SCHWIMMWESTE 10-30 B2 was used extensively by RA. Courtesy P. Marzetti Archive

The RA units equipped with Ju 87 dive-bombers used German kapok life preservers. Courtesy P. Marzetti Archive

Some Cobelligerent Air Force units used this variant of the RAF "MAE WEST" type 22C/447. This model was also used by the ITAF SAR units until the early-1960s. *Below*: High visibility cap contained in the "MAE WEST" emergency equipment.

Shown here are rare images of the individual life raft type BPA-1 taken from the operation manual.

CHAPTER TWELVE

OXYGEN MASKS

Front cover on one of several operation manuals regarding the O.M.I. oxygen system.

RA oxygen mask on display at the NASM in Washington, D.C.

Oxygen mask designed by Prof. Margaria, produced by Pirelli, and used by a pilot of the 97th FG of the 4th FW in 1942.

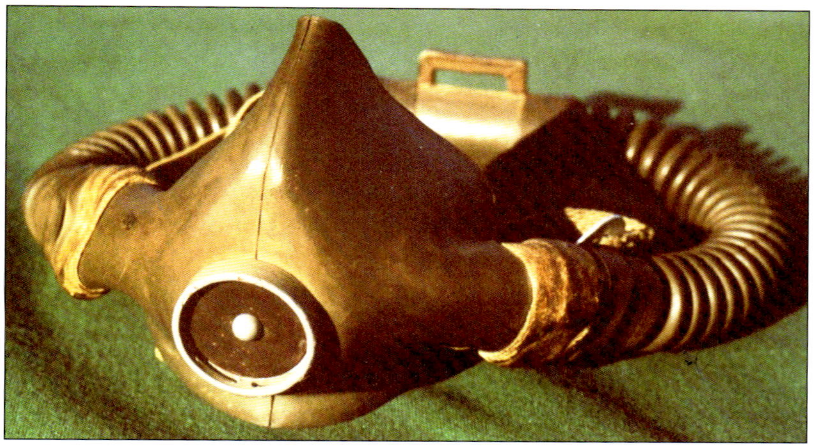

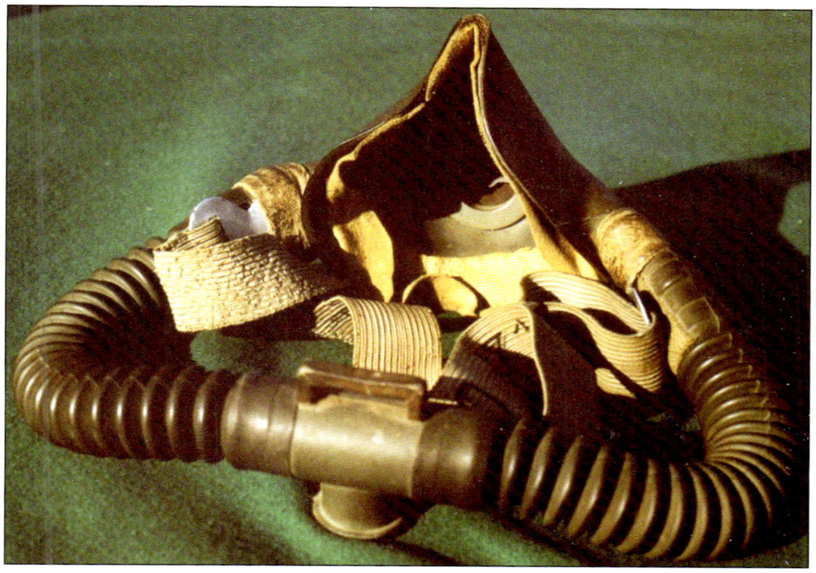

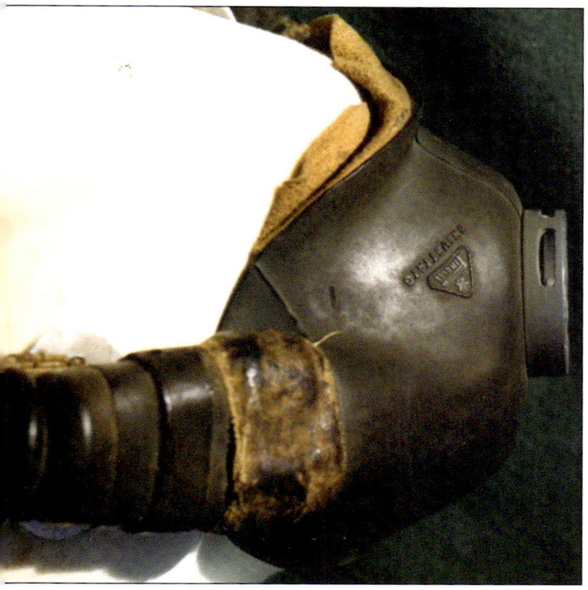

Detail of the manufacturer's mark.

Pirelli oxygen mask coupled with a SAFAR APP 8120 summer flight helmet.

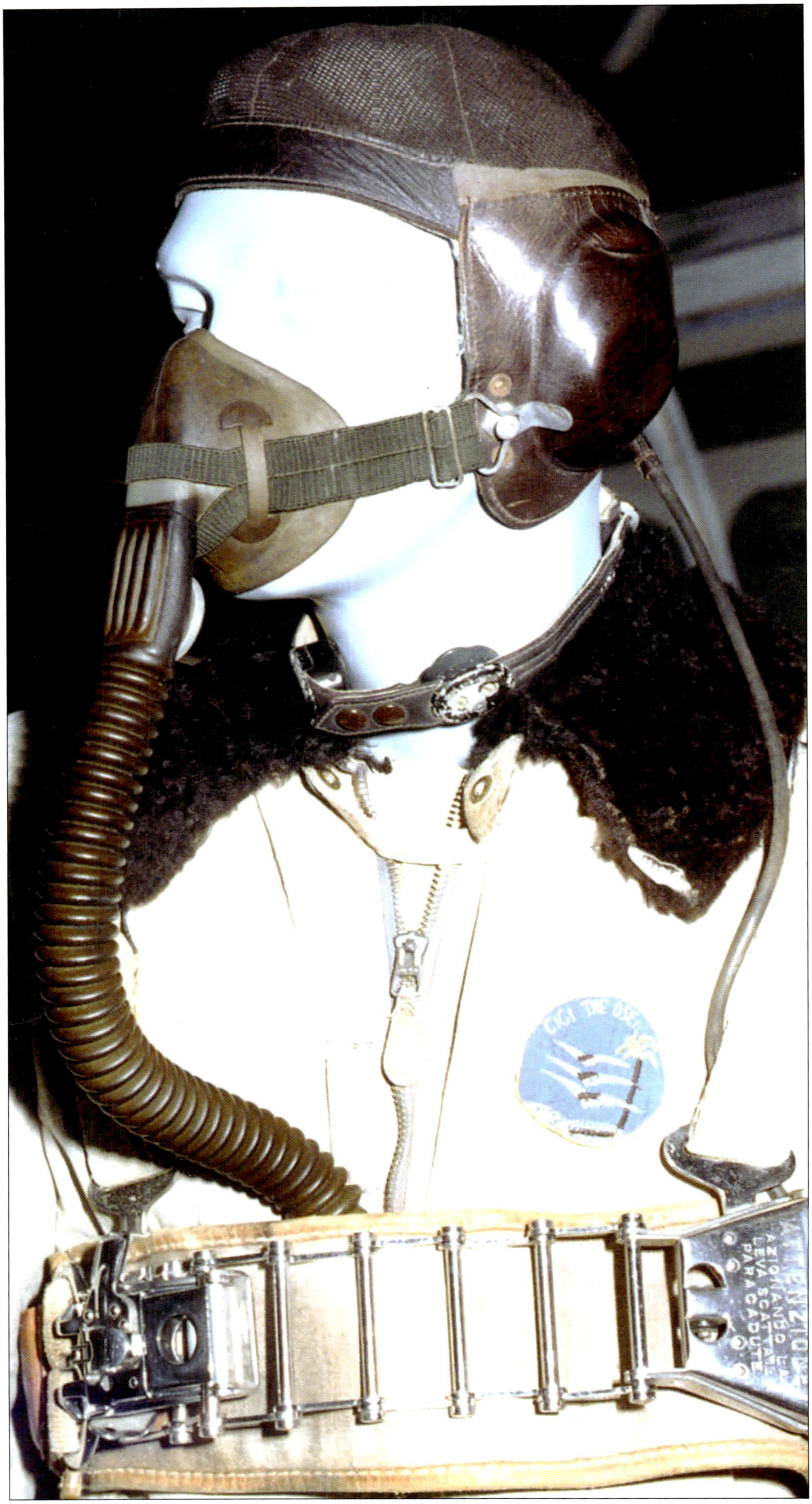

German AUER HM-5 oxygen mask used by a pilot of the ANR in 1944-1945. Courtesy MUSAM-ITAF

German oxygen mask with two fitting hooks used by RA pilots.

German Draeger oxygen system fitted in a Macchi MC.202 fighter displayed at the ITAF Museum of Vigna di Valle. Courtesy MUSAM-ITAF

Automatic oxygen system by OMI.

Draeger oxygen system fitted in a FIAT G.55 fighter. Courtesy MUSAM-ITAF

Standard fitting of a OMI oxygen system in a RA fighter. Courtesy MUSAM-ITAF

A mint and complete Margaria patented oxygen mask. Courtesy NASM, via Alex M. Spencer

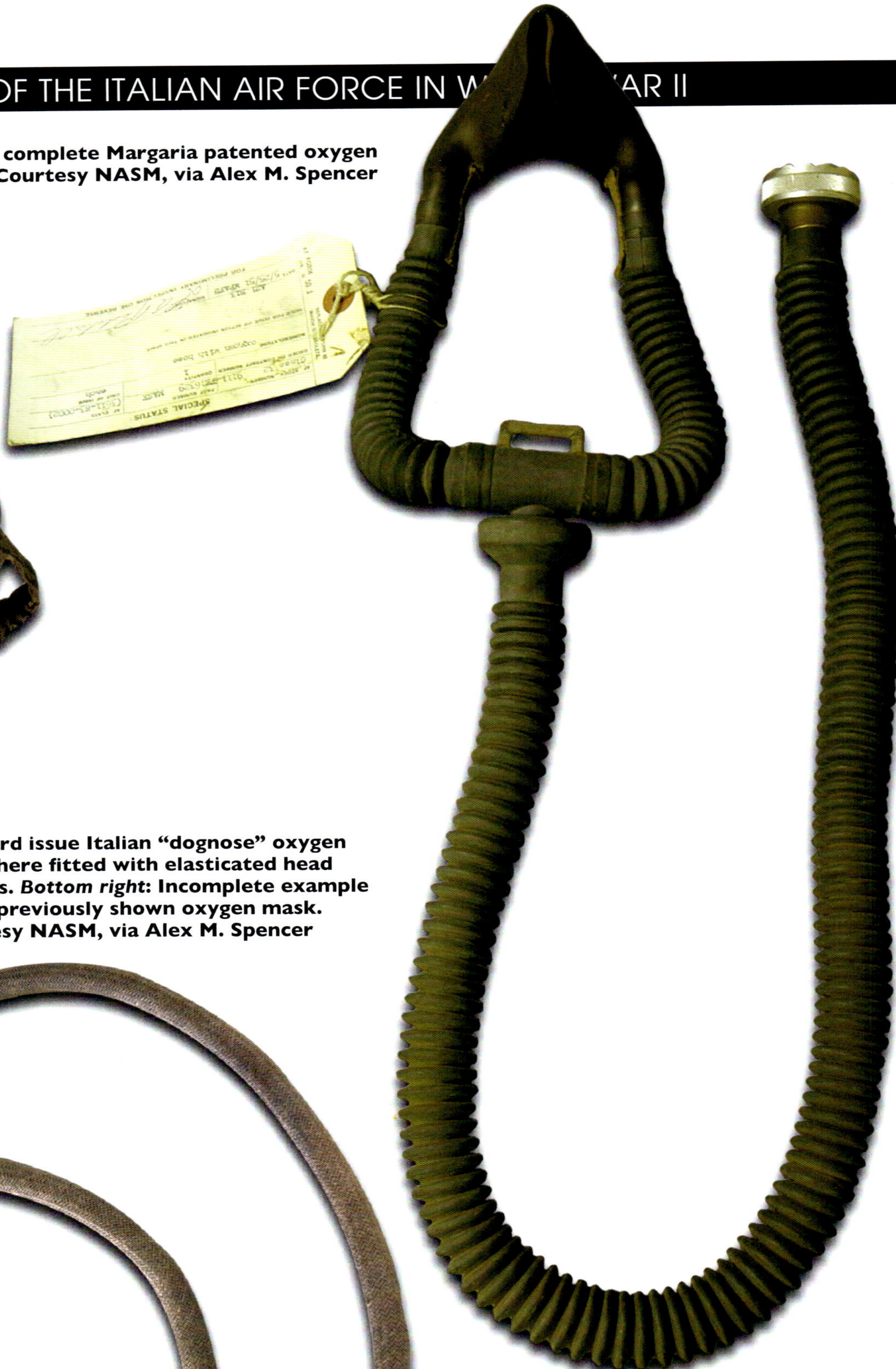

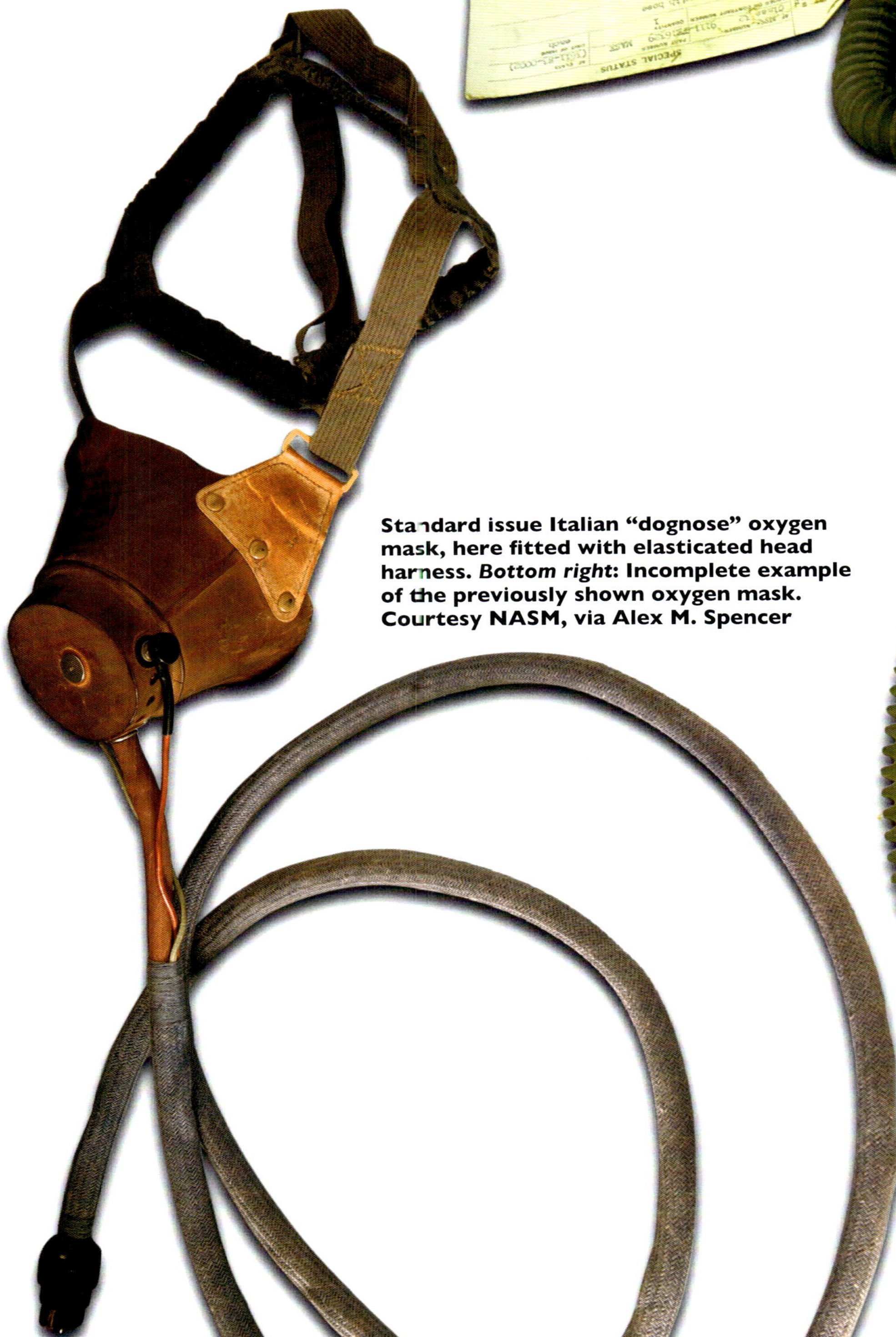

Standard issue Italian "dognose" oxygen mask, here fitted with elasticated head harness. *Bottom right*: Incomplete example of the previously shown oxygen mask. Courtesy NASM, via Alex M. Spencer

CHAPTER THIRTEEN

BOOTS AND GLOVES

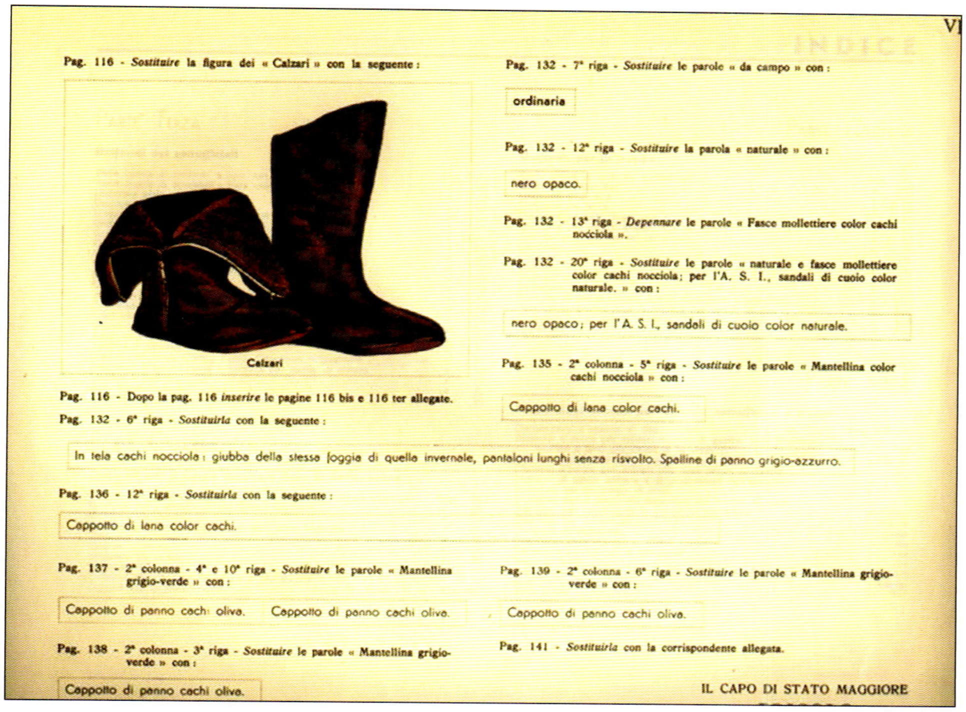

VI

Pag. 116 - *Sostituire* la figura dei « Calzari » con la seguente:

Calzari

Pag. 116 - Dopo la pag. 116 *inserire* le pagine 116 bis e 116 ter allegate.

Pag. 132 - 6ª riga - *Sostituirla* con la seguente:

In tela cachi nocciola: giubba della stessa foggia di quella invernale, pantaloni lunghi senza risvolto. Spalline di panno grigio-azzurro.

Pag. 136 - 12ª riga - *Sostituirla* con la seguente:

Cappotto di lana color cachi.

Pag. 137 - 2ª colonna - 4ª e 10ª riga - *Sostituire* le parole « Mantellina grigio-verde » con:

Cappotto di panno cachi oliva. Cappotto di panno cachi oliva.

Pag. 138 - 2ª colonna - 3ª riga - *Sostituire* le parole « Mantellina grigio-verde » con:

Cappotto di panno cachi oliva.

Pag. 132 - 7ª riga - *Sostituire* le parole « da campo » con:

ordinaria

Pag. 132 - 12ª riga - *Sostituire* la parola « naturale » con:

nero opaco.

Pag. 132 - 13ª riga - *Depennare* le parole « Fasce mollettiere color cachi nocciola ».

Pag. 132 - 20ª riga - *Sostituire* le parole « naturale e fasce mollettiere color cachi nocciola; per l'A. S. I., sandali di cuoio color naturale. » con:

nero opaco; per l'A. S. I., sandali di cuoio color naturale.

Pag. 135 - 2ª colonna - 5ª riga - *Sostituire* le parole « Mantellina color cachi nocciola » con:

Cappotto di lana color cachi.

Pag. 139 - 2ª colonna - 6ª riga - *Sostituire* le parole « Mantellina grigio-verde » con:

Cappotto di panno cachi oliva.

Pag. 141 - *Sostituirla* con la corrispondente allegata.

IL CAPO DI STATO MAGGIORE

In this list of updates and variants to the RA flight equipment contained in O.D.4 of 1937. The depicted flight boots are named "overshoes."

RA flight boot "overshoes."

Another pair of flight boots that were worn over the normal shoes.

Flight boots used by RA airmen, and probably "made in Germany." Courtesy A. Gaiani

Standard flight boots in black leather. Courtesy P. Marzetti Archive

Rare variant flight boots produced in the 1920s and used by seaplane crews.

Italian electrically heated flight boots. Note the snap buttons that connected the boots to the flight suit heating wiring system.

Sandals for hot climates were often used by RA aircrews in Africa and Southern Italy. Courtesy MUSAM-ITAF

Two different models of German flight boots used by Italian flyers with the C.A.I. expeditionary force in Belgium during the Battle of Britain, and in the late-war years by ANR fighter units.

"Three finger" leather gloves with fur lining, and patterned after the well known O.D.4 of 1937

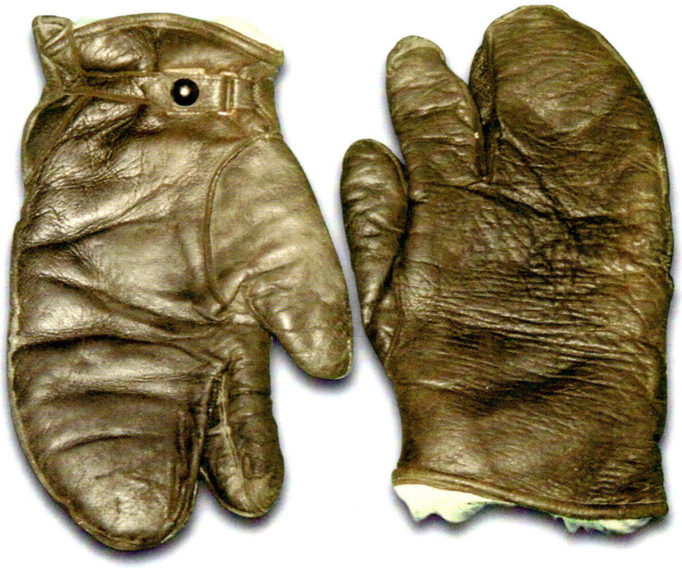

Commercial "three finger" gloves.

Gloves used with the electrically heated flight suit. They were connected to the flight jacket sleeves' inner snap buttons. Courtesy Museo dell'Aviazione-Rimini

MARUS electrically heated gloves. Courtesy G. Tugliani

CHAPTER FOURTEEN

PILOT BADGES

Pilot wings Model 30 without ROYAL crown.

Pilot wings Model 30 with military pilot crown.

"Atlantic" pilot wings, Johnson manufacturer, Milan. Courtesy S. Crinò

"Stratospheric" pilot wings by Johnson of Milan. Courtesy S. Crinò

"High speed" pilot wings by Johnson of Milan. Courtesy S. Crinò

Military pilot wings by Breccia.

Military pilot wings by D'Angelo Bros. of Naples.

Military pilot wings by Breccia.

Decorations belonging to an Italian pilot. Military pilot wings by Coruzzolo and Luftwaffe fliegerführer abzeichen.

Military pilot wings by Johnson, adopted in 1944 by the ANR.

"High speed" pilot wings by Johnson of Milan, belonging to General Silvio De Giorgi. This wing was modified after September 8, 1943 by removal of the fascist symbol and later on, after the Republic was promulgated, trimming the crown. This wing was a personal gift to the author from General Giorgi.

Embroidered flying observer badge.

Military pilot wings made by Picchiani & Barlacchi.

Military pilot wings by Danieli of Padua. Courtesy S. Crinò

Civilian pilot wings by Danieli, also used by student military pilots. Courtesy S. Crinò

Embroidered military pilot wings.

Embroidered student pilot wings.

Embroidered G.I.L. air cadet (italian fascist youth) badge.

The entire career of an Italian pilot is shown in this display. Starting from below: fascist student pilot wings, RA military pilot wings, ANR military pilot wings, postwar ITAF military pilot wings.

Below
Pilot Badges of the Italian expeditionary air force of the Spanish Civil War.

ANR military pilot wings of uncertain provenance, probably a postwar copy or a type not officially issued.

Official, original ANR military pilot wings by Johnson.

CHAPTER FIFTEEN

MISCELLANEOUS

Embroidered World War II 4th FW badge for flight suit.

RA 6th FW "Red Devils" badge painted over silk.

Flight suit embroidered badge of 16th BW whose nickname was "Green Rats," c.1930. Courtesy L. Di Gabriele

Embroidered 13th BW badge with the unit motto, sewn over a MARUS Model 40 winter flight jacket. Courtesy N. Pavan

RA 15th Wing badge.

Embroidered 21st FG badge.

The famous "Scarecrow" (SPAVENTAPASSERI) of the 22nd FG painted over silk adopted during the Russian campaign and designed by Lt. Bepi Biron. Personal gift to the author from Attilio Sanson.

Embroidered badge of the 50th Assault Wing.

The "Black Cat" of 51st FW. Courtesy Biccolini

Another embroidered variant of the 6th FW " Red Devil."

Handpainted leather badge of the 18th FG during the Spanish Civil War. Personal gift to the author from General Vittorio Merlo.

Badge of the RA "Loreto" battalion.
Courtesy L. Di Gabriele

Badge similar to the previous in rayon.
Courtesy L. Di Gabriele

Silk embroidered badge of the 7th BW.

Embroidered badge of the 3rd SQN, 2nd FG of the ANR.

Badge of the 214th BS of the Italian expeditionary air force during the Spanish Civil War.

Flight jacket badge of the 154th FG. Courtesy G.P. Rao

Embroidered badge of the 5th Assault Wing.

Officer uniform cap of the RA technical services. Courtesy A. Gaiani

RA pilot officer cap in tropical variant.

Lt. uniform cap belonging to an ANR pilot.

NCO pilot summer uniform cap.

Major pilot cap, note the brass badge.

Officer pilot tropical cap.

Staff Lt. forage cap, tropical variant. Courtesy A. Gaiani

Enlisted man's forage cap. Courtesy A. Gaiani

Italian expeditionary air force cap used during the Spanish Civil War. Courtesy MUSAM-ITAF

Fabric waterproof cap with fur lining used during the russian campaign.

M-33 helmet used in Belgium by the C.A.I. expeditionary air force. Courtesy P. Marzetti Archive

First aid kit still containing some medications. This type was used aboard RA multi-engine aircraft.

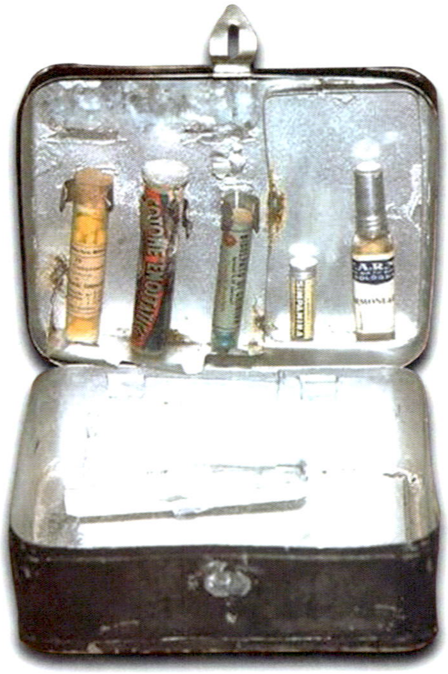

Cadet's dagger of the RA Academy.

Beretta 7.65 M34 pistol of the RA as noted by the RA mark on its case. Personal gift to the author from Amleto Monterumici.

Fabric cartridge belt containing emergency flares that was worn around the pilot's thigh. Courtesy P. Marzetti Archive

RA flight clipboard. Courtesy MUSAM-ITAF

Transparent case for flight maps. Courtesy S. Santucci

Navigator clipboard. Courtesy MUSAM-ITAF

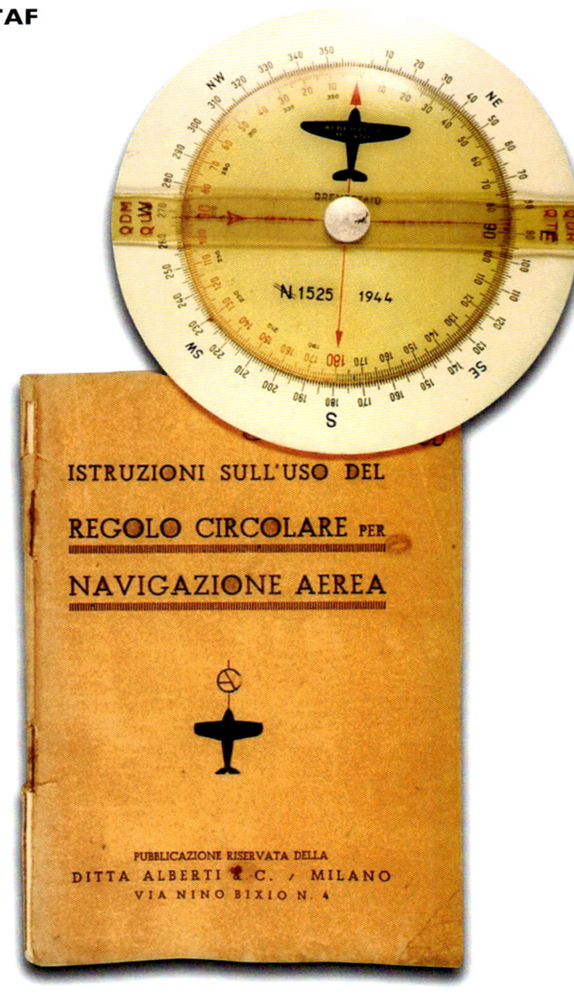

Two different navigation computers used by Italian aircrews.

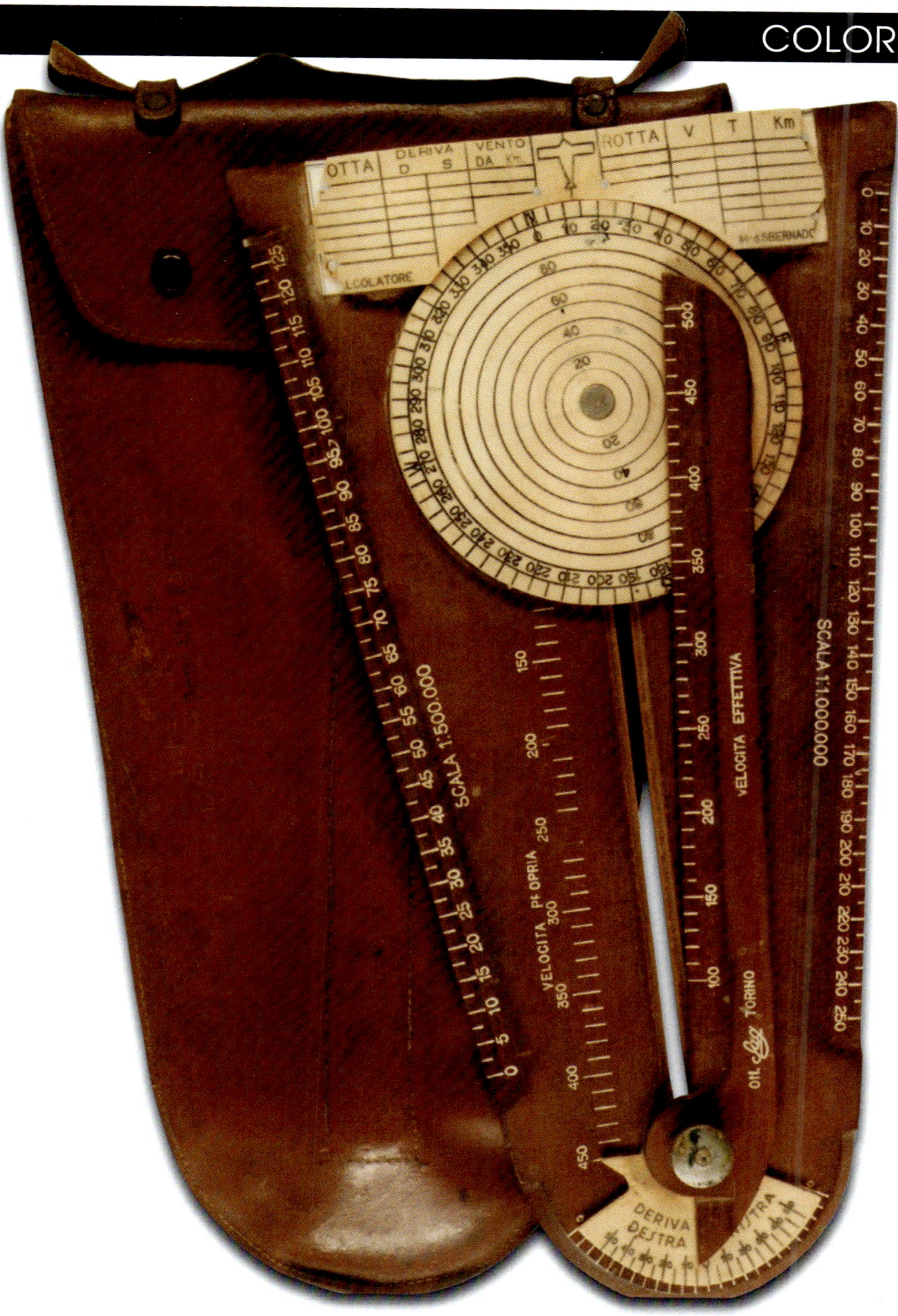

Sbernadori navigation computer. Courtesy MUSAM-ITAF

Sensitive altimeter made by the Agolini workshops of Padua. It was worn by student pilots during flight checks to receive their flight licenses.

The LEONIDAS "a ritorno" chronograph, was used by bomber crews to calculate the bomb dropping time with the IOZZA bombsight. Its leather belt allowed it to be worn over the flight suit. Courtesy S. Santucci

Another LEONIDAS "a ritorno" chronograph.

A fine example of a watch by Boselli, and often issued as gifts to RA pilots.

Radio receiver apparatus Model AR-18 made by the Ducati factory and used in RA multi-engine aircraft. Courtesy A. Gaiani

Italian carbon throat microphone.

First type of personal logbook.

Second type of personal logbook.

Squadron metal badge for service uniform belonging to a pilot of the 2nd Fighter Group of ANR-RSI.

Carrying bag for the electrically heated MARUS flight suit.

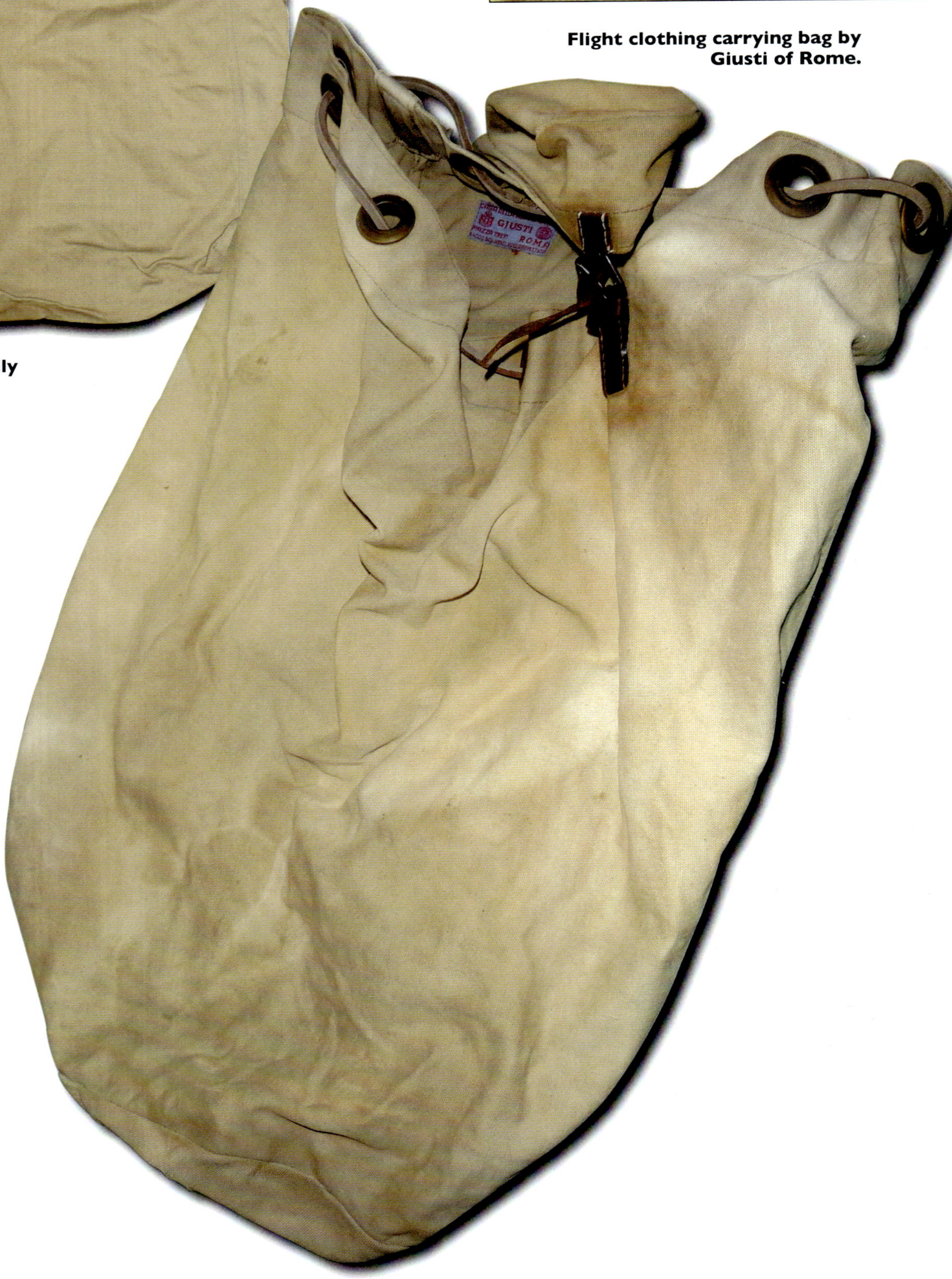

Flight clothing carrying bag by Giusti of Rome.

Crew comfort and survival kit used in RA multi-engine aircraft. This one belonged to the 3rd ZAT (3rd Air Region) and has "SPECIAL RATIONS FOR AIRCRAFT" printed on the box cover.

White summer great formal uniform colonial "Grande Uniforme" for a high rank pilot officer. Courtesy F. Burgio

Pilot officer field service uniform jacket (uniforme da campo) with overseas cap. Courtesy F. Burgio

NOTES

NOTES

NOTES

NOTES

NOTES

BIBLIOGRAPHY

P. Marzetti: *Tenute Di Volo Della Seconda Guerra Mondiale.*

A. Viotti: *Uniformi E Distintivi Dellar. Aeronautica.*

A. Spaziani: *Caschi Radiotelefonici Della Regia Aeronautica.*

N. Virgilio: *Sciacca 1940-43 L'aeroporto Fantasma.*

Nei Cieli Di Guerra: *Editoriale Aeronautico 1942.*

Cacciatori-Editoriale Aeronautico 1942.

Various issues of *Wartime Magazine.*

L'ala D'italia 1939-1943.

Manual Instructions For Use and Maintenance of Flight Gears, and other Equipment, Published By Air Ministry.